Ways of Hearing

Ben Thompson started writing about music in 1985, when a teenage infatuation with the anti-Thatcherite northern soul of The Three Johns and The Membranes prompted him to produce a scruffy ten-page fanzine called *The Devil's Music*. When some Goths in St Albans bungled the production of the second edition, he forsook guerrilla publishing for the mainstream media. Since then he has written for *Sounds, NME, New Statesman & Society*, the *Observer, The Wire*, the *Independent*, the *Independent on Sunday*, the *Face, GQ, Mojo, Midweek, Spin, Request*, the *TLS, Australian Vogue*, the *Journal of Oral History* and the *Saturday Telegraph Magazine. Ways of Hearing* is his second book.

By the same author

Seven Years of Plenty: A Handbook of
Irrefutable Pop Greatness 1991–1998

Ben Thompson

Ways of Hearing

A User's Guide to the Pop Psyche,
from Elvis to Eminem

ORION

First published in Great Britain in 2001 by Orion
An imprint of Orion Books Ltd
Orion House, 5 Upper St Martin's Lane, London WC2H 9EA

A CIP catalogue record for this book is available
from the British Library

ISBN 0 575 06809 4

Some of these words have previously appeared in the *Saturday Telegraph Magazine,*
the *Independent On Sunday,* the *Independent, The Wire, Midweek, Mojo, The Face, NME,
Sight & Sound* and *New Statesman & Society,* but generally in a different order.
Rough and ready prototypes of 'The Cautionary Tale of the 13th Floor Elevators' and
'Film' were previously published as the sleevenotes to *The Best of the 13th
Floor Elevators* (Nectar Masters 1995) and 'Pop and Film: the Charisma Crossover' in
Celluloid Jukebox: Popular Music and the Movies Since the 50s, eds Romney,
Wootton (BFI 1995) repectively.
All (well, almost all) quotes were given to the author unless otherwise specified.

Typeset in Great Britain by Deltatype Ltd, Birkenhead, Merseyside

Printed and bound by Clays Ltd, St Ives plc

'These voices – they're a kind of a bridge back to the human world'

Aldous Huxley

Mission Statement

It's the mid-nineteen nineties. The Chemical Brothers are on the turntables at the Heavenly Social. Someone comes up and asks them where he can buy a copy of that brilliant new song they've just played. The song is The Beatles' 'Tomorrow Never Knows', released some thirty years earlier, its alchemy still fully intact.

The simultaneous accessibility of the whole of pop history is both a daunting prospect and a thrilling challenge. How can we make sense of that history without undermining its magic? How can we experience the weight of the past as an energy rather than as a burden? These are two of the questions *Ways of Hearing* seeks to answer.

Hopscotching gleefully across the decades, other, still more fundamental, conundrums present themselves. Since the personality of the pop performer is an ideal – projected on to a screen inside our heads to elicit admiration or opprobrium, according to taste – then how it is constructed raises issues for everybody. What is the nature of the connection between the people who make music and the people who listen to it? And why, when scientology claims to open up the hidden chambers of the intellect, does pop offer instant access to areas of the mind L. Ron Hubbard could only dream about?

Inspired by a vision of a better world in the mirrors on Lee 'Scratch' Perry's hat, *Ways of Hearing* will employ Lemmy's opposeable thumb, Neil Young's facial hair and Missy 'Misdemeanor' Elliott's overcrowded trainer drawer as building blocks in the construction of an actual sonic cathedral.

From Slade's film career to Simon Bates' adventures in artificial insemination; from the psychedelic madness of *Stars in Their Eyes* to the secret impact of The Rolling Stones on shop-lifting in east London in the late nineteen sixties, it aims to take the reader as deep into the social and aesthetic mystery of pop as any book ever published.

Introduction

pop (pop) *n.* **1.a.** music of general appeal, esp. among young people.
psyche ('saiki) *n.* the human mind or soul.

On hearing particular music at particular times, the listener does not just feel like a better person, the listener *is* a better person. This transformative power is an article of faith which, like all articles of faith, demands thorough investigation.

In his autobiography *My Last Breath*, the great surrealist film-maker Luis Buñuel compared the making of the perfect dry Martini with the passage of the holy ghost through the hymen of the Virgin Mary at the moment of Jesus Christ's conception. This striking equation of sacred and profane was no doubt meant to shock, but by pinpointing the influence of the celestial in the most everyday pleasures, it actually supplied an image of divine inspiration applicable to believers and heathens alike.

In his stern and schoolmasterly book *What To Listen For In Music*, the American composer Aaron Copland (the man who gave the world *Fanfare For The Common Man*, later to be so memorably covered by Emerson Lake and Palmer) observed: 'The composer cannot write into his music a value he does not possess as a man . . . his character may be streaked with human frailties [at this point he cites Wagner, but Craig David would do just as nicely] but whatever is fine in this music will come from whatever is fine or valuable in him as a man.'

Beyond the outrageous assumption that the composer can only be a man, there is something else about this statement which does not quite ring true. While obviously correct in a physical sense, in a *meta*physical sense maybe music is a way of gaining access to the values you do *not* possess as a person – or at least can only possess for the sound's fleeting moment.

In his pioneering analysis of schizophrenic mental disturbance, *The Divided Self*, R.D. Laing wrote of a young psychotic redeemed by the sound of horns. 'There was only one situation as far as I could judge in which he could let himself go without anxiety about not recovering himself, and that was listening to jazz.' While not everyone will share the musical taste of the individual concerned, most people will know where he was coming from. Perhaps we *all* have divided selves – one part of which is listening to music, and the other part of which isn't.

Once, when outer space jazz ambassador Sun Ra performed for patients at a Chicago mental hospital, a woman who was said not to have moved or spoken for many years, got up from the floor, walked directly to his piano and shouted out 'Do you call this music?'[1] Any one who has ever listened to the second Stone Roses album will know how she felt.

At this point it would probably be helpful to establish what it is exactly that this book calls music. Where the broadest and most practical definition might be 'any sound that human beings enjoy hearing' – from the chink of a cash register to a starling imitating a car alarm – the musical sub-set addressed within these pages is (for the most part) song. That is, music in which words play a part, music which communicates not simply through pure sound or meaningful utterance of the human voice, but a complex and sometimes mysterious inter-relation of the two.

It's not just song that will concern us, but song as experienced through the filter of what is sometimes rather off-puttingly termed The Pop Process. That is why the subtitle of this book starts with Elvis who – however deeply his music might have been rooted in sounds and styles that preceded him – defined that process as we understand it.[2] (It ends with Eminem for reasons that go beyond the purely alphabetical, but more of that later.)

As well as being *about* the pop process, this book is also, in its own modest way, a part of it. Its raw materials were gleaned through the sinister business of writing interviews and record reviews for newspapers and magazines, and inevitably – and properly – bear the mark of those devious mechanisms.

Just as electrical feedback adds character to guitar-playing, so the distortions and compromises implicit in the business of mass mediation add depth and intrigue to the pop personas they impact upon. When we listen to someone's music we hear these things just as clearly – sometimes *more* clearly – than the song itself. And it's in seeking to unravel the intricacies of the performer's identity that we often find out most about our own. Which is why this book is called a user's guide, because recourse to the pop psyche is the ultimate means of self help – for artist and audience alike.

In *The Faber Book of Pop*, Jon Savage recalls an encounter with pioneering British pop svengali Larry Parnes – the man who changed Ronald Wycherley into Billy Fury and Clive Powell into Georgie Fame. He points out that however exotic they might have sounded to audiences on this side of the Atlantic, the names of rock and roll pioneers Elvis Presley and Jerry Lee Lewis were the ones on their birth certificates.

'Parnes,' Savage asserts perspicaciously, 'made it clear that pop was about one thing: self-recreation. You could be an inner-urban child with a boring circumstance, yet by one simple act – changing your name – you could be transformed for ever into an electronic deity.' The sense of starting from scratch which British pop would derive from setting out into the world under an alias would be crucial to its distinctive character.

But this transformative impulse did not originate on the Eastern side of the Atlantic. One reason for the enthusiasm with which the British pop audience has traditionally greeted black American musical forms – from blues to soul to house – that have previously been undervalued in their homeland, is an intuitive understanding of their urge to self-recreation. Black blues players and jazzmen called themselves kings and dukes as a means of overturning the social – and racial – hierarchy. And when white musicians started to imitate their music, things got really complicated.

The complexities of this inter-relation were foreshadowed in the alarming nineteen-century phenomenon of minstrelsy, wherein white performers would darken their faces with burnt cork to ape black musical traditions, in a grotesque parody that was at once travesty and tribute. In his book *The History of the Blues*, Frances Davis cites the extraordinary case of the first black minstrel, who was himself expected to black up, and whose billing promised not just 'imitation of white minstrels' but also 'imitation of himself'.

As offensive as it is to present-day sensibilities, minstrelsy, Davis argues, provided 'an entry into a world in which black could be white, white could be black, anything could be itself and simultaneously its opposite'.

The resonance of this bizarre tradition extends to the present day, and not just in Davis's catty definition of Mick Jagger as 'the most famous of contemporary minstrels'. It is hard to resist the notion that the terrible saga of another, still more famous, MJ might actually be minstrelsy in reverse, and many a gangsta rapper – dead or alive – might raise a wry eyebrow at the phrase 'imitation of himself'.

One of *Ways of Hearing*'s chief underlying concerns is the way ideas of 'blackness' and 'whiteness' bleed into and out of each other through pop history. The fluidity of this interaction seems to mirror the way music's power is at once contained and not contained within the other media through which we experience it. It also points to the true nature of music's place in a broader social arena – cause and effect, symptom and cure, tangent and crux – and its similarly paradoxical double life as both an outgrowth and a component of individual identity. But it would be a mistake to swim any further into such murky conceptual waters without a deep draught of clean pure oxygen from Pete Townshend's aqualung.

The Shock of The Who

'When I got close up to him, I could see he was wearing my true face . . . the face I always wanted.' This is how one hard-core Who fan felt when he first saw Pete Townshend on stage at a Shepherd's Bush church hall in 1962.[3] The epiphanous effect might seem to be undermined by his qualifying statement – 'Everything would have been perfect if I had a nose like this geezer' – but actually it isn't, because The Who's very distance from conventional pop-star ideals was one of the things that made them so important to people.

Nothing would appear to have been more inimical to the band's original spirit than 1994's four-CD boxed set, *The Who: Thirty Years of Maximum R&B*, but whatever you might think about The Who swapping pop's renegade thrill for rock's monumental self-regard, the chances are that the eternally querulous Townshend thought of it first. In the sleeve-notes he wrote in *Rolling Stone* magazine for their brilliant 1972 singles compilation *Meaty, Beaty, Big and Bouncy*, Pete Townshend observed presciently that this was 'the greatest of Who albums', bearing in mind that when the band started out, 'albums were what you got for Christmas, singles were what you bought for prestige'.

That The Who's heftiest consumer durable should come adorned with pictures of vandalised amplifiers seemed like a final irony, but the band's contradictions had always been deeply ingrained. When Townshend first wrote the words 'Hope I die before I get old', he was proclaiming the joy of the moment, not looking to the future. It wasn't The Who's fault that their celebration of built-in obsolescence was built to last.

Even the classic Pop Art identity crisis which the band's name appeared to embody was not as clear-cut as it appeared. Townshend, the art-school theorist who should have been delighted by such a notion, preferred the rather less conceptually pleasing The Hair. This was not the end of the confusion. Townshend's nervy, volatile lyrics were to be given voice by the lusty Roger Daltrey, a former apprentice welder. The band's outstanding instrumentalist was their drummer, and much of the credit for their extravagant guitar sound was due to their relatively unassuming bassist, John Entwistle.

Furthermore, for all The Who's air of street-gang solidarity, outsiders – first pill-popping mod avatar Pete Meaden, then flamboyant co-managers Kit Lambert and Chris Stamp – were crucial in formulating their identity. 'Pete was the only one of us you could really describe as a mod,' Daltrey remembers. 'It's quite hysterical to think that John Entwistle or Keith Moon could ever be described as mods, and I was just a ted in mod's clothing, as simple as that.'

Somehow, though, they managed to make a sound that captured

the mixture of outward flash and inner turmoil that was the mod condition, at the exact moment that the movement went nationwide. A decade and a half later, when *Quadrophenia* came out, the beat which slams into the recycled Kinks riff at the start of 'I Can't Explain' could still jerk the most sceptical head into a Phil Daniels nod. A fully-fledged mod revival was set in train, and it would be some years before squirrels could again walk safely in the streets of east London.

If ever there was to be a case of band frozen for ever in a celluloid paperweight, The Who and *Quadrophenia* should have been it: like sleeping beauty, except ugly. But twenty years on, the slumbering monster was awoken with a kiss. In the summer of 1999 the sublimely off-beat US high school comedy *Rushmore* featured a virtuoso sequence in which an escalating feud between Bill Murray and the film's charismatic teenage lead Jason Schwartzman was cut to The Who's 'A Quick One'.

Writer/director Wes Anderson explained in the sleevenotes to the soundtrack album that he had originally intended to employ only the music of The Kinks, on the grounds that they 'played loud angry teenage rock songs and wore blazers and ties', but later 'expanded this concept to include the whole British invasion, because they all basically dressed like that'. Thus the shock of The Who was experienced anew, and with one more good rhyme, we'd have a limerick.

When Spike Lee's *Summer of Sam* came out a few months later, Townshend and co's cinematic renaissance took a strange new turn. In putting their music at the centre of his mischievous paean to the punk rock summer of '77 (the film's climactic sequence is brilliantly choreographed to 'We Don't Get Fooled Again') Lee seemed to be making a deliberate mistake – perhaps hoping to get under the skin of a new super-annuated punker constituency, in the same way that his bungling small-time hoods were calculated to annoy his friends in the Italian-American community.

In fact, his depiction of The Who as punk pioneers was not entirely without foundation. Earlier in the seventies, they had challenged fellow British road-pigs Led Zeppelin and The Rolling Stones as setters of new standards – if that is the right word – in old-school rock debauchery. By the time punk hit, they should have been the enemy, but The Sex Pistols still cut their teeth on the primal garage angst of 'Substitute' and 'I'm a Boy'. And in a memorable chance encounter in a Soho drinking establishment, Pete Townshend once ranted at Paul Cook and Steve Jones that The Who were 'prostitutes'. 'Don't break up,' came the earnest reply. 'You're our favourite group.'

A third film released in the UK in this same halcyon five-month period – Sam Mendes' Oscar-winning *American Beauty* – also used the music of The Who. But not in an especially clever or interesting way. Oh well, as Meat Loaf would have it, 'Two out of three ain't bad.'

The important thing is the way true pop genius lurks in the collective subconscious like seeds in the Namib desert patiently waiting to be fertilised.

In Bed With Madonna

In heroic contravention of Jung's Iron Law Of Pub Conversation (there's nothing more boring than other people's dreams), Kay Turner's book *I Dream of Madonna* details fifty women's night-time encounters with the queen of pop.

In her theoretical introduction, Turner speaks of Madonna appearing to people as a 'sisterly companion' rather than a superstar. This is not strictly true, since even in the many dreams here where Madonna does not acknowledge her own celebrity, the dreamer is always aware of it. Yet the complex relationships between dreamers and dreamee illuminate aspects of fandom that clichés of unthinking dependency obscure.

Most of the contributors are not teenagers but mature women, from the author's circle of professionals and academics. They feel protective of Madonna, and take pleasure in her success. Erica (35) dreams of her speaking at a charity function: 'They know she isn't an idiot and are interested in what she has to say on this subject.' Monica (27) approaches Madonna and says: 'Let me take you away from all this' (the great woman's reaction to this rather disreputable pick-up line is not recorded). All is not cosy sisterliness, though. A grandmother (61) feels at a low ebb, and Madonna tells her she looks a mess.

Even the most bizarre of the dreams – Janet (33) worries about Madonna and Sandra Bernhard working in a frozen chicken factory; Michelle (27) fetches her a baby sheep – seem perfectly logical next to some of the responses she elicits from people who are awake. One of the collages with which Kay accompanies her dream texts features a cutting from an American tabloid, in which a psychic medium claims to have spoken to Madonna's dead mother, who has informed her that her daughter is cursed by the devil and will burn in hell.

A Brief Note on Titular Inspiration

(Those of a nervous disposition should probably proceed directly over the page to the place where it says At Last, To Business.)

From the moment of its first publication in 1972, John Berger's slim volume *Ways of Seeing* was acclaimed as an intellectual landmark, and would one day become a cornerstone of the bizarre and unnatural practice of cultural studies – an outrageous confidence trick perpetrated on the taxpayer by those cunning enough to build careers out of the stuff that everybody else does for a hobby.

Of course, there is nothing implicitly wrong with building careers out of the stuff that everyone else does for a hobby – in fact it is one of the chief objectives of modern life – but those who are lucky enough to have pulled it off should at least have the decency to own up to it. Simon Frith defines popular culture as a field wherein 'no one needs to be licensed by study or qualification to speak authoritatively', which puts those whose *job* it is to speak authoritatively about it in a pretty difficult position. And quite right too. In other respects their lives are easy enough.

Anyway, coming upon Berger's ground-breaking investigation into the effects paintings and photographs have on us in a museum bookshop almost three decades on, the first reaction of the idle peruser (well, this one anyway) was how forbidding and arid it seemed to the contemporary reader. The second was what a good idea it would be to use it as the springboard for a similarly far-reaching survey of pop aesthetics, based on an entirely contradictory set of critical principles, thereby doing for music what you might imagine John Berger's *Ways of Seeing* did for the visual image, if you hadn't actually read it.

The intent of this unauthorised companion volume would not be to disparage Berger's work. *Ways of Hearing*'s assumptions and prejudices will no doubt seem just as ridiculous to readers in thirty years time (if not sooner), and playing chicken with posterity is at least half the fun of any critical judgement. But by rediscovering the links between art and individual personality which *Ways of Seeing* was blind to, it would hope to free the fun-loving spirit of intellectual critical inquiry from academe's tyrannical harness. As well as providing the perfect platform for expressing anxiety about the plinky-plunk totalitarianism of Jools Holland's turn of the century TV persona (see pages 23–4).

WOH vs SYOP

While this author's first book, *Seven Years of Plenty: A Handbook of Irrefutable Pop Greatness 1991–1998*, focussed on a specific time-frame in the hope of giving the recent past a bit of well-earned mythic resonance, this second volume reaches back deep into pop history in pursuit of the eternal present. (Any readers with philosophical objections to the concept of temporal dislocation are directed, as Austin Powers was by Michael York's Basle Exposition in *The Spy Who Shagged Me*, to 'just relax and enjoy it'.) It both ends where its predecessor starts, and picks up where it finishes.

The two books are intended to be mutually complementary rather than dependent on each other for survival. It is hoped that their relationship will be that of egg and chips – able to stand on their own but combining to magical effect – rather than that of the two tubes in a pack of Araldite, which have to be mixed together in order to stick properly.

At Last, to Business

Ways of Hearing is split into three sections. It begins with five preliminary investigations into some of the indirect means by which we tap into the pop psyche (and it taps into us). At a time when progress is constantly blurring the boundaries between previously distinct media, ultimately promising to deliver all cultural sustenance through a single screen, this seems a topical area of enquiry. Not in an I-remember-when-all-this-were-nobbut-fields type of way, but as a challenge to future technologies to match their predecessors for depth and multiplicity of nuance.

In *Ways of Hearing*'s middle segment, the pop psyche takes human shape in the form of a celestial chorus. Neil Young rubs shoulders with Lee Perry, Kelis makes out with Sir Cliff Richard and Lemmy from Motorhead gets down with The Beta Band. Five further essays then expand underlying themes upwards and outwards, drawing them back together in the hope of broadening an understanding of how music helps us define ourselves, both inside our heads and out in the cruel world.

Kodwo Eshun's book *More Brilliant Than the Sun* coins the memorable phrase 'the import ear' to describe the way in which the weedy voices of early eighties UK synth pop were able to speak directly to underground black music-makers in Detroit at the dawn of the Techno epoch. In tribute to the perspicacity of this formulation, and in grateful acknowledgement of the fundamental simplicity of the act of listening, the third part of *Ways of Hearing* will be, quite literally, all ears.

Where the Cover of Pink Floyd's *The Dark Side of the Moon* Comes Into It

This book's essential dynamic is – like so many aspects of life – most easily understood with reference to the cover of Pink Floyd's *The Dark Side of the Moon* . . . the single light beam coming in from the left being the different conduits via which music is delivered to us, the central prism being the personality, the soul even, of listener or performer, and the rightward-flowing spectrum being the way music relates to its broader human context.

What was that Bit at the Very Beginning About a Sonic Cathedral Again?

The phrase 'sonic cathedral' had a brief – and instantly debased – currency in the British music press of the early nineties. It started life as a means of describing music that aspired to achieve something which words could not express, and then mutated into a joke about the high levels of pretension often inherent in such projects, and in writers' attempts to interpret them. A tacit admission of the inadequacy of the critical apparatus thereby became – as it has done so often – a means of undervaluing creative endeavour.

In the attempt to right this wrong, and atone for all those moments when a critical judgement is made with less energy and scrupulousness and sense of wonder than went into the artefact it refers to, *Ways of Hearing* really does want to build a sonic cathedral.

BT
Hackney Downs
Easter 2000

n.b. This book is respectfully dedicated to all those who fall within the clammy embrace of its overheated rhetoric, and with thanks for their input – witting or otherwise – to Nicola Barker, Eugene Manzi, Mark Heley, Tom Baker, Craig McLean, Jon Savage, James Brown, Dennis and Edna, Russell Davies, Shabs, Mark Sinker, Carlton B. Morgan, Laurence Earle, Simon Petty, Jessamy Calkin, Heather Hodson, Nick Coleman, Francesca Ryan, Mark Wilson, Matt Reynolds, Chris Sharp and last, but not least, Ian Preece.

Contents

The Beam/The Conduits/The Nave

.

Radio

'Who knows but that, on the lower frequencies, I speak for you?'
Ralph Ellison: *Invisible Man*

Travelling in New Zealand, when 'Our Tune' was still little more than a twinkle in Satan's eye, Simon Bates had a job artificially inseminating cattle. 'The insemination process,' Bates explains, clutching the cafetiere in which he makes his own coffee, 'demands rubber gloves, a certain amount of muscular activity with your right arm, and sensitivity towards the cow, because the intrusion isn't always welcome.'

The intrusion isn't always welcome . . . if the story of the radio DJ could be said to have a moral, this would probably be it. A proper history of the medium of pop radio would delve back to its beginnings in Martin Block's pioneering 1940s California DJ show – resonantly named 'The Make-Believe Ballroom' – and move through rock 'n' roll and Alan Freed's death by payola to the seminal moment in Otley in 1946 when Jimmy Savile invented turntablism,[4] onto the British pirate radio explosion of the late eighties and early nineties.

But that history already exists, in the form of Bill Brewster and Frank Broughton's highly entertaining and deceptively exhaustive *Last Night A DJ Saved My Life*, so this one is going to strike out into less well charted and – cynics might argue – tautologous territory, by endeavouring to penetrate the DJ's very soul. In order to do this, it will be necessary to spend a while longer in the company of Simon Bates.

At the time of the encounter recorded here, the erstwhile Radio 1 coffee-time overlord addresses the issues of the moment every weekday on Talk Radio UK. Earlier this particular morning, his familiar treacly tones could be heard delivering an unexpectedly seditious sermon on the subject of a graffiti tagger who has been sent to prison. 'What is the law if it is not an ass? What is society if it is not stupid? Is that contempt of court? Yes it is. Good.'

Simon Bates' first job at the BBC was as a Radio 4 newsreader and continuity announcer. 'I was very bad at it too,' he admits. 'I never mastered the art of saying "Radio 4" between the end of one programme and the start of the next. If you try it, it's really very difficult.' He tries it. It really is very difficult.

He had problems with newsreading too. 'I'm not very good with facts. And Michael Aspel once told me that to be a good newsreader the stuff has to go in through the eyes, out through the mouth and bypass the brain, otherwise you'd realise the enormity of what you were saying.'

But isn't that – if you leave out the enormity bit – the essence of radio DJ-hood: that he or she should have their personal opinion, but somehow it wouldn't be relevant?

Bates guffaws. 'I think that's the most intelligent thing I could say about 17 years at Radio 1. The broadcaster's opinion doesn't matter.'

But how does that make a man feel?

'You mean, does it seem like a negation of yourself? No, not at all . . .'

Talk Radio UK's original daytime schedule showcased the razor-sharp mental reflexes of Caesar the Geezer, a man once heard to say, 'People think I'm stupid but actually I'm a member of Mencap.' Needless to say, the station got off to a rocky start.

'When this station started there was obviously a strong trans-Atlantic influence,' Simon Bates continues. 'The Americans came over here and said, "Well, this works in Dumbfuck, Idaho [Warning: an off- air conversation with Simon Bates will contain some sexual swear-words]" . . . Of course it won't work here, why in God's name would they think it would?

'The difference between the corporate structures of British and American radio,' Bates explains, is that ours 'stems from a Protestant ethic in the thirties, a propaganda effort in the Second World War, a sense of oneness and a sense of nation.' America, on the other hand, was the only country in the world where radio wasn't identified from the beginning as a branch of government. Consequently, radio there is 'much more accessible: it's all about being open to all-comers. If you take the two skeletons,' Bates concludes, 'I don't think there's any connection between them.'

What about the original pirates?

'The pirates believed they sounded American, but actually they always sounded just like British people – they were slightly . . . *nervous.*'

John Peel was a pirate once – enjoying a short-lived spell at Radio London before becoming Radio 1's voice of the underground when the national station launched in 1967. In the early sixties, his dad had sent him to America because he thought he lacked direction. It didn't take him long to find one.

'I was driving back from New Orleans,' Peel recalls in that familiar scouse mumble. 'I'd gone there with a couple of mates. We used to follow the fortunes of a girl called Chris Colt: The Girl With the Two 45's – we'd trail her from awful strip joint to awful strip joint, getting deservedly ripped off along the way. Anyway, I'd wearied of Chris Colt and I was driving home through the Piney Woods of Texas and the road was dead straight through the trees with the moon at the far end of it, so I was driving along this kind of silver ribbon through the woods, and it was fantastically beautiful.'

This is not the first time John Peel has told this story (apologies are due to anyone who has come across it elsewhere), but as he tells it his face is lit from within by an almost religious radiance. 'I was listening to [legendary US DJ] Wolfman Jack and he played a great song by Elmore James called "Stranger Blues", which I hadn't heard before. The words go "I'm a stranger here, I just drove in your town" and just as I heard them for the first time, I drove over a ridge into this little town, and I thought, "This is the most perfect moment."' He pauses for a long overdue breath. 'Even the fact that I can describe it now in such wearisome detail shows how clearly I remember it. And I've always hoped that some of the music I play might have the same effect on other people.'

He looks up from the Peel Acres kitchen table and smiles at his wife, whom he habitually addresses by the ungallant soubriquet 'Pig' on account of her infectious snorting laugh, though she's actually on the willowy side of slender. (In fact the only member of the household with any tendency toward the porcine is the man who sits down at the table and begs her for an extra piece of cheese. 'I wish she was a crap cook and didn't make such good sandwiches,' Peel says, disingenuously, 'then I should be slim and lovely.')

The reason this conversation is taking place inside John Peel's lovely home is that a previous attempt to speak to him at his Radio 1 studio has ended in disaster. To say that he goes completely to pieces would be a slight exaggeration, but only after he has endeavoured to remove several singles in mid-transmission, misplaced a session tape and had to play two tracks in a row from the same Captain Beefheart record because he's forgotten to get the next selection ready, does Peel reveal that he can't cope with strangers in the studio while he's working. After all, he's only been doing this job for a third of a century.

On reflection, perhaps his strangely disembodied studio demeanour is a proper reflection of his calling: why should he waste time talking to strangers when so many friends out there in the ether require his undivided attention?

Enough of the people who have underestimated John Peel in the past are currently sleeping with the fishes to make one suspect that his bumbling, slightly curmudgeonly public image is a cunning smoke-screen designed to lull potential rivals into a false sense of security. Behind the lovingly maintained (and oh so conveniently true) myth of the regular guy whose greatest indulgence is the odd trip to the football and a mushroom biryani, lurks one of the most splendidly devious careers in the history of media manipulation. If Madonna and Peter Mandelson went to college, John Peel wrote all their text-books.

This, after all, is the punk-rock hero who began his show-business career in America, cashing in on Beatlemania by swapping his public school accent for homespun Liverpudlian; the presenter of an award-winning Radio 4 programme about family values who was once (again, in his US wildman period) briefly married to a fifteen-year-old girl; the untainted icon of underground integrity who paid for his tennis court by doing adverts for Andrex toilet tissue.

The apparent inconsistency in Peel's approach to his own career and those of the people whose music he plays (or doesn't) does not seem to trouble him.[5] 'There's nothing wrong with inconsistency,' Peel insists, 'if I was consistent I'd still be playing Melanie records. Around the time of my return to Britain,' he continues, 'music had . . . I think the proper word is bifurcated. One minute there was nothing inconsistent in buying a Pink Floyd single and, oh, I don't know, a Ruby Murray single, the next you had Led Zeppelin refusing to release anything on 7-inch.'

That kind of thing seems pretty stupid now, doesn't it?

'I agreed with it at the time, though,' he laughs, 'and when people go to gigs they should sit on the floor and listen in reverential silence . . . but then you grow up a bit and you realise that's all bollocks.'

Joe Strummer once said, 'Listening to John Peel is like having a dog be sick in your face.'

'Ah,' Peel smiles knowingly, 'but it depends at what stage in his career he said it. If it was around the time of The Clash's first album, he might have meant it as a compliment . . . if it was later on, he might have been annoyed that I'd stopped playing his records.'

You don't have to fully agree with his friend and former producer John Walters' assessment of Peel as 'the single most important individual in the development of British rock music' to see a vital heritage that would not have existed in the same way without him. The root of Peel's loyalty to the people he's stuck with – the Beefhearts and the Mark E. Smiths and the Ivor Cutlers of this world – is that 'in their own different ways they have a poetic vision that goes way beyond anything I've ever had or could have . . . they just *know* more than I do.'

In the light of this, it's strange that he's always seemed hostile to anything too clever. 'I've tended to follow the words of John Lennon,' Peel grins, '"the avant-garde is French for bullshit." I'll hear two records that to the casual listener would sound pretty much the same, but some people do things because they kind of have to, and others will do them as an art statement.'

And the work of the latter wouldn't be as appealing to him?

'Not really no.'

So does that make John Peel a bit of a philistine on the quiet?

'There's nothing on the quiet about it: I'm quite happy to be called a philistine. I like rousing vulgarity and distortion and excess. I've never made a conscious effort to find stuff that was weird and unlistenable, it was just what I liked.'

The Peel–Bates Schism: Manichean Dichotomy or Faustian Smokescreen?

The antipathy between Simon Bates and John Peel is the stuff of legend. One of many arresting anecdotes in *The Nation's Favourite*, Simon Garfield's riveting journalist-on-the-wall account of Matthew Bannister's brutal purge of Radio 1's *ancien regime*, concerns the infamous occasion on which Peel and a group of drunken colleagues lay in wait for Bates in a BBC car-park after a Radio 1 Christmas Party in the hope of engineering a physical confrontation. As seductive as the prevailing view is of Peel versus Bates as a straightforward battle between good and evil, everyman bluntness and showbiz insincerity, it does not really tally with the facts of the case.

Before you can understand why, you've got to consider Garfield's book in greater depth. On first sight, its heady mix of voices seems to replicate the casual chaos of the turning radio dial. The format – all direct speech, like a screenplay without stage directions – takes a bit of getting used to. The sudden cuts between edited interviews, radio transcripts and overheard meetings are hard to keep pace with, but gradually the reader learns to stop trying, and a compelling momentum begins to build up as different streams of language[6] – the calculated outrageousness of self-aggrandising broadcasters, the anodyne cruelty of official memos, the fatal innocence of the focus group – come together in a single river. What emerges is a strange and intriguing parallel universe; a place where tabloid showbiz editors talk intelligently and in sentences and the wisdom of the ages comes from the mouth of Dave Lee Travis.

But it's when you start to separate these streams back out again that things really begin to get interesting, and that's where the Manichean dichotomy bit comes in.

When Simon Bates appears at the start of a hired video warning viewers that the film they are about to watch contains 'some sexual swear-words', no one has any reason to doubt that he means it. (This purity of identification does have its compensations: thanks to the hard work of the video pirate community, the Bates visage has – in fact *is* – global currency. 'I can get a free meal in Delhi or a free drink in Moscow anytime I want,' he says happily, and the supreme frugality of his radio show's travel tips – 'Guess how much I paid for that insurance!' – suggests this might be more than just a figure of speech.)

For Peel on the other hand, separating his voice from his soul has enabled him to sell one without mortgaging the other. Any questions hanging in the air about the propriety of such enterprises as being the voice of the Marmite baby are deflected in the classic Peelite manner. He didn't do an advert for Ford dealers because he 'doesn't like people who drive Fords', but then he was very happy to do Vimto, 'because it is the only thing you can drink with chips . . . it has that chemical quality to cut through the layer of fat that forms on the inside of your mouth.'

Pepperami and Andrex followed ('that went on for so long that every time people heard my voice they wanted to wipe their bottom'), even Threshers wine merchants – 'My mother used to spend a good deal of her money there,' Peel explains, 'and I wanted some of it back.'

The common and crucial feature that unites Peel's many commercial clients is that they have nothing to do with music. 'If someone wants to buy Vimto because I suggest they should, that's fine,' Peel explains, 'because it's got nothing to do with me. But if someone listens to my show and thinks there's a certain oafish honesty to it, then it would be wrong for me to use that to convince them to buy records by a band I don't like.'

In the Faustian separate-your-voice-from-your-soul contract, it is important – both for yourself and others – to set some kind of limit from the start (as all those who have filled their homes with dodgy indie compilations advertised by Steve Lamacq or Jo Whiley will sorrowfully testify).

Nose to Nose With the Radio Incubus

The American 'shock-jock' Howard Stern takes pride in setting himself no limits whatsoever. Monstrously tall and improbably good-looking – far from the self-confessed über-geek of pre-infamy infamy – this is the man of whom Cher has said, 'I hate him, he's just a creep.'[7] As a hairdresser fluffs up his luxurious curls for the benefit of a passing photographer, Stern muses on the distinction between the incubus and the succubus (the former is a male demon who has sex with sleeping women, the latter is a female demon who has sex with sleeping men).

Stern's radio career has been built upon the proposition that a woman's value to a largely male listenership is inversely proportional to the number of clothes she has on, while his private life has been a model of domestic probity and responsible parenthood. So how does he maintain the obnoxious façade that has endeared him to millions?

'It's in real life that I feel like I'm role-playing,' Stern explains gravely. 'It's only when I'm on the radio that I feel like I'm really me.'

So the public mask *is* the real man, it's the home-loving private individual who is the despicable fake?

'It is, it is, I know that. I mean, where do you think the stuff I do on the radio comes from? All day I walk around with that shit locked in my head and I'm really controlling it. I can't even pick up the phone and complain to the phone company – I have my wife do that. It's only when I get on the air that I finally get to be the man that I am inside.'

The conventional lapsed liberal position on Howard Stern is that his are the dark impulses that lurk inside all of us, and even though the social consequences of airing these feelings on a daily basis may not be entirely beneficial, it would be more dangerous to bottle them up. Howard Stern's position on Howard Stern is that the man is truly evil and the world would be better off if he was in a Turkish prison. 'That's right!' He leaps out of his seat in his excitement, all but head-butting his hairdresser in the process, 'That is the correct assessment.

'It's not like I've only stayed with my wife because I want to say "Hey, fuck you" to everyone who thinks I'm a sleazebag,' Howard continues. 'It's just interesting that this is the one thing they can't attack . . .'

But he does conciously use his squeaky-clean domestic profile to wind people up?

'Oh yes, sure. Absolutely.'

This will not come as news to those lucky enough to have caught Stern's memorable barbecueing of Chris Evans on *TFI Friday*. Britain's most notorious Howard Stern wannabe could have had a long-lasting marriage like his inspiration, Howard counselled him, 'but you had to go and be with all your sluts.'

Listening to Mark Radcliffe sitting in for the aforementioned Mr Evans on the Radio 1 breakfast show in late 1996, it was hard to escape the conclusion that the nation's pop radio culture was in an uncommonly healthy state.

Before getting listeners to fax in translations of the Welsh-language coda to the classic Gorky's Zygotic Mynci single, 'Patio Song', Radcliffe played a sophisticated (no, really) game called 'Bird or Bloke'. Contestants were asked to guess the genders of the following – AA Milne, BB King, Ce Ce Peniston, Dee Dee Ramone and ee cummings – and the first caller got it right. Would this have happened in Mike Read's day? It seems unlikely.

Sitting in was one thing and taking over was another. In many ways Radcliffe's eventual appointment as full-time replacement for Evans was the logical culmination of all the changes Matthew Bannister had wrought at Radio 1. In its blend of irreverence, erudition and enthusiasm, the grizzled Mancunian's late-evening show epitomised all that was best in the revitalised network; and to shift him into the key early-morning slot was a bold stroke typical of the one-time *Newsbeat* reporter who was now calling the shots.

'It's always struck me as odd,' Radcliffe observes, just after coming off the air in his first week in the job, 'that the people who are let on air to talk with a free microphone and no script should have nothing to say. On Radio 4 you've got a load of people with Oxbridge degrees reading words that are scripted for them by Oxbridge-degree people 20 years younger than them. Then in the past on Radio 1 you've had people – mentioning no names here obviously – without an intelligent thought in their heads, being encouraged to say whatever they want. I think the powers that be have cottoned on to the fact that if you're going to have people talking live without scripts it's better to have someone who knows something.'

The appointment to the highest profile position in British radio of a man who could be brought to book by a tabloid newspaper for 'encouraging Blur's Damon Albarn to talk about Herman Hesse' was always going to have its controversial side (especially once Radcliffe and his sidekick Mark 'Lard' Riley had decided to strike a blow for the power of the regions by refusing to move down to London). 'There is very little evidence of culture in the programme so far,' Radcliffe maintains defensively, 'though sometimes I'll turn to Lard with a minute and a half to go to the news and say: "What about Le Corbusier's *Modular*?" And he'll come straight back with: "It's ill-conceived."' Lard smiles. 'Or I might just say "bollocks". . . We can be childish and inane. We do make the effort.

'There's really only one way things can go from here,' Radcliffe admits, 'and that's down, but that's really liberating in a way. There's something rather compelling about failure on a grand scale. It's like if you're in a band: you can't help but be fascinated by the idea of going on at Madison Square Garden and being shit.'

Unfortunately, once the novelty of hearing a Radio 1 breakfast show being trailed as 'the best way to start the day – apart from listening to other radio stations, reading a newspaper or just not saying anything at all, really', had worn off, the British public began to take Radcliffe's self-deprecation at face value. People would set off to work in the morning muttering 'If he plays another boring record by David Devant and his Spirit Wife I'm going to kill myself', and it was left to Zoë Ball – Noel Edmonds' spiritual daughter – to restore the nation's equilibrium with insights into her exciting showbiz lifestyle and jokes about going to the toilet.

Radcliffe came through his ordeal relatively unscathed, if with cause to reflect that while popular culture might theoretically embody the tension between genius and democracy, it is democracy that tends to take up the slack. Sympathetically relocated to an early afternoon slot more conducive to their combined vocal timbre, he and Lard (whose supporting role had been eerily prefigured by his fine 1983 single 'Shadow Figure' in the guise of Mark Riley and The Creepers) accepted the iron discipline of the playlist, and focussed their energies on institutionalising underachievement with their band The Shirehorses and characters such as Fat 'Arry White – a lubricious soul lothario whose obscene Walrus-of-Love-style innuendo gradually degenerates into a comedy Northern accent.

While not being in himself in any way amusing, Fat 'Arry White sheds an eerie new light on one of the fundamental issues in the history of pop radio. In 1947, *Ebony* magazine noted the new vistas opening up to black Americans in radio broadcasting on the grounds that 'a voice has no colour'[8].

If subsequent developments in the medium (from the raft of white DJs – including Peel's inspiration Wolfman Jack, and Memphis legend Dewey Phillips and his mad gorilla-masked performance artist associate Harry Frizius – who successfully adapted black DJs' jive talk to their own specifications, to the bizarre case of Vernon Winslow, a black man employed to teach the white DJ whose job he'd been turned down for how to sound like him) were to prove anything, it was the inaccuracy of this observation.

Half a century or so later, erstwhile Kiss FM breakfast overlord Steve Jackson took his former employer to court, alleging that the pioneering expirate dance station had sacked him, their only surviving black DJ, on the grounds of his colour.[9] By a happy twist of fate, as Kiss doggie-paddled desperately towards the mainstream, Radio 1 was striking out boldly the other way, employing ace black UK Garage mechanics the Dreem Team – Mikey B, Timmi Magic and DJ Spoony – to bolster their weekend schedules' proud claim to be the home of the UK dance underground.

The Dreem Team broadcast on a Sunday morning, when – like all self-respecting scions of the UK dance underground – they are somewhat prone to tiredness. But their genially hungover blend of rap, garage and contemporary r'n'b is so sublimely engaging that, at the dawn of the twenty-first century, The Make-Believe Ballroom is again made a wondrous reality.

TV

Documentary film-maker Molly Dineen, trying to comfort a little girl moved to tears by the imminent auction of Geri Halliwell's clothes: *But these are only Geri's clothes – the things she wore – all of her isn't here.*
Little girl: *Most of her is though.*

Geri, Channel 4, 1999

'*My mind is tuned to more TV channels than exist in your world.*'
Without Conscience: Charles Manson in his own words, With Nuell Emmons

In 1985, unemployed Holloway club-goer Richard West 'visualised' himself on *Top of the Pops*. Seven years later, that visualisation became a reality, as with recourse to a new identity (Mr C of The Shamen), a bizarre codpiece and a still more outrageous cockney accent, he performed the immortal chorus 'E's are good e's are good 'e's Ebeneezer Goode' to an audience of millions.

The fact that the BBC's flagship TV pop show was at that point subject to one of its innumerable changes of format – specifically designed to keep people like him off the screen – only made Richard West's triumph more complete. The memory of his gurning visage demanding 'Has anybody got any Veras?' overshadows all other recollections of that particular edition, except one of the presenters at the time – a large man who used to say 'Laters' a lot – despairingly proclaiming, 'Tasmin Archer is going to be really big.' (Which, of course, she was.)

'If you have a dream,' Mr C says a few years afterwards, 'don't hope it's going to come true, *know* it's going to happen. Say hypothetically, on a material level, you want a car: don't just think you want a car, know what car, what make, what model, what colour, even visualise the registration on the plate – the more specific you are, the more chance there is of it becoming a reality.'

Richard West gives much of the credit for his transformation from teenage gluesniffer to TV folk devil to a book called *The Power of Positive Thinking*, which his step-father gave him for his eighteenth birthday. The role of self-help literature in the history of pop music is hard to overestimate (honorary Beach Boy Charles Manson first met his future ghost-writer Nuell Emmons while trying to convince him of the benefits of scientology in a California prison yard; Rastafarian hardcore legends The Bad Brains took inspiration from Napoleon Hill's *Think and Grow Rich*).

But the traffic went both ways, as the true story of scientology's floating showband makes clear. In the latter stages of his extraordinary career – some time after he tried to take over the Rhodesian economy but before the publication of his last novel *Battlefield Earth* – godfather of dianetics, L. Ron Hubbard, found himself in charge of his own private navy. The flagship of his motley fleet, a handsome 3280 ton vessel called *The Apollo*, was moored off the port of Funchal in Portugal, when the commodore decided the time had come to put ashore and lure new recruits with the music of the young people.

As Russell Miller recalls in his admirable history, *Bare-faced Messiah – The True Story of L. Ron Hubbard*, L. Ron believed himself to have a great understanding of popular music, and encouraged those of his followers with pretensions to musical ability to form a band – The Apollo Stars – who would serenade the youth of Portugal from the deck of the ship with music designed to the commodore's specifications.

One of the musicians described what happened: 'The band was terrible, awful; it was the most embarrassing thing I have ever done.' The Portugese were not too keen either: in the ensuing riot two of the ship's crew's cars were overturned and thrown into the sea amid scenes of mayhem that would not be equalled until the Jesus and Mary Chain played the Camden Electric Ballroom.

In other matters L. Ron Hubbard's judgement was more or less infallible. What was the root of his musical misapprehension? His theories of pop music were, Miller explained, based on 'hours of watching TV in Queens'. Historical proof, if more were needed, that the experience of music through television is not – whatever the makers of Nicam digital stereo would have you believe – the same as the experience of music on its own.

A random burst of early nineties Tuesday-night TV. Eastender Sharon Mitchell, temporarily off the leash from her possessive husband Grant, goes to a college rock gig with Michelle Fowler and learns to like the band as she gets drunker. Later a male student (just the sort of dangerous middle-class interloper of whom the denizens of Albert Square have always had good reason to be suspicious) woos her by singing 'Time To Go Home', the closing theme from *Andy Pandy*.

Half an hour on, in a repeat of *Citizen Smith*, an old schoolfriend of Wolfie's returns to Tooting claiming to be a successful rock impresario, and plunges the Popular Front into chaos by holding auditions for a band he intends to manufacture with a view to cornering the American market. They will be called Rat and (in ever more eerie prophesy of eighties LA false-metal legends Ratt) will be 'a cross between punk rock and the Osmonds'. The shrewd understanding of music business practice demonstrated in this episode is further compounded by the fact that the impresario turns out to be on the run from the law.

Without getting into a pointless – if enjoyable – argument about which of our two pre-eminent cultural manifestations (music and TV) is ultimately the more potent, there can be no doubt about which is wearing the trousers when one is being broadcast as an aspect of the other.

But the fact that music on TV is an integral part of a larger experience does not mean that it has no life of its own. When an anguished letter in the *Daily Mirror*'s weekly TV supplement mourned 1991's sacriligious up-dating of the theme to *Emmerdale*, this was plainly part of a larger disquiet about the dropping of the key 'Farm' element in the programme's title, the new racy storylines and the depopulation of rural areas; yet the musical complaint was strong enough to stand on its own. Aesthetically, this *was* something of an outrage – new brooms having done away with the Vaughan Williams sweep of the original and replaced it with a charmless Brooksided-up electro hiccup, lacking even the Orchestral Manoeuvres in the Dark pizazz of the original Mersey soap theme.

Who better to speak to about this regrettable turn of events than Tony Hatch, author of not just the original *Emmerdale Farm* theme but twenty other instantly recognisable TV signatures? Hatch – formerly *New Faces'* 'Mr Nasty' – and his wife Jackie Trent (showbiz legend knows them together by the happier domestic soubriquet of 'Mr and Mrs Music') moved to Australia in the 1970s to escape top-rate taxation. Even on the other side of the world, rumbles of discontent from the Yorkshire Dales still reached him.

'I heard that some members of the public aren't too pleased with it,' Hatch admits gruffly of the *Emmerdale* remix, 'but I haven't heard it myself so I can't comment.'

Does it upset him to have his work messed around with?

'The great danger for me is that if they do change it and people don't like the new version, they might get rid of my theme altogether.' Never one to undervalue the importance of a repeat fee, Hatch's personal favourites from his TV canon are the longest runners: the original 'Emmerdale', which would now be in its twenty-first year, and 'Crossroads', which notched up twenty-four years of active service before Central wielded its callous axe (and also had the distinction of being re-recorded by Paul McCartney as a track on *Venus and Mars*).

Perhaps the biggest adrenalin rush of all Hatch's themes is *BBC Sportsnight*. 'That one is brilliantly played,' he notes contentedly. 'It was an eight man brass section – four trumpets and four trombones. I think Tony Fisher was the lead trumpet, and he was really bursting bloodvessels.'

Does Hatch himself have any set working methods?

'Just to get it done as quickly as possible – I normally have some idea of how the tune is going to go from the minute I've finished being briefed by the client.'

This speed of operation was integral in Tony and Jackie's most spectacular colonisation of global consciousness – the theme from *Neighbours*.

When *Crossroads* creator Reg Watson sought submissions for a signature tune for his Grundy Corporation's new down-under soap, a time limit of six weeks was set. Drawing on their own experiences as expatriate Brits warmly welcomed into an Australian community, Hatch and Trent had their tune on Watson's desk the next morning, and the rest was history.

Does he get the same thrill from a TV theme's ability to survive endless ceremonial repetition as he does from the enduring appeal of his classic sixties pop hits 'Downtown' and 'Don't Sleep In The Subway Baby' (as exquisitely performed by Petula Clarke)?

'The two kinds of repetition are different, but yes, definitely. I do view theme writing as an art form. It's very important to set up an interesting motif within the first few seconds, a call signal if you like, to entice the audiences from the other room to the one where the television is.'

Hatch is living refutation of the widely-held belief that TV theme music is the place where pop careers go to die. For subsequent generations, writing TV theme and incidental music has been a merciful release, particularly for those – the Other Two from New Order say, or Eric Clapton – for whom upfront charisma and personal involvement have always been the hardest of pop's qualifications to fulfill. The music they make under these circumstances is the sound of musicians at peace – left, like the masked sonic crusaders of the BBC Radiophonic workshop, to just get on with it.

An artefact like *The Man From Uncle* – a compilation of classic TV themes from 1959's *Danger Man* to *The Tomorrow People* twenty years later (the original, not the remake with Todd from *Neighbours*) – might be marketed as part of the global baby-boom brain-rot conspiracy, but it actually reveals just how worthy a craft is the building and sustaining of small-screen momentum. Listening to the work of such perennially underrated TV composers as Edwin *The Saint* Asteley and Laurie *The Avengers* Johnson alongside more established names like Barry Gray and Lalo Schiffrin, a disciplined heritage of tourniquet-tight arrangements and flamboyant horn and string flourishes comes through loud and clear.

Leaving its televisual baggage in an airport locker, the theme from *Mannix* takes flight as the extraordinary piece of music that it is. It doesn't do to take these things too far out of context though. When

Barry Gray's work for Gerry Anderson's TV puppet shows – some of the first TV themes to be upgraded in status to a musical experience in their own right – was given the symphonic treatment by the Royal Philharmonic Orchestra, the results were not entirely happy.

Formerly accompanist and arranger for Dame Vera Lynn, Gray's experiments with pioneering electronic music devices like the Ondes Martenot (also used by Olivier Messiaen in his Turangilia symphony) and the Miller Spinetta matched the low-budget frontier technology of the series he wrote for. Forsaking that Heath-Robinson charge for the dubious allure of the concert hall made the whole thing seem a bit pointless.

Music that's been made to measure for TV should submerge happily within the medium, not be grafted clumsily over the top, otherwise the viewer is left with the unwelcome sense of being manipulated by an intrusive outside force. The right song in the right place can be devastating – the lovely Noel Gallagher tune at the end of *The Royle Family* gets a lump in the throat almost every time it strikes up – but those making half-assed attempts to half-inch pop resonance can sometimes get their fingers caught in the till.

You're watching some dreary Lucy Gannon TV drama about a teenage runaway when Pulp's 'Babies' comes on the soundtrack at an inappropriate moment, and you can't help but notice how many hundreds of times more cinematic the song is than the wretched assemblage of warmed-over narrative clichés whose impact it is supposed to intensify. This is not an isolated case but an evermore frequent occurence in the increasingly pop-saturated world of TV drama.

In the nineties, soundtrack commodification spread from big screen to small like a nasty case of shingles (oh, all right then, singles). First *Beverley Hills 90210* and *Dawson's Creek* in America, and then *Heartbeat* and *The Lakes* in the UK jumped on the *Reservoir Dogs* and *Trainspotting* bandwagons with their own compact disc accoutrements. Even though it never got its own commemorative album (unless you count Portishead's *Dummy*), the defining moment in Britain's very own TV soundtrack demographic lifestyle conspiracy was probably *This Life*.

One of the many deliciously inauthentic features of Tony Garnett's mercilessly entertaining drama series about a motley crew of young lawyers was the fact that they all had identical taste in music. Not only was this taste far more directional than could reasonably be expected of a group of young legal professionals (whose long working hours and sheltered social backgrounds have historically been more conducive to a fondness for the Eurythmics than Tricky), it was also instrumental in establishing the notion that *This Life* was somehow edgy, risk-taking contemporary drama, rather than the shallow froth we all knew and loved.

When TV professionals realised this meant they no longer had to make series about vets and firemen but could focus on people just like themselves, joy was unconfined. In the ensuing tidal wave of celebratory *bourgeoiserie*, many of society's basic moral guidelines were cruelly swept away. Though the scene in *Cold Feet* where John Thomson and his annoying Irish friend went to a club and tried to buy drugs reached levels of sub-cultural nous not seen since the legendary episode of *Quincy* where the pathologist came face to face with the full horror of LA punk.

It's not just in drama that the linkage of music and visual images has unexpected ramifications. Consider that controversial innovation in TV sports coverage – the pop soundtracked highlights medley: the snooker player's trick shots and crowd-pleasing facial tics martialled to the sound of Elton John's 'I'm Still Standing'; the darts champion's triumphant march through the qualifying round, choreographed to Joe Cocker and Jennifer Warnes singing 'Up Where We Belong'. Initially this seemed like an insult to the purity of sporting endeavour, but now it is an accepted part of the TV experience, which has started to impact on pop history in strange and magical ways.

It is unlikely that Big Beat would have ever existed in the form that we eventually came to know it in the late nineteen nineties without the need to design music for *Match of the Day*'s 'Goal Of The Month' medley. Something was happening inside the grounds too. As stadium PA technology improved, the old days of the club secretary's hand-held tape recorder playing 'We Are The Champions' at half-time gave way to a new era of sonic exactitude and 'Wonderwall'.[10]

While the beneficial effect of acid house (or more properly Ecstasy) on terrace etiquette has already been widely noted[11], the equally dramatic impact of the communal experience of music in football crowds on the wide-screen tendencies of late-nineties pomp pop – from The Verve to The Stereophonics – is one avenue of intellectual enquiry that remains resolutely unexplored.

TV's sense of pop communion is a more private matter. When a familiar but external musical theme emerges organically in a TV soap – Len Fairclough's niece on *Coronation Street* turning out to be a Joy Division fan, or Truesteppers on the radio in the *Eastenders* café – the excitement we feel is immense. This is because they the characters are listening to the very same thing as we the audience, and the music has taken us momentarily inside their magical world. For some reason only music can do this: outside broadcasts just don't have the same effect.

Watching an open air music festival on the small screen is a strange and (unless it's raining heavily) faintly unsatisfactory experience. Once upon a time, when music on TV was such a precious resource that otherwise sane and reasonable people were happy to video the pop segments of *TV-AM*, the idea of a live broadcast from Glastonbury would have seemed an outlandish fantasy. Now the bands are hardly booked for the Virgin-sponsored two-day festival in Colchester and Staffordshire before the whole thing is parcelled up and pre-sold to one of the profusion of TV channels desperate to pack its late-night schedules with low-cost entertainment.

If you agree with William Burroughs (and there is no reason not to) that a live pop or rock show 'is in fact a rite involving the evocation and transmutation of energy'[12] the exact nature of that transmutation becomes problematic in the case of the televised festival. Those who are sitting at home have simply not made the same commitment to the occasion as those who will be sleeping face down in the mud, and the technical arrangements – cameras, sound booms, etc – which pander to the latter over the former, compromise the integrity of the event.

It's not so much a question of whether the nature of an experience is changed by knowing it will be televised; turning on ITV late at night to see Nirvana's magical version of 'All Apologies' at the 1992 Reading festival is a thrill it would be churlish to deny anyone. But the idea (defined by global multimedia events such as *Live Aid*) of TV acting as a conduit out of the arena and into a broader community raises a number of insurmountable difficulties, as anyone who remembers David Bowie's rendition of the Lord's Prayer at the Freddie Mercury Tribute Concert will sorrowfully testify. Suffice to say that when Joe Strummer attacked the BBC cameras at the Glastonbury Festival in 1999, he was making a political gesture a good deal more prescient than the bandanna he wore on the cover of *Combat Rock*.

For specialist pop TV shows filmed indoors, the key problem has always been the crowd. Given that the audience in shot are representatives – ambassadors, emissaries even – of the audience at home, how they look and how the production treats them are vital factors in the sort of mood the programme will generate.

Watching *Top of the Pops* in the seventies and eighties, before proper zoom lenses had been invented, you would constantly see the camera dolly scything through the crowd, taking out small children and the unfit in some awful paradigm of Darwinian evolution. Happily, the importance of the show as a weekly ritual was sufficient to justify this sacrifice, and the horrific injuries incurred by those who were lucky enough to attend the show's recording could be worn with pride – like battlescars, or a Yakuza's severed finger.

The empty space at the back and sides of the studio audience is the one thing the viewers at home must be stopped from seeing at any cost. It reminds them of a coach station and their own mortality, though not necessarily in that order. An early edition of *The White Room*, Channel 4's short-lived rival to *Later*, featured an old clip of The Specials in some packed club and it was the most exciting thing imaginable, then the shot switched back to the grim white studio with its supposedly postmodern podium dancers and the spaces in the crowd were like air bubbles in the bloodstream.

Of those programmes with the good sense to cram their audiences in tight, Pete Waterman's late-lamented *The Hitman and Her* made instant stars of its stylish local club-goers, *The Word*'s human zoo was a grim realisation of Mrs Thatcher's dream of there being no such thing as society, *CD-UK* hilariously puts its courageous hosts Ant and Dec under actual physical seige from a horde of frenzied pubescents, and *TFI Friday* embodies the cruel class distinction of turn of the century VIP culture by its rigid stratification of the pit – where the bands play and the crowd are herded like recalcitrant camels – and the bar, where predatory women in low-cut tops compete to catch Chris Evans' eye.

Of all the studio crowd scenarios, perhaps the one most urgently demanding remedy is that of the *Later* audience, wherein coachloads of self-satisfied professional types who no longer have time to go to gigs stand around looking unbearably smug and occasionally waving at the camera over Paul Weller's shoulder.

How Jools Holland's Personal Descent into Unalloyed Hubris Mirrored a Subtle Shift in Television's Broader Cultural Economy

'One of the things I don't like about TV,' John Peel has been heard to glower, 'is the preposterous dignity it accords to even the most transitory of programmes.' When he used to host *Top of the Pops* with Kid Jensen in the mid to late nineteen-eighties, the delight the pair took in undermining the medium's spurious pretensions to gravitas was utterly infectious. Did Peel ever regret introducing Big Country as 'the band who put the tree into country'?

'It's wasn't exactly Oscar Wilde,' Peel admits, 'but I did used to enjoy phoning up costumes and saying, "We'd like to do it in the costume of the seventeenth-century French court," because nobody ever asked "why?"'

It was a similar instinctive irreverence that made Jools Holland such a folk hero as presenter of *The Tube*. Never mind how dreadful some of the music he introduced was, this man said 'fuck' on live TV before nine o'clock when it still meant something. But then British television changed, and in the beginning of this change was *The Word*, wherein the frequently thrilling live music counterbalanced the abysmally dispiriting character of almost everything else.

At the time of writing, the new sly sneer which came in around this time is still the dominant tone of terrestrial TV pop discourse – from Steve Wright's supercilious voiceover on *TOTP 2*, to the identity parade round on *Never Mind the Buzzcocks*, where minor pop luminaries whose time in the sun is passed are paid five hundred pounds for the privilege of being humiliated by Sean Hughes.

While *Later*'s apparent devotion to the ideal of musicianly authenticity might seem the polar opposite of this supercilious tendency, it embodies its own brand of contempt in the delusion that there is no form of music so subtle or multi-faceted that it cannot be improved by the addition of Jools Holland's boogie-woogie piano. In later series – around the time Jools was voted twelfth greatest jazz musician in history by a Channel 4 poll – no excuse (Elastica didn't turn up, BB King's head has fallen off) was too flimsy for Jools to whisk on members of his big band.

This trend reached its gruesome apogee on the occasion of Herbie Hancock's *Later* appearance, when Jools insisted the great man should play a duet with him. Obviously for the one-time Miles Davis sideman and all-round musical legend whose band The Headhunters gave us the immortal 'God Made Me Funky', the opportunity to match his talent with the man responsible for the piano solo on 'Cool For Cats' was not to be missed.

Two grand pianos were pushed together and as Jools' valiant barrel-housing could be heard striving valiantly to hold its own against his guest's extraordinarily complex chord structures, the quizzical expression on Hancock's face was magnificently hard to fathom. An educated guess would place its true meaning somewhere between 'A cat may look at a king' and 'I have come to eat your young'.

Ice-T Dream Sequence

In a Channel 4 dressing room, Ice-T is dressing up as a Black Panther. He is powerfully built and his boxer shorts are light in colour, with a subtle stripe. The trousers procured for him by the producers of *Baadasss TV* (the six-week Friday-night series of which he is at this point the co-presenter) are a little on the tight side, but what else would he expect from the makers of *Eurotrash*?

Excepting the odd vital discovery, like the episode of *The Partridge*

Family in which David Cassidy hangs out with a gang of Black Panthers led by Richard Pryor, *Baadasss TV* generally inclines towards the less revolutionary end of the entertainment spectrum.

There is still a subversive element in Ice's ability to juggle different roles for different audiences, to play off reactionary fears against liberal hopes, and vice versa. You don't have to put words into his mouth, you just have to take what he actually says at face value. Harvard lecturer on the topic of free speech and hardcore player from the streets, Ice-T dons an absurd Afro wig and moves from costume to make-up.

As the studio calls him, Ice-T is warming to his now complete Black Panther identity. Under the harsh lights of the set, his leather coat creaking amid a sea of fun-fur, he accepts an offer of a doughnut with humourful bad grace: 'The Man wants me to eat the doughnut,' Ice proclaims with a rhetorical flourish. 'He knows that the vanilla extract is going to bring about heart failure in the black male.'

The Company of Cameramen

While for the viewer the alleviation of loneliness is arguably the greatest of television's many contributions to general social well-being, there is a quality of superstar isolation occasionally captured on the small screen that transcends anything accessible elsewhere. There is something about the presence of a camera crew that can, in the right conditions, act like a magnifying glass to the sun's rays, intensifying the experience of solitude to a supernatural pitch.

When Robbie Williams and Geri Halliwell left Take That and The Spice Girls, they defined themselves from the outset as existentialist paradigms: Robbie by having the cheek to cover George Michael's 'Freedom' when everyone thought they had him pegged as the Andrew Ridgley of the group, Geri by her winningly brazen attempts to make off with Lady Di's wardrobe as a UN goodwill ambassador. But the exact conditions of their respective individual odysseys were captured for ever by two moving TV documentaries, *Geri* and *It Ain't Half Hot, Mum: Robbie Williams On Tour In America*.

There is something about the artificial authenticity of the fly on the wall documentary form that marries perfectly with the deliriously disembodied character of the pop promotional experience. The look on Geri's face when she found out her family hadn't bothered watching her UN address on Sky TV, or the sound of Robbie's mum's answering-machine messages hoping that he was OK, are the most affecting representations of the loneliness of the long distance pop star since David Bowie's in *The Man Who Fell To Earth*.

Over a long period, the company of camera-crews can have an intriguingly intoxicating effect, placing the individual in a heady articifial state, simultaneously isolated and centre stage. This might explain why when an embarrassing Canadian radio interviewer asks Robbie if as 'part of the boy band phenomenon' he has any advice for members of The Backstreet Boys who might be considering going solo, Mrs Williams' favourite son replies, 'When you're going onstage just after one of your fans has given you a blowjob, don't forget to wipe your dick on the curtain.'

Film

3 Minute Screenplay: Junction of Doom

Pontius Pilate (David Bowie) has been cryogenically frozen in a vat of pork-pie jelly. He wakes, showers to rid himself of the sticky residue, and unzips a beautifully cut suit from its protective carrier. He puts the suit on, admiring himself in the mirror to the sound of Roxy Music's 'In Every Dream Home, A Mealtache' and walks down a hotel corridor. The barman (LL Cool J) serves him a drink, accompanied by a wry observation on the fleeting nature of human love. The bellhop (Sting) carries his baggage across the foyer, but Pilate does not tip him. He pays his bill in crisp notes, and the woman on reception (Madonna) gives him a sly look. Outside is a sweltering street in the Deep South. The camera zooms in inexplicably through the courthouse window to find a judge (Whitney Houston) ferociously banging her gavel. On the streetcorner, a madman (Mick Jagger) quotes from the book of Leviticus, and three prostitutes (All Saints) argue on a graffiti-covered stoop.

A car pulls up – it's a small battered family saloon, perhaps a Honda Civic. At the wheel is Elvis Presley (as himself). Elvis shifts – with some difficulty – into the passenger seat and Pilate gets in. The car pulls away, kangarooing slightly. The two men are looking for something, but they don't know what. The radio plays U2's 'I Still Haven't Found What I'm Looking For'. At the second intersection, Presley and Pilate collide with a busload of famous actors. At the moment of impact, the camera focusses on the face of the driver (Cliff Richard). As the credits roll, Posh Spice reads Robert Frost's 'The Road Less Travelled'.

'Some of those other writers,' Jerry Butler remembers, entirely accurately of his friend Curtis Mayfield's soundtrack to *Superfly*, 'had big movies that the music was in. Curtis had big music that the movies were about'.[13]

The tradition of pop as film is an honourable one that thrives to this day – Jim Jarmusch's *Ghost Dog* and Paul Thomas Anderson's

Magnolia being just two examples of movies whose writer-directors give credit to the composers of their soundtracks (Wu-Tang Clan mastermind The RZA and Aimee Mann respectively) not only for a job well done but also for their screenplays' original inspiration.

Film can work as pop too – from jungle and hip-hop dreamscapes infused by snatches of scary dialogue from *Predator 2* or *Jacob's Ladder*, to Madonna's 'Erotica' imagining itself as the soundtrack to some dubious Warholian stag movie, or Lee Perry's fantastic spaghetti-western inspired concept album *The Return of Django*.[14]

In fact once you start thinking about the felicitous interactions of music and celluloid, it is very hard to stop yourself. The incendiary opening statement that Public Enemy's 'Fight The Power' makes in the title sequence of Spike Lee's *Do The Right Thing*. The clunk of the 'Be My Baby' drumbeat as the light comes in through Harvey Keitel's curtains in Martin Scorsese's *Mean Streets*. The moment The Chemical Brothers' 'Block Rockin' Beats' barrels through the carnage in Adam Sandler's American football comedy *The Waterboy*. The way *Shaft*'s street scenes seem to be cut to the rhythm of Isaac Hayes' 'Soulsville'. The loping stoner's swagger Aerosmith's 'Sweet Emotion' gives to *Dazed and Confused*. The way the soundtrack of *Rushmore* brings back the magic of the film every time you put it on. The list of happy conjunctions goes on and on.

There is one area, however, in which difficulties arise, and that is in the transfer of an individual performer's charisma from one medium to the other. Like a mischievous malfunction in the Star Trek teleport system that sends the crew of the enterprise down on to the surface of a strange planet without any trousers, the attempted crossover from pop to film stardom all too often results in ridicule and contumely.

Sometimes the reason for this is obvious: pop stars get film parts for which their abilities as actors do not qualify them, and on the big screen there is no place to hide. But the situation is often much more complicated than this. After all, when you look into the hidden recesses of their personal histories, a disturbing number of pop and rock icons turn out to have spent their first ten years at stage school. Perhaps our innate hostility to celebrity over-reach stops us accepting someone in a film whom we have happily embraced on disc or video.

Feedback from one career to another can also be damaging: even if Sting was a truly great actor, people would still hate him in films for his musical misdemeanours. Madonna could star in the most erotic Hollywood film ever made (admirers of *Shanghai Surprise* might argue that she already has done) and commentators galled by her successful exploitation of her own sexuality as a pop star would still claim that people laughed at her sex scenes.

The two types of career do not share the same dynamic and – as Ringo Starr knows only too well – a ticket to ride in one world is not necessarily transferrable to the other. A pop persona works in a different way from a film persona: it is more complete, which means it is harder to submerge, and has a disturbing tendency to pop up at the wrong moment.

When David Bowie is unconvincingly buried alive at the end of *Merry Christmas Mr Lawrence*, the dramatic impact of his cruel demise is still more cruelly softened by thoughts of 'The Laughing Gnome'. This is part of the reason so few pop luminaries – Kris Kristofferson and Cher excepted – have ever made the transition to authentic film stardom, and even when they have done, this separation of identity has only been achieved at some cost to their credibility as musical performers. It's not that pop fame and film fame are incompatible, just that they interact in an extremely complex way.

A Boring History Lesson

Pop and film were bound together from the beginning. In Jimmie Rogers' 1929 landmark *The Singing Brakeman*, or pre-pop 'race movies' starring Bessie Smith or later Louis Jordan, the charisma crossover seemed relatively straightforward. (Though in the 1950s, the campaigning US civil rights organisation the NAACP were petitioned to get the original print of Smith's remarkable appearance in the twenty-minute my-man-done-me-wrong-but-I-don't-give-a-shit-because-I'm-the-coolest-woman-alive 1927 epic *St Louis Blues*, destroyed on the grounds that its representation of black people was stereotypical and demeaning. What they would have made of Ice

Cube's 1998 directorial debut *The Player's Club*, we can only guess at.)

One of rock 'n' roll's earliest defining moments happened in the cinema, as teenagers possessed by the devil rioted in the aisles to Bill Haley's 'Rock Around the Clock' over the credits to *The Blackboard Jungle* (Richard Brooks, 1955). By *The Girl Can't Help It* (Frank Tashlin, 1956) the pop cameo was an established art form[15], as was the suitability of the burgeoning music industry as a case for film treatment – sympathetic or otherwise. It was only a short step for pop stars to take lead roles, with not only Elvis and Tommy Steele but also Pat Boone, Cliff Richard, Frankie Avalon, and Adam Faith making it a standard career move in Britain as well as America.

From *Jailhouse Rock* (Richard Thorpe, 1957) to *GI Blues* (Norman Taurog, 1960), Elvis led the way as primal raunch was sanitised into social responsibility. Cliff Richard, moving with deceptive ease from the hoodlum's brother of *Serious Charge* (Terence Young, 1959) to the budding entrepreneur of *Summer Holiday* (Peter Yates, 1963), was not far behind. The Beatles of Richard Lester's *A Hard Day's Night* (1964), however, were not using film as a stepping stone to respectability. 'I fought the war for your sort,' chides an irate commuter as the young rascals invade his railway carriage. John Lennon replies, 'I bet you're sorry you won.'

Lester's snappy cinematic sensibility helped The Beatles onto the next phase of their career, just as they were defining what it meant to be a pop group. Anything The Beatles could do, The Dave Clark Five could do not quite as well, and in John Boorman's weirdly compelling *Catch Us If You Can* (1965) they confirmed the emerging truth that inferior pop stars tend to make better film actors. *Help!* (Richard Lester, 1965) had left The Beatles feeling like extras in their own film, so they made *The Magical Mystery Tour* themselves. Shown on British TV on Boxing Day 1967, it elicited a profoundly unfavourable critical reaction. Paul McCartney defended it feistily – 'The Queen's speech was hardly a gasser,' adding 'it is better to be controversial than to be boring.' (This was a message he would unfortunately have forgotten by the time he got round to making *Give My Regards to Broad St.*)

On the other side of the Atlantic, *Head* (Bob Rafelson, 1968), the intended cinematic coming of age of ersatz Beatles The Monkees, ensured itself eternal cult status by alienating an even higher proportion of its prospective audience. Psychedelia broke up narratives and widened the generation gap, as well as nourishing the ideal of rock stars as Dionysian figures. This notion found its purest cinematic expression in the casting of Mick Jagger in *Performance* (Donald Cammell/Nic Roeg, 1970) and David Bowie in *The Man Who Fell To Earth* (Nic Roeg, 1976).

As the rock 'n' roll and film industries huddled together in the fading embers of the sixties counter-culture, James Taylor and Dennis Wilson broke the speed limit but no acting records in *Two Lane Blacktop* (Monte Hellman, 1971). Kris Kristofferson ambled out of the soundtrack of *The Last Movie* (Dennis Hopper, 1971) and into a starring role in *Cisko Pike* (Bill Norton 1972), and Sam Peckinpah cast him and Bob Dylan in *Pat Garrett and Billy the Kid* (1973). Meanwhile David Essex was giving Brit-grit a good name with *That'll Be the Day* (Claude Hawtham, 1973) and *Stardust* (Michael Apted, 1974) but The Who – with a little help from Ken Russell – lost it with *Tommy* (1975).

The rock star as auteur was never meant to be. Performers who remained true to flighty musical muses over the span of several decades proved unable to transfer that maverick spirit on to film. Neil Young's *Journey Through the Past* (1973) and *Human Highway* (1978, both directed pseudonymously as Bernard Sharkey) and Bob Dylan's *Renaldo and Clara* (1978) all endure as landmarks of maverick hubris but little else. David Bowie's inability to sustain a film career after the success of *The Man Who Fell To Earth* prefigured the inabilities of Prince and Madonna – the eighties megastars he influenced so greatly – to build lasting cinematic personas on their twin triumphs *Purple Rain* (Albert Magnoli, 1984) and *Desparately Seeking Susan* (Susan Seidelman, 1985). All three consoled themselves by excelling at promo clips, but however energetically they blurred the line between cinema and video (and, in Madonna's case, however many films they made), there was no getting away from their sense of themselves as matinee idols *manqués*.

True matinee idol status was reserved for Björk, Will Smith, Dolly Parton in *9 to 5* (Colin Higgins, 1980) and Whitney Houston, who resurrected her recording career and broke box-office and soundtrack sales records by playing a pop star in *The Bodyguard* (Mick Jackson, 1992). This was a performance worthy of Elvis. As he was in *Clambake* (1964).

At the turn of the new century, Mariah Carey set off in pursuit of her good friend Whitney by proclaiming her intention to executive produce and star in a romantic comedy about an early eighties girl group. Much to her chagrin, Mariah met Jennifer Lopez coming back the other way. Lopez' successful leap from film siren to Latino pop megastar was pretty much unprecedented, though anyone willing to countenance the possibility of romantic involvement with Puff Daddy in connection with an artistic or material goal was always likely to prove pretty unstoppable.

The Stars Speak

Mick Jagger: 'Acting is just as natural as singing – you can either do it or you can't.'

Tom Waits: 'Moving from music to films is like going from bootlegging to watch repair.'

Elvis Presley: 'Just as soon as I could get out of those film contracts, I wanted to get back to live performance.'

The Beatles in Flashback

For those whose memories are all in colour, The Beatles are a bridge back to a black and white world – and not just because *Magical Mystery Tour* got a black and white repeat a few days after its original colour broadcast. So there is no reason to object when the 1994 Beatles biopic *Backbeat* opens with the stock narrative device of a black and white historical montage – the Matthews Final, dockyards with people working in them – fading into colour.

The biggest challenge facing the makers of *Backbeat* was to create a world on which The Beatles had yet to make their mark. The burden of hindsight has weighed down many a biopic with disingenuous dialogue and this one was no exception – 'Liverpool: home of . . . Liverpudlians,' Ian Hart's John Lennon notes sarcastically, surveying an anonymous Mersey cityscape. Later on he tells his artistic best friend Stuart Sutcliffe, 'We're going to be too big for our own good.'

The interesting thing about Lennon and Sutcliffe's relationship is the idea of someone being too cool to be in The Beatles rather than – like the unfortunate Pete Best – not cool enough. John's insecurity and aggression in the face of the Continental sophistication which his friend both metaphorically and (in the person of Astrid) literally embraces when the band go to Hamburg suggest a sense of cultural inferiority shared by even the sharpest of pre-Beatles youth[16].

Stephen Dorff's gentle transatlantic accent appeals even to those whose appreciation of Liverpudlian charm has been dulled by generations of TV Scousers. *Backbeat's* soundtrack too boasts healthy American input. The music featured is not The Beatles' early grapplings with rock and roll – which tend to sound pretty dreadful to today's ears – but an approximation of their spirit by a stellar scratch band of US alternative rock luminaries featuring members of Nirvana, REM, Sonic Youth, Soul Asylum, Gumball and The Afghan Whigs[17].

There is a satisfying echo in this of The Beatles' original cinematic incarnation, as it was an American who created the fresh film language which helped sell their white British take on black American rhythm and blues back to the US. Richard Lester was an American TV director who came to Britain in the fifties to work with Spike Milligan and Peter Sellers (whose influence on The Beatles' trademark banter cannot be overestimated). He also made *It's Trad, Dad*, a brave stab at establishing the trad-jazz exploitation film as a viable genre.

A Hard Day's Night stands up well four decades on. The extent to which it was a step forward from the standard UK pop star vehicle, as driven by Tommy Steele or Cliff Richard, was fully appreciated at the time of its original release. The sense of a cultural conflict between old ways and new could be glimpsed in Alexander Walker's newspaper location reports. If that reporter was to be believed, when the train on which The Beatles were being filmed pulled into the previously peaceful Somerset seaside town of Minehead, the crowds of waiting teenage girls were charged by local schoolboys holding banners proclaiming 'Vivat Brahms'.

Some of the film's dialogue was improvised, but most was scripted by a young Liverpudlian playwright called Alun Owen, who got an Oscar nomination for his pains. When the actor playing George Harrison in *Backbeat* quotes as his own dialogue written for the real George by someone else – 'Oh yes, I'd be most prepared for that eventuality' – he hints at the mixture of flagrancy and elusiveness that makes The Beatles of this period so intriguing.

The enduring sensation left behind by *A Hard Day's Night* is one of unfettered motion within new enclosures – The Beatles' jerky speeded-up movements recalling the title of Lester's 1960 short *The Running, Jumping And Standing Still Film*. By the time of *Help!*, their second collaboration with Lester a year or so later, all sense of constraint had gone. Perhaps that's why this film was not so universally liked – these people no longer knew their place, having broken out into denim, colour, Caribbean locations and an absurd *Carry On*-style plot about a sacrificial ring and the murderous Oriental cult of a goddess called Kylie.

The Beatles' subsequent avowal of Eastern mysticism adds a certain piquancy to their disrespectful spoofing of it here, but the film's most celebrated and resonant moment comes, appropriately enough, right near the beginning. Two old women, one of whom is Gretchen Franklin, *EastEnders'* Ethel, wave them in through their separate doorways to a slyly knocked-through pad of breathtaking opulence. 'Lovely lads,' observe the gossiping innocents, 'so natural ... Still the same as they were, before they were.'

What the Big Bopper Might Have Said About It All If He Was Still Alive

When you consider former Eighth Wonder vocalist and Haircut 100 video star Patsy Kensit's lead role in *The Mia Farrow Story*[18] – playing the woman who had played her mother when she appeared as a small child in *The Great Gatsby* – it is hard to stop a small headache developing. Or how about the young Ashley Judd, narrating the fictionalised lifestory of her actual, real-life, singing mother and sister in the classic country bio-pic *Love Can Build A Bridge*, and then going on to have a big Hollywood career playing beautiful women people suspect of being serial killers? No wonder she became sufficiently disoriented to go out with Michael Bolton.

Casting pop stars in proper films and not just biopics constantly prompts similar confusions of identity, as inevitably the stars are themselves and not themselves in varying proportions. But these confusions of identity are as likely to open up new areas of intrigue as to prove a source of frustration.

Four Areas of Intrigue

1. The age of innocence There wasn't one. The cinema's idea of rock 'n' roll started out as cynical as it was ever going to get (the idea of a new branch of the entertainment industry more venal than itself was just too good to resist). While films like *The Girl Can't Help It* captured the excitement of early rock 'n' roll, they did so through a filter of condescension and contempt that would not really be removed (and then not for good, mentioning no names Ken Russell) until Richard Lester met The Beatles. Compared with the ideas about the relationship between music's production and its consumption in *Expresso Bongo*, Malcolm Mclaren's Svengali fantasies in *The Great Rock 'n' Roll Swindle* are the work of a playground innocent.

2. Pre-pop film stars playing variants of a pop self not yet fully formed cf Meat Loaf in *The Rocky Horror Picture Show*, David Essex 'hitching a rollercoaster ride in search of fish and chips and freedom' in *That'll Be the Day* and then making his friend's dog abort by giving it LSD in *Stardust*. Not to mention Hazel O'Connor in the criminally underrated *Breaking Glass*. (Who could forget that unforgettable moment in the old Rainbow theatre when there's a power cut and the crowd all wave candles while Hazel performs acoustically?) Though subsequent real life pop careers were shot though – in Hazel's case, fatally – with memories of a celluloid preface.

3. Aspirational casting In which an established star or stars take a role because they want to tell us something, but end up telling us exactly the opposite, often to very entertaining effect. Diana Ross as Billie Holiday in *Lady Sings the Blues* and Kylie Minogue as a bad girl with a heart of gold in *The Delinquents* spring to mind, but these transparent career moves pale into respectability compared to The Monkees in *Head*. In their desperation to prove they were hip to what was happening in the psychedelic underground, The Monkees forgot that they were, in fact, a great pop group and buried themselves six feet down: 'Changing your image, darlings,' observes a passing waitress, 'and while you're at it, why don't you have them write you some talent?'

4. Paying your dues The seeming modesty of a judicious blend of cameo and low-budget major roles can actually represent the ultimate in long-term status enhancement (if things go wrong though, life can get ugly, especially if you're Adam Ant). Isaac Hayes and Debbie Harry showed the way, and the letter's supreme performance in John Waters' *Hairspray* will probably never be bettered (though Iggy Pop's frontier transvestite in *Dead Man* was pretty good too). The ultimate dues-payer though is Tom Waits, whose bulging portfolio of drunkards and low-rent psychopaths have inspired a generation of rock character turns from Nick Cave to Lyle Lovett. For those with an eye to the main chance, John Waters, Jim Jarmusch and Robert Altman are the directors to look out for. If Alex Cox calls, you're not in.

The Courtney Love Story

'It seems that in every film, from *Man on the Moon* to *The People vs Larry Flynt*, and now her recent casting as William S Burroughs' wife, she's doomed to play dead celebrities' middle-aged wives. With a little more plastic surgery perhaps she might make a good Yoko Ono.' With these cruel but undeniably provocative words – thoughtfully posted on his Internet site towards the end of 1999 – Marilyn Manson moved his remorselessly entertaining feud with Courtney Love on to another level. He also pointed up a fascinating tension between the two strands of the great woman's career.

As a pop star, the combination of fascination and repulsion with which Love addresses myths of the destroying rock wife has been the engine for some of her most inspired creative coups. Watching Courtney onstage, trampling the sour grapes of patriarchy into a most excellent whine and singing made-for-cinema couplets like 'Someone should tell Anne Boleyn/Chokers are back in again', you'd think she was made for movie immortality. Yet as a celluloid presence, she seems to embrace all the restrictions her musical career has sought to break free of. Suitably abysmal in Alex Cox farragos *Straight To Hell* and *Sid & Nancy* (playing Nancy Spungen's friend), a fine cameo as – what else? – an inspiring woman of easy virtue in Julian Schnabel's underrated *Basquiat* seemed to propel her film career into its mature phase.

Unfortunately, the roles she took once she'd made it seemed to project an acceptance of female subservience entirely at odds with everything people who liked her thought she stood for. The scenery-chewing stay-at-homes Love gave us in *Man on the Moon* and *The People vs Larry Flynt* were exactly the kind of two-dimensional clichés great Hole songs like 'Twenty Years In The Dakota' and 'Celebrity Skin' had seemed to lay to rest for ever.

It was a fitting irony then that Courtney's greatest and – to date – only worthy film role should come in a documentary about her and her late husband Kurt Cobain that she did everything in her power to stop[19]. Where Nick Broomfield's usual film-making methodology is to fix on a famously unsympathetic subject and then make ever more disingenuous attempts to get under their skin, *Kurt and Courtney* (1998) saw even his notoriously elusive moral core pricked by the drama of Kurt Cobain, to the extent that in his desperation to pin Cobain's death on his wife he seemed to be making some kind of belated stab at personal redemption.

Broomfield's willingness to give screen time to anyone – however disreputable – in the hope that what they say might make Courtney look bad, rebounds strangely in her favour. The psychotic sado-masochist singer of notorious LA shock-rockers The Dwarves (who died in suspicious circumstances shortly after claiming to have been offered $50,000 to 'whack' Cobain) supplies the film's undoubted highlight, when he dares to suggest that Bloomfield himself 'may not be a reliable witness'.

As *Kurt and Courtney*'s subtext – the hypocrisy Bloomfield thinks he perceives in Love's perfectly justifiable determination to stop him making his grubby little film – moves nearer centre stage, Courtney assumes more and more of the iconic lustre she has always craved. Her decision to deny the director access to Nirvana's music for the soundtrack somehow makes the shock of Kurt's absence all the more unbearably poignant.

Shortly before he engineers a thrillingly inconclusive face-to-face confrontation at a meeting of the American Civil Liberties Union, Bloomfield tracks down an old boyfriend (disreputable Seattle punk leftover Rozz Rezaback). He produces a lovingly-preserved five-year plan with the intriguing title *Here's how Courtney will make it*, written long before anyone had ever heard of her. When he gets to the part where it says 'Become friends with Michael Stipe', discerning cinema audiences have been known to get up and cheer.

Rappers' Annexe

No one seems to have a problem with rappers having film careers (the same applies to country singers and the French). The relationship between what they do and what they are is subtly different to that of a conventional pop star, and not just because their day job is all about delivering lines anyway. Ask LL Cool J about his role as Michael Gambon's son in Barry Levinson's *Toys* and he says, 'There's no growth in doing that [hip-hop characterisation]. I *already* do that.'

Ice Cube's Doughboy in John Singleton's *Boyz N The Hood* – one of a series of successful hip-hop transitions to the big screen, including Tupac Shakur's in *Juice* and *Gridlock'd* – proved otherwise. In establishing that black rage and white corporate profit did not have to be mutually exclusive, rappers had facilitated the emergence of a new generation of black film directors, so it was only fair that they should also reap some of the benefits.

Ice-T did this apparently without effort (establishing a thriving career as an action hero in *New Jack City* and *Ricochet*, after a shaky start in some terrible breakdance movies, and duking it out with Ice Cube to enjoyable effect in Walter Hill's ghetto *Treasure of the Sierra Madre* rewrite *Trespass*). At a press conference in London in 1993, he outlined his thespian principles:

'I'm not an actor, I have absolutely no idea how to act, I just read the script. If the script says, "Open the door", I open the door, and the director tells me how wonderful I am . . . Not being an actor by trade, I have the luxury of being able to pick which movies I do. So I try to do the kind of stuff that I'd go to see myself. Give me a cool movie about something stupid and I might like it: I'm not trying to do anything super-dramatic. I'm a b-movie fan – I like action movies, horror movies, shit that's not good. If I read a script and it says, "You're a schoolteacher but you might get an Oscar", I'm like, "Save that Oscar, I want to go shoot some shit up."'

Save That Oscar – I Want To Go Shoot Some Shit Up

It's not just rappers who make good criminals on the big screen. The pop star–gangster interface is the exception that proves the general rule of charisma-cross opprobrium. The early identification between rock and roll stars and juvenile delinquency is probably one aspect of this. But shared outsider status and the common need to present a bold face to the world seem to enable even the least convincing pop stars to pass muster as celluloid gangsters.

Phil Collins' *Buster* might have been reprehensibly sanitised, but that was what the film demanded (if they'd wanted a darker portrayal they would have asked Peter Gabriel), and Spandau Ballet's Kemp Brothers were memorably nasty in *The Krays*. Quasi gangsterdom gave Elvis arguably his best role in *King Creole*, and Jimmy Cliff produced one of the most electrifying performances in the whole pop film canon as Ivan the reggae-hopeful-turned-outlaw in Perry Henzell's *The Harder They Come*.

Jagger & Richard

Performance made the link between rock stardom and gangsterhood as explicit as it was ever going to get. Turner – Mick Jagger's amphibian rock star archetype – mingles identities over Notting Hill hallucinogenics with Chas, James Fox's East End gangster on the run. 'Comical little geezer,' Chas observes prophetically. 'You'll look funny when you're fifty.' Jagger's definitive rock star on film performance makes an intriguing comparison with an earlier showing by a similarly enduring British pop icon: Cliff Richard's as Bongo Herbert in *Expresso Bongo*, Val Guest's caustic adaptation of Wolf Mankowitz's hit West End play.

Both were London films and both were controversial in their own time. *Expresso Bongo* revelled in its steamy Soho setting; the strip club scenes passed the censors on the grounds of their 'documentary' style, and Laurence Harvey's fast-talking manager Jonny Jackson just talked too fast for them. The release of *Performance* on the other hand was delayed for two years because Warner Brothers thought it was 'evil'.

Jagger's is certainly an effectively louche personification of sensual licence. He carries off his blues number with great aplomb and the 'Memo From Turner' sequence – in which he slicks up and invades the hood's life as an equal – is one of the best rock videos of all time, some eight years before such things were formally invented.

By Turner's own prescription however – 'the only performance that matters is the one that achieves madness' – it is Cliff Richard's embodiment of manufactured teen idol Bongo Herbert that carries the honours. Cliff plays Bongo as a noble savage: 'I've got the rhythm, kind of natural like!' The unnerving blankness of his performance inpressed people then as much as now. 'He is either such a clever actor,' wrote contemporary critic Isobel Quigley, 'that he actually persuades one he isn't acting, or else a boy of such transparent and alluring simplicity that the whole of *Expresso Bongo* has rolled off him like water off a duck's back.'

All around him is infectious cynicism (the dialogue was toned down a little from the original stage play, but this film is still the nearest thing we have to a British *Sweet Smell of Success*), yet Cliff refuses to be brought down by classic barbs like: 'Recordings, variety bookings, why he'll even open up shoe shops for cash.' And his resolute asexuality in all dealings with shifty love interest Yolande Dolan is kookier and more disturbing than anything Mick Jagger and Anita Pallenberg can cook up for James Fox in *Performance*.

'Bongo is under age,' someone reminds Jimmy Jackson shortly after his protégé has royally shafted him. 'To me,' Jackson replies, 'he looks all of a sudden very grown up.'

Individuals and Community: In Praise of Oncoming Vehicles

The charisma swap debate focusses most easily on questions of individual identity, but collective crossover can be just as intriguing. The Ramones in *Rock 'n' Roll High School*, for example – 'Driving down Fifth Avenue, eating chicken vindaloo' – are not 'acting' in any sense other than that in which they always are, but theirs is still a pivotal film performance. And anyone lucky enough to have seen the semi-legendary robot replicants scene in Hanna Barbera's *Kiss Meets the Phantom of the Park*, in which a mad scientist tricks a theme park full of kids into accepting – nay embracing – an *inauthentic* Kiss, will have to think long and hard about the divide between fantasy and reality[20].

The Spice Girls in *Spiceworld*, bombing round London in a Union Jack bus driven by Meat Loaf, play out the impending drama of manager Simon Fuller's dismissal with chilling documentary accuracy. In *Take It or Leave It*, Madness play themselves in their early days. The impact of this shockingly honest saga of instrument and record theft, fare dodging, fights and musical incapacity is somewhat mitigated by the fact that some members of the band appear to be struggling not to laugh, but it still makes a fascinatingly charmless counterpoint to the band's more calculatedly endearing video persona (see **Video**), and there are a number of poignant insights into the development of a group identity ('You said we were playing up here in the bedroom, not out in the poxy garden').

The mother of all nuts and bolts portrayals, however, is Slade's, in *Flame* (1974). The story of a group plucked from the obscurity of working mens' clubs and groomed for stardom by a suave London executive – played by a young Tom Conti with a disturbing hint of Al

Pacino – only to break up quickly under the pressure of fame might seem a rudimentary one. But the background of cramped dressing rooms, unsavoury canal tow paths and squalid pirate radio station interiors has the pungent whiff of authenticity about it, and the band's collective acting performance is a triumph of West Midlands naturalism. Rarely, if ever, have the harsh truths of most pop and rock lives – if you've got drums you're the drummer, if you've got a van you're the roadie – been so clearly and compellingly on display. If you haven't seen it, just imagine Vic Reeves and Bob Mortimer's immortal 'Slade At Home', but without the showbiz trappings.

Slade in *Flame*: Noddy Holder's Eye-Witness Testimony

Originally it was our manager, Chas Chandler's idea. He'd always planned our career in stages and once we'd had a bit of success with records and touring, he thought it would be a good idea to do a film. We got quite a lot of scripts in. There was a rough draft for a spoof of the Quatermass films – The Quite A Mess Experiment *it was going to be called – that was quite funny, but Dave Hill, our guitarist, wasn't quite so into doing it because he got eaten by a triffid in the first reel. Because none of us had any acting experience, we thought it would be best if we were a band, so in the end we decided to go for more of a documentary approach. The director Richard Loncraine and the writer Andrew Birkin sent us a script which was not really what being in a band was like – it was like people that weren't in a band's idea of what being in a band was like. So they came with us for several weeks on our American tour and learnt a bit about our backgrounds. We told them stories about ourselves and other bands and they amalgamated them into a script, so* Flame *was a cross-section not just of us but a lot of bands at the time. Everyone had these experiences of crooked promoters, small time managers, etc. Although we were thought of as a seventies band, we set the film in the late sixties, because that was the time when all this sort of thing was most rife. The characters they wrote were basically our characters – the names have been changed to protect the innocent – so we didn't really have to act.*

When the film came out, I don't think people knew what to make of it – everyone expected a slapstick sort of thing with lots of costumes and running about with speeded-up film, but we'd obviously taken it seriously and tried to get a realistic picture of how things were. We wanted to make a real nitty-gritty, down to earth, working-class movie. There were some good actors in it too: Kenneth Colley, Tom Conti – it was his first film. The critics were very nice about it – even Barry Norman gave it a good review on Film '74 *– but the fans were a bit baffled because we didn't give them the glamour. It wasn't all tomfoolery in the dressing room, there were some very heavy scenes, and a lot of it was filmed heavier than it came out, but it got toned down a bit because we were worried about getting an X certificate.*

Unfortunately, what remained was still too close to the proverbial bone for Slade's fanbase, and *Flame's* critical kudos never translated into commercial success. Sadly a later project involving *Airplane* writers Zucker and Abrams, the Two Ronnies, Slade and a plot which sounds strangely similar to the former team's later goofball gem *Top Secret*, came to naught.

With the benefit of hindsight, what does Noddy Holder think of *Flame?*

Well, the last time I watched it on Channel 4 in the late eighties I thought, 'Bloody hell, this is quite good.'

END CREDITS

Five Pivotal Moments in Pop/Film Charisma Cross History

I've Got A Horse (Kenneth Hume, 1965). Billy Fury co-stars with his own racehorse.

Privilege (Peter Watkins, 1967). Manfred Mann's Paul Jones is a fascist state pop star construct (but we knew that already).

That's The Way of the World (1974). Harvey Keitel meets Earth Wind & Fire.

Ladies & Gentlemen – The Fabulous Stains (Lou Adler, 1982). Steve Jones and Paul Cook invent punk rock. Again. But this time with a little help from Laura Dern.

Spiceworld (1998). So many noteworthy incidents it is hard to pick just one, but beating off stiff competition from Victoria's performance on the assault course is the moment when The Spice Girls rush to a hospital bedside to bring a young child out of his coma and the sisterly cry goes up: 'Take your top off, Geri.'

Roll of Honour

BEST PERFORMANCE AS A NUN: Madonna in *Shanghai Surprise*.

BEST PERFORMANCE AS A TOASTER: Aswad's Brinsley Forde – former *Double Decker* – in Franco Rosso's *Babylon*.

BEST PERFORMANCE NOT ACTUALLY BY A ROCK STAR WHICH SHOULD HAVE BEEN (THOUGH HE DID MAKE IT INTO THE CHARTS EVENTUALLY, WITH BLUR'S HELP): Phil 'you've killed my scooter' Daniels in *Quadrophenia*.

Hall of Shame

BUTTOCKS: Art Garfunkel in *Bad Timing*.

HUBRIS: David Bowie in *Absolute Beginners*.

BEING RUPERT EVERETT'S LOVE RIVAL: Bob Dylan in *Hearts of Fire*.

Video

Freeze Frame One[21]: The Irn-Bru Pop Video Exhibition of 1992

The idea of a major gallery exhibition devoted to pop video was never
going to go down well with those who regard the medium as a
sinister mind-rotting force that has caused an entire generation to
enter chronological adulthood blessed with the attention span of a
baby marmoset. But even for those of us to whom it is the very stuff of
life, the notion is a strange one, as the idea of setting off to seek pop
video pleasure outside the home runs counter to the classically
passive, domesticised nature of the experience.

The Museum of the Moving Image has certainly done its bit to
remind everyone that this is a field of artistic endeavour in which the
tug of war between art and commerce is more than usually one-sided.
The exhibition is obtrusively sponsored by a Scottish soft-drinks
firm, whose awful television and cinema ads – in which the viewer is
invited to laugh along with 'groovy pop stars' who accept money
from an advertising company – exemplify the knowing vacuity of the
video medium at its worst.

Weightily subtitled 'The Story of Song on Screen', the show does not begin, as you might expect, with Queen's 'Bohemian Rhapsody', but rewinds a rich and distant heritage back to the early sychronised animations of the German Oskar Fischinger (who went on to work on Disney's *Fantasia*), then forward through Jazz 'Soundies' and Ethnic Shorts (not a fashion item but fifteen-minute films made specially for black Americans of the forties and fifties), to The Monkees' TV series and The Beatles' films for 'Penny Lane' and 'Strawberry Fields Forever'.

In the end, all this historical context seems like an unnecessary intrusion. Most pop videos were not built to last. The images fragment and break up as they enter your mind, in the manner of the biodegradable wrapper on the toilet rim-flush refill. Which is why when something good turns up on *The Chart Show*'s Video Vault, it is rarely quite as you remembered it. For instance, many people are still surprised by the scene at the end of Lionel Richie's 'Hello', where the blind girl beats Lionel to death with her stick.

The time before video-makers realised that their creations might have a life after people stopped buying the singles they were made to promote, was a true age of innocence. It is this very unguardedness that makes, say, a Duran Duran video compilation such a poignant socio-historical document. In the welter of cheerfully debased imagery which made pop a visual as well as a musical Esperanto, inspiration turned to cliché at the press of a pause button.

Freeze Frame Two: Cheerfully Debased Visual Esperanto in Close Up[22]

The Exploding Lightbulb The video innocent would just think 'why?' The video literate knows that is one question you should never ask. The Exploding Lightbulb is the archetypal sensory jolt mechanism, designed to hammer home key points in song-structure without concession to literal meaning. A distant relative of the much-loved Slow Motion Falling Glass of Red Wine, it was a logical progression from the notorious Swinging Lightbulb, a classic early video director's ruse, allowing the star to appear cast in a sudden and stark light when in fact he or she had been in make-up for several hours and was in any case illuminated from within by the inner light of celebrity. This sort of thing seemed to go into decline after The Cars split up, along with other classic gambits like The Venetian Blind and The Woman in a Négligé Looking Rumpled on a Motel Bed, so when Curtis Stigers revived not one but both lightbulb techniques in the video for his single 'Sleeping With The Lights On', public joy was unconfined.

The Location as Destiny Delusion This reached its zenith with Anton Corbijn's U2-trying-to-look-spiritual-in-the-desert epics, which The Stone Roses and The Inspiral Carpets sought to emulate a couple of years later, on considerably smaller budgets, by making their breath condense in chilly English beauty spots to demonstrate their affinity with rave culture and its psychic connection to the great outdoors. There are few sights more absurd than a band shivering on a mountainside trying to look spontaneous while lip-synching a seventh take in a blizzard. Especially when that band is Ultravox. Midge Ure and co's more hedonistic New Romantic brethren Duran Duran favoured warmer, more exotic video-shoot destinations, not realising that they were footing the bill, and The Cure struggled to get their message across from inside a cupboard that a passing music lover had pushed off a cliff. Only the last of these seemed to appreciate the truth of Louis Armstrong's immortal doctrine 'It's not where you are, it's where you're at'.

The Fibre-glass Phallus In which a large sleek metal object moves elegantly (or not so elegantly, depending on the budget) across the screen, easily pulling a not wholly invisible trailer-load of pyscho-sexual baggage. ZZ Top's three-part big-red-car video cycle was elegantly crafted techno-sexism with its tongue in its beard. AC/DC's 'Heatseeker', in which the camera followed a huge missile into a forest and eventually crashes through a wall, is not so subtle. The role of subliminal phallic imagery in early pop promos – the questing camera, slipping down alleyways and into darkened nightclubs to find its subject – is too horribly large and obvious to contemplate at length; but Cher gave the whole business a novel twist with the classic video for 'If I Could Turn Back Time', in which she pointed up the connection between warfare and the male libido by performing athwart one of the cannons of the *USS Missouri*.

The Scientific Smokescreen In which up-to-the-minute technology is employed to divert the audience's attention from unpalatable truths. The most celebrated example being the video for Peter Gabriel's 'Sledgehammer', in which effects-boffins contrived a procession of visual diversions so dazzling that millions of people forgot that this man had once been in Genesis and was therefore an outcast from respectable society. This technique is not only applicable to career blemishes. Thanks to 'Money For Nothing', Dire Straits – no oil paintings in anyone's visual language – were made safe for MTV by the miracle of shoddy computer graphics. See also Def Leppard's 'Let's Get Rocked', which went one step further by giving the virtual makeover treatment to a hypothetical metal fan.

Freeze Frame Three: 'It is I, Mike Judge.'

Dick Zimmerman, a California state lottery winner who used his winnings to set up an anti-*Beavis and Butt-head* hotline, described MTV's long-running cartoon staple as 'pure societal poison, glorifying losers, violence and criminality'[23].

In the post-*South Park* epoch, it is hard to remember just how shocking the pre-lapsarian world of 1992 found the notion of two culturally and morally bankrupt fourteen-year-old boys roaming the information highways in search of cheap thrills. What upset people most about *Beavis and Butt-head* was the supposed lack of any moralising voice of redemption or come-uppance. (This, of course, was exactly why other people liked it – whether as an adjunct or an antidote to MTV's disingenuous synthesis of amoral product and self-righteous sixties sermonising.) This was strange, because they were meant as a vehicle of retribution.

Telephoning their (then) thirty-year-old creator shortly before his creations made their controversial Channel 4 debut, his air of beleaguerment was plain for all to hear. 'It is I,' a tired Texan voice proclaims wearily at the other end of the line, 'Mike Judge. There are always people who don't get satire,' he acknowledges. 'They don't understand you can portray something without condoning it.'

The 'hatred and loathing' Judge felt for the blank generation whose spokesmen he unwittingly created was there for all to see. Butt-head – the smarter of the pair – he gave hideous, uncontrollable adolescents' hair, permanently flared nostrils, protuberant gums and mean, piggy eyes. (Judge had started out trying to draw a guy he knew when he was a kid and couldn't quite get him right but 'liked the way he turned out anyway'). Beavis' lightning-flash eyebrows and unsavoury leer had no specific human template.

'I'm not a great artist,' Judge explains, 'but when I first drew them I probably did it a little bit less well than I could have. I wanted them to be an animated version of what I used to draw in high school; there's a way people draw when they've been in art class for too long – they want to draw things from other cartoons, not as they are in reality. Like for an eating place they'll always do a fifties diner, but I just drew *McDonald's*.'

Judge's brutal realism had a savage and unexpected consequence, as Beavis and Butt-head's halting speech patterns and moronic, stuttering laughter made them instant folk heroes. When fox-hunting enthusiast and part-time philosopher Roger Scruton fulminated apocalyptically about popular culture 'replacing the dialect of the tribe with the grammarless murmur of the species', he might have had Judge's creations in mind[24], but while he would no doubt have approved of such practices as frog baseball, the chances are the sophistication of the duo's critical apparatus was probably lost on him.

Their division of all artistic phenomena into two categories – 'stuff which is cool' and 'stuff which sucks' – bespeaks an evaluative aesthetic of inspirational directness. Furthermore, Beavis and Butt-head's commentary on the videos that are their prime source of entertainment also supplies the kind of critical voice which Scruton and his elk are constantly insisting is absent from contemporary culture, mercilessly exposing not only their own limited parameters ('Look at all those butts!') but also the unwarranted pretensions of bands and videomakers ('I think it's only cool if you, like, go to college').

Whether you agree with Jon Savage that 'it is tempting to view Beavis and Butt-Head as a Janus-faced Candide'[25] or take the Mike Judge amendment ('Huh-huh . . . he said Janus') there is no denying the extent to which the gruesome twosome were bringers of enlightenment. Only their superhuman simple-mindedness could match and overcome the monolithic dumbness of the pop video medium as it existed in the early nineties. And just as their weirdly fragmented narratives had the power to lift you out of MTV's seamless flow and make you think, so the very advent of *Beavis and Butt-head* inspired a new generation of video-makers to raise their creative game.

Fast Forward to Video Auteurhood: Hype Williams and Spike Jonze

Pop video is to film as checkers is to chess, as Boyzone are to Take That, as Peter Kay is to Johnny Vegas. When Barry Norman came down from the mountain carrying this particular tablet of stone, Hype (real name Harold) Williams jumped out from behind a burning bush, wrestled Barry to the ground and smashed the tablet into a thousand pieces with a single snap of his clapperboard. Spike Jonze could have helped him but didn't. He was lurking behind a cactus, disguised as the back end of a pantomime camel.

Unfairly described in Armond White's Tupac Shakur biography *Rebel For The Hell Of It* as 'the hip-hop video director specialising in Hollywood knock-offs', Williams has actually reversed the traditional subordinate relationship of pop video to film. While Hollywood has become ever more dependent on soundtrack-led marketing strategies, Williams has turned the supposedly debased creative environment of the promo video into the launch pad for some of the most startling and audacious cinematography of recent years. From Missy Elliott's giant inflatable suit to Tupac Shakur's decadent empire of the Californian sun to Kelis' homicidal wronged woman, the images he has come up with have been as enduring as anything on the big screen in the same period.

Watching MTV over the last few years (something Williams

himself never does, preferring to spend time away from the camera with his infant daughter, rather than keeping an eye on how every video-maker and their dog is trying to rip him off), the transformation he has effected has been mesmerising. A few years back, your standard r'n'b or hip-hop video would feature a small party scene and some low-rent booty shaking with the odd cut-away to the rapper and his mates hanging around in a car-park looking shifty. Now, well, the hackneyed phrase 'production values' doesn't really cover it – Williams' videos are science fiction cornucopias choreographed by the black Busby Berkeley; a Dino De Laurentiis docusoap of the last days of the Roman empire.

From mainstream stars like Mariah Carey, Usher and Brandy, to crossover mogul Puff Daddy, to edgier talents like Busta Rhymes and the Wu-Tang Clan, Williams' svelte and startling visualisations span a broad musical spectrum, but it's his work in the hip-hop field that has had the most dramatic impact. Given that it was the early eighties Breakdance exploitation film cash-in cycle that gave him his intoxicating first taste of showbiz (Williams' Queens high school got a week off to supply extras for *Krush Groove*), this was entirely as it should be.

A stocky, soft-spoken, nappy-headed individual in Rough Ryderz T-shirt and very wide jeans, Williams is not in the best of moods on the day I meet him. Apparently there was congestion on the roads which delayed his taxi. This hardly rates as an outrage in central London at nine o'clock on a weekday morning, but for someone who is used to stopping traffic as a matter of course, it seems to threaten long-term psychological damage.

'Colour was the biggest thing,' says Williams, grouchily, of what he learnt in the four years as a gopher on shoots for Big Daddy Kane and Biz Markie, 'the palette was so drab.' In the videos he makes now, the sumptuous cinematography of his long-term collaborator Malik Hassan Sayeed (also responsible for the stunning look of Spike Lee's *He's Got Game*) is illuminated at every turn by Williams' trademark colorific intensity. 'The reds, the greens, the olives, the golds . . .' Hype enthuses. 'I just want everything to look as good as it does in real life.'

Real life has not always looked as good in hip-hop as it does in the year 2000. Working with people on both sides of the East Coast–West Coast divide in the era of Biggie Smalls and Tupac Shakur's deaths, Williams must have been party to some pretty heavy duty goings on. How does he feel about that era in retrospect?

'It was . . .' Williams chooses his words carefully '*historical:* there was a lot of misfortune, but what Death Row did was a blueprint of success for anyone with a dream.'[26]

Were things as scary as they seemed from the outside?

'There was a time when who you kept company with became a matter of life and death. It was dangerous to go anywhere,' he remembers. 'Only towards the end of '98 did it honestly feel like those days were in the past.'

Even then though the shadow of violence never entirely lifted. Williams is understandably reluctant to talk about the incident in the spring of 1999 when rapper Nas' manager was beaten up with a champagne bottle after MTV showed the version of Williams' epic video for his single 'Hate Me Now' which featured Puff Daddy being crucified (Puff had changed his mind about this aspect of the video on the grounds that it might alienate his new Christian fanbase, and retribution was extracted along the lines of the rarely quoted verse in the Book of Revelations where it says 'And he who doth release a version of a video of which you disapproveth shall receive many blows from the Krug receptacle').

The alarming tension between conspicuous consumption and extreme peril embodied in the Puffy champagne attack is miraculously resolved in Williams' video canon. In a time of clear and present danger the director's breathtaking sci-fi scenarios – the sensual cyber-feminism of TLC's 'No Scrubs' or Janet Jackson and Bustah Rhymes being reconstructed entirely from tin foil – took hip-hop's biggest stars off the street and gave them a place of safety. Not for the first time in the history of black American music, futurism had proved the ultimate refuge.

Cloaking himself in a protective dustcloud of wilful disinformation and either blowing out interviews at a moment's notice or, when he does deign to give them, restricting his answers to 'I don't know', Spike Jonze's manner in person is that of a prairie dog or meerkat –

out in the grassland for the moment, but liable to disappear into his burrow at any time.

He is certainly a far cry from the ebulliently relaxed character who appeared on *Mirrorball*, a late-night Channel 4 TV series offering the world's most fashionable video directors a platform to be as pretentious as they wanted. Where others spoke in high-flown terms of the congruence between their ideas and their art, Jonze chose to pose as an amiable redneck, tooling around LA in his red Chevrolet while offering such heartfelt observations as, 'There's way more to life than cool cars.'

How did the programme's makers react to this?

Jonze smiles. 'I just sent it over to them – there wasn't a great deal they could do about it'.

Perhaps they had cottoned on to the fact that Jonze seems able to talk about himself only in terms of other people. Asked which of his video work he would put on his showreel, he says 'mostly Michel Gondry's' (Gondry is a stylish and innovative member of Jonze's video-making peer group, best known for his work with Björk).

What is it about what Gondry does that Jonze likes?

'Just that every time he makes something, he invents something new – each video is an invention either conceptually or technically, and then he puts the whole thing together and executes it in a really charming way.'

It is probably no coincidence that this generous assessment of a potential competitor applies just as well to Jonze's own oeuvre. From the delirious cop-show spoof he created for The Beastie Boys' 'Sabotage', to the MGM-style choreography of Björk's 'It's Oh So Quiet', to the dog cut off from human society by the music on its ghetto blaster in Daft Punk's 'All Around The World', Jonze's best videos transcend the straightforward pastiche for which the genre is justly notorious to create their own imaginative worlds. His assertion that a great pop video 'can be as satisfying as a really good piece of cinema' will seem less outrageous to those who are familiar with his work than those who aren't.

There's something about the way The Beastie Boys interact in that 'Sabotage' video – the way Mike D's character 'the chief' taps his head knowingly – which sums up everything that is fun about them. And the doughnuts thrown up in the air are a moment of true genius.

Jonze's most public coup to date (if you don't count his Oscar-nominated feature film *Being John Malkovich*) was the video for Fatboy Slim's 'Praise You'. It starred 'The Torrance Community Dance Troupe': a music and movement commando organisation from an unglamourous LA suburb, whose gleefully a-rhythmic dancing leaves passers-by outside a shopping mall looking comically bemused. By the time their leader – an enigmatic and highly committed individual called Richard Koufey – made his moving 'best video' acceptance speech at 1999's MTV awards, ('We've been together for seven years, and this is by far the most exciting thing that has ever happened to us'), it had become clear that Koufey was, in fact, none other than Jonze himself, whose deliciously twisted imagination had created the whole Torrance Community Dance phenomenon.

Aliases are nothing new to Jonze. He is already using one. It was his penchant for tonsorial disarray which first earned him the nickname Spike, as a teenager working at a BMX bike shop in Rockville, Maryland. No one knows where the Jonze bit came from, but his real name – Adam Spiegel – though admirable in many ways, does not quite have the same ring to it as his adopted one, which simultaneously doffs a cap to the Afro-American cool of Spike Lee, acknowledges the historical precedent of madcap forties comedian Spike Jones, and exudes that special touch of pizzazz which only a z in your second name can bring.

Dave Grohl and the Robot of Pop: Together in Electric Dreams

Every edition of British MTV's American Top Twenty concludes with a tune from 'the robot of pop' (a small automated toy who dances to a Moby-penned electro-doodle proclaiming 'I am the robot of pop, feel me rock'). Hair-gel heir Toby Amies runs the show as some kind of deliciously deranged fiefdom. His catchphrases – 'ladies and gentlemen, boys and girls, players and playa-haters' – are not especially funny in themselves, but there is something about his devotion to them which is profoundly endearing.

Amies even makes entertainment capital from the night-time VJ's eternal dilemma – how to cover up the fact that you yourself aren't watching the videos as all your contributions are filmed in one go and then chopped up into little pieces for slotting in between the clips – by treating the videos as an unwelcome intrusion, bringing the viewer back down to earth from whatever half-assed goofball farrago he has concocted for them with an exaggerated, 'Let's find out, what's going on . . . *in the charts*.'

On leap-year night in February 2000, former Nirvana drummer Dave Grohl is helping Toby through his links with a series of delightfully underwritten insights into his fictional career as a *fashionista*. As the notoriously unaffected Grohl strikes a series of ludicrously vain poses while essaying a surprisingly passable Naomi Campbell impression, the ineffably image-conscious Amies looks up at him in the adoring manner of one of Jesus' lesser known disciples. Something about their enjoyment of this absurd routine is utterly infectious – perhaps it has to do with the humility Grohl has shown in continuing his career without ever seeming to want to usurp Kurt Cobain's glory.

Before the robot of pop puts in his final appearance, 'Learning to Fly', the current video by Grohl's amiable bubble-grunge outfit The Foo Fighters, gets a well-deserved airing. The band star not only as themselves – boarding an internal US flight – but also as air-hostesses, stewards, passengers and crew, all of whom are thrown into turmoil when a consignment of concealed drugs leaks into the coffee machine, incapacitating all on board bar the irresponsible rock 'n' rollers, who have prudently opted to drink only whiskey and are consequently in a position to land the plane with the help of a handy manual.

'A lot of people's criticism [of the pop video] is that now they can only see those pictures when you hear the song, and the song really made you dream.' David Lynch said this[27], and given that he made *Wild At Heart* – which might fairly be described as the greatest extended pop promo of all time – you'd think he would know what he was on about. But Lynch also claimed the medium was limited because it had no dialogue, silences or interim sound effects, and this was after the advent of John Landis' landmark video for Michael Jackson's 'Thriller', in which Michael's werewolf tells his victim he's 'not like other guys', so perhaps in this instance it would be best to ignore him.

The truth is that in its highest and most evolved form – from the unspoilt pre-MTV literal-mindedness of The Specials' 'Ghost Town' or The Undertones playing Subbuteo in 'My Perfect Cousin' to the irresistible later hi-tech phantasms of Bone Thugs & Harmony's 'Tha Crossroads' or Aphex Twin's 'Come To Daddy' – the pop video not only *makes* you dream, it actually is a dream. A dream of magic and mischief. A dream of a world in which there can be two Mariah Careys – a good one and an evil one – and they can get in a fight in a cinema toilet. A dream of a world in which Robbie Williams can fly.

Interviewed on *CD-UK* in his American hotel room shortly before the release of 'She's The One', Robbie was so obviously – and poignantly – in the grip of serious depression that even Cat Deeley noticed. The conjunction of huge personal turmoil and a beautifully judged soft-rock ballad would have been hard enough to resist on its own. But the video in which Robbie's lovelorn ice-dancing coach flies into the breach to produce a medal-winning skating performance was a pop moment which he (indeed anyone) will do well to surpass in the future.

The ambiguities in his feelings for his younger dance partner are beautifully observed in their own right, but also function as a perfect allegory for an increasingly cynical Robbie's relationship with his fanbase. The video ends with an astute comment on the post-imperial Torvill and Dean-style patriotism reflected in Williams' own new-found superstar status. All the marks on the scorecard are 5.8s, 5.9s and maximum sixes, until the wise eye of commentator Barry Davies lights on a patriotic 6.1 from Williams' adjudicating fellow-country-man, causing him to observe sympathetically: 'I think the British judge has got a bit carried away.'

Books

In his introduction to *The Faber Book Of Pop*, the distinguished novelist and screenwriter Hanif Kureishi described pop music as 'a form crying out not to be written about'. This observation raised eyebrows on a number of counts; not least in appearing to undermine the whole point of the book he was supposed to be introducing.

If something being 'physical, sensual, of the body rather than the mind' means you shouldn't write about it, where does that leave sex or shopping or scenery? And surely there is more than a hint of condescension in Kureishi's attempt to identify pop as the "new literature" Tom Wolfe demanded in his introduction to *Bonfire of the Vanities?* Pop music does not aspire to the condition of literature, it aspires to the condition of pop music[28].

The New Journalism Wolfe pioneered in the sixties and seventies was in itself a pop phenomenon: his account of, say, lunchtime dancing on Oxford Street in *The Pump House Gang* has the magic spark of a great single by The Shirelles. His later fiction on the other hand is quite another matter. In its grim determination to embrace the *zeitgeist*, it suggests the predatory Christmas party advance of a drunken technical services manager[29].

Wolfe is one of a number of literary heavyweights to get in the ring with pop music and come out with a bloody nose: the unworthy groupie clichés that bog down the vaulting prose of Salman Rushdie's *The Ground Beneath Her Feet*; the uncharacteristic factual laxity of the, as a rule, heroically anal Bret Easton Ellis[30], referring to that notorious techno duo 'The Aphex Twins' in *Glamorama*. The list goes on and on. It's not that pop isn't a fit topic for novelistic consideration, just that too many literary grandees seem to take it as an invitation to let their standards slip.

The spectacle of music journalists berating famous writers for the slapdash nature of their pop references is no more edifying than its traditional counterpart – literary critics deriding the bookish pretensions of rock lyricists. And such insider efforts as Tony Parsons' *Platinum Logic* and Barney Hoskyns' *Lonely Planet Boy* have done no more to advance the credibility of the 'rock novel', than Bob Dylan's *Tarantula* or that book by the bloke out of Belle And Sebastian[31].

The interesting question is whether there is some fundamental incompatability between musical and literary endeavour. Returning to the *Faber Book of Pop* – which is, for all Kureishi's soft-sell, pretty much the ultimate cornucopia of pop literature – the answer would seem to be a resounding 'No Way'. Excerpts from such pop-informed literary landmarks as *Lucky Jim, A Clockwork Orange* and Ralph Ellison's *Invisible Man* make sense not only on their terms, but also as a context within which the value of the greatest specialist music writing can be formally appreciated.

The words of Jack Good or Penny Reel or Greg Tate open up new imaginative worlds in the same bold and sure way that the best fiction does – you can almost feel the ground shifting beneath them. There is a strange and perhaps unexpected poetry, too, in early tabloid pop writing, for example the *Sunday Pictorial*'s 'Is Johnnie Ray a mass hypnotist?' ('What Ray does is break down self-consciousness, to make his fans feel that they are no longer mere cogs, no longer alone'), and even the *Sun*'s first vision of Boy George – 'the sensational singer who looks like a girl, sounds like a fella and behaves like something strangely in between' – has acquired a certain mythic snap to it.

Why is it then that, since the halcyon early days of Colin MacInnes' *Absolute Beginners* and James Baldwin's *Just Above My Head* and Nik Cohn's *I Am Still the Greatest Says Johnny Angelo*, so little of the best writing about pop has been fictional? Perhaps because in this particular field, fact pursues fiction in the hope of rendering it irrelevant.

'All I had in mind when I started,' remembers former Farm manager Kevin Sampson of the band in *Powder*, his entertaining *ur-pulp* romp through the British rock'n'roll infrastructure, 'was a vaguely melancholy Northern four piece. I knew what their influences would have been and how they'd sound. Then, in Easter 1997, The Verve's "Bittersweet Symphony" came out of the radio and it seemed to sum up everything about the feel and the mood and the attitude I was thinking of.'

Is the reason successful fictional pop creations are so hard to come by that all the best pop stars are fictionalising themselves anyway?

'I think that's right,' Sampson grins, 'as was never more clearly seen than in The Beatles cartoon, where the cartoon Ringo is more Ringo than Ringo is.'

To put it in a slightly more pretentious way, perhaps the range of possibilities contained in pop's actuality is too valuable to be traded in for the fictive, except by those who were born to it with that special gift of imagination that transcends merely arranging real-life events and people in vaguely different shapes.

The greatest pop fictions use music in the same way that we all do – as an atmosphere that not only adds colour and texture to day-to-day life but also transports us to different times and places. For example, Philip K. Dick's record shop and radio station novels *Mary and the Giant* and *The Broken Bubble* allow the modern reader to breathe the gasoline-tinged air of fifties California as surely as if they grew up there.

And when Nicola Barker's *Reversed Forecast* magically captures the innocence of pre-Britpop London at the last moment before Blur's *Parklife* destroyed it for ever, or Irvine Welsh's *Trainspotting* simultaneously taunts and succours its AIDS-ravaged Edinburgh junkiedom with the antediluvian opiate hymns of Lou Reed and Iggy Pop, the writers concerned have the skill to leave you thinking that they are not so much using the music as the music is using them[32].

The best way to understand how books like these can *be* pop rather than merely being *about* it, is to consider a couple that aim for the same goal but don't quite score. Nick Hornby's novels *High Fidelity* and *About A Boy* both incorporate substantial musical motifs, but for all the obvious affection and knowledge which underpin them, the underlying tendency within these themes is to regard pop and the culture which surrounds it as one element (and not an especially helpful one at that) in a broader process of personal development: as an index – a means of measuring up or not measuring up – to some abstract standard of normality. This, surely, is exactly the *opposite* of what pop is supposed to do.

High Fidelity's lovelorn record shop owner has a theory about making compilation tapes. He thinks that you should never put white performers on a tape with black performers on it, unless the white singers are trying to sound black. Compare this virtual musical apartheid to the state of mind depicted in *Space Is the Place*, John F. Swzed's inspiring biography of outer space jazz-eminence Sun Ra. Whether pioneering the consumption of vitamin tablets or dressing in the style of an ancient Egyptian, Mr Ra's day to day life seems – like all the best pop role models – to establish a template for the quotidian application of the extraordinary and the remarkable.

Defending himself against accusations of draft-avoidance in an unsympathetic Southern court, Sun Ra proclaims, 'I don't see how the government of anyone else could expect me to agree to being judged by the standards of a normal person.' The judge, using a racial epithet, states that he never saw a defendant like Ra before. 'No,' proclaims the musician, 'and you never will again.'

Henry Rollins' gruelling five-year tour diary *Get in the Van* tells a story from the other end of the musical spectrum altogether, but with a similar epic ring to it. Rollins' life on the road with US hardcore punk heroes Black Flag was, famously, no picnic, but though his general tone is on the sepulchral side of dark, there is affecting light relief in his battle-hardened assessments of the people around him ('At Dave Slut's house – the Meat Puppets are a great band, but they are children') and especially in his valiant attempts to keep up his own perpetually flagging spirits. 'Having no girlfriend,' he asserts pluckily but without real conviction, 'is better.'

Next to drama on this scale, the ideals of American alternativeness projected in such recent US novels as Jeff Gomez' *Our Noise*, Pagan Kennedy's *The Exes* or even Dennis Cooper's gay indie porn rhapsody *Guide* inevitably seem to playing on rather a small screen. In the same way that theatre audiences will laugh at things in Shakespeare or Alan Ayckbourn that would probably not strike them as remotely amusing in the world outside, these books seem to be striving to capture an elusive spirit more readily accessible via a quick flick through the pages of *Spin*.

Just as real fiction eschews or surpasses autobiography, so a great pop story does not have to be told in the actual voice of the participants. In fact sometimes the participants are best kept out of it. Anyone looking for the definitive history of The Sex Pistols will almost certainly favour the impassioned erudition of Jon Savage's *England's Dreaming* over the hectoring tone and obsessive self-validation of John Lydon's *No Blacks, No Irish, No Dogs*[33]. And the grim tenor of a brutal first-person excoriation like Charles Mingus' *Beneath the Underdog* might well leave you gasping for the heady fabulations of Nick Tosches' *Hellfire*.

At other times the participants just need a helping hand.

'Dolly has never talked openly,' it says on the cover of Dolly Parton's *Dolly: My Life and Other Unfinished Business*, 'until now,' which might leave those with a clear memory of earlier autobiographies feeling somewhat short-changed. But it would be churlish to quibble about this, or the fact that a certain Buddy Sheffield is thanked for the use of his computers ('the one on your lap and the one on your shoulders'), since the voice the book speaks in – whether individually or collaboratively arrived at – is 100 per cent Dolly. For those unable to afford a visit to the magnificent Dollywood theme-park, and with no prospect of purchasing products from the Dolly Parton Beauty Confidence collection, this book could well prove to be a lifesaver.

The well from which the bulk of Partonian wisdom is drawn is her harsh but fair upbringing as the fourth of twelve children in a family of poor Smoky Mountain share-croppers. She is not afraid to dig into the earthier side of farming life: the moment when, poised over the slop bucket, she felt the un-welcome intrusion of a raccoon's nose, or the time a brother was found substituting a taboo part of his anatomy for the bottle when hand-rearing a calf ('Damn, dad, are you just going to stand there and let this thing eat me up?').

Dolly's favourite childhood haunt was a derelict chapel, where she would alternate between playing hymns on the old piano and examining the dirty pictures graffiti'd on the wall. Identifying the three most powerful forces in her life as God, music and sex (that pecking order being 'subject to change without warning'), *My Life and Other Unfinished Business* pinpoints the time-honoured nexus between old-time religion and sexuality with a poetic clarity academic analysis could not hope to match.

As a young girl, Dolly would sit in church – 'Trying to be holy . . . all the while being aware of the boys looking at me, the woods behind the church and the possible combination of all these things' – and conclude that she and the devil had one thing in common: 'We were both horny.' At her baptism at twelve years old 'these body parts that were destined to become my calling-card in life . . . were already well in evidence.' In the course of the service, the white cotton dress became transparent in the rushing water 'and the boys on the bank were moved to shout "Hallelujah."'

Frankness – *Straight Talk*, to borrow the title of Dolly's entertaining cinematic two-hander with James Woods – is central to Dolly Parton's myth. It comes as no surprise when she confesses to having stolen from room service trays as a star-struck but starving Nashville teen, or stopped her car to streak through Tom Jones' backyard just for the hell of it. Yet there is still something exhilarating about what is aptly referred to on the jacket as Dolly's 'tell-it-like-it-is style'.

It's not only the force with which she speaks her mind ('Being a woman in showbusiness is like being a birddog in heat: if you stand still, they'll screw you, if you run they'll bite you in the ass'), but the elegance with which she translates such hardwon knowledge into practical advice, that makes Dolly such an enduring source of inspiration. 'A smart woman,' she counsels, 'can take a man who thinks with his small head and quickly turn the would-be screwer into the screwee.'

Another downhome upbringing – across America to the left and then up a bit – is the foundation of our next essential pop document. The early stages of Iggy Pop's *I Need More* (with Ann Karz) find the young James Newell Osterberg growing up in a trailer home in the outskirts of Ann Arbor, Michigan, which would have been a one-horse town if it had a horse.

Raised not so much on the sizzle of his mum's frying pan as the comforting whirr of the fan heater and the warming glow of the little red light on an aluminium plug, Iggy was a pupa in an electric cocoon. ('The sheer presence of electricity in large doses,' he remembers, always made him feel 'real comfortable.') And when he sprouted wings and took flight, the music that drove him on was 'a sweeping sound like Mongolian hordesmen charging in; thousands of little tartars with swords – frequencies only a geek can hear'.

When American punk prophet Lester Bangs heard the frequencies on Iggy and The Stooges' *Raw Power*, he hailed 'the advent of a star with not one shred of dignity or mythic corona left'. Time passed and, as Bangs would probably have predicted if he could have been bothered to think that far ahead, this very supposed absence of mythic corona became one of the biggest mythic coronas of all. The same would be true of Bangs himself, in that it was his very willingness to acknowledge the possibility that the music he loved might be 'a bunch of garbage . . . everything your parents said it was' which enabled him to submerge himself so utterly in the beauty of its rushing many-streamed complexity.

You don't have to have an obsessive interest in The Godz or The Count Five or whichever delinquent reprobates Bangs was ranting on about at any given moment to understand why he was special. It wasn't just his ability to write about music that most people would probably approach with at best a sceptically raised eyebrow, as if it were the only thing keeping him alive (in any case – as *Let It Blurt*, Jim Derogatis' well-researched and compassionate biography confirms – it quite often *was* the only thing keeping him alive); Bangs' identification with his subject matter was absolute. Not in the manner (well, not always anyway) of his English acolyte Nick Kent, whereby the writer competes to be even more of a decadent egotist than his subject, but in trying to bring the same creative energy to reacting to the music as was – or should have been – put into making it in the first place. Observing that some of the pieces he wrote about Lou Reed's music in the seventies were 'probably better art' than the records themselves, Bangs' tone is not so much vainglorious as regretful.

Greil Marcus' introduction to the seminal anthology *Psychotic Reactions and Carburettor Dung* says that what the book demands from the reader is 'a willingness to accept that the best writer in America could write almost nothing but record reviews'. Like all the best bizarre statements, this one has a kernel of truth in it, but for all his bluster ('Who was better?' he once demanded, 'Bukowski? Burroughs? Hunter Thompson? Gimme a break. I was the best') Bangs seems to have had as much trouble swallowing that kernel as anyone else.

It shouldn't have mattered that his occasional stabs at novel-writing were as undistinguished as Salman Rushdie's later foray into the world of rock songcraft as a guest lyricist for U2. For in his visionary description of 'incredible unglimpsed horizons of master-fully abstracted sound', Bangs had already found his own fiction, which was also his own truth. And in the pursuit of such sacred objectives, great musicians don't just walk the same paths as great writers (or great painters or great architects come to that), they wear the same built-up shoes.

Afterword

As evidence to support the above proposition, and in tribute to an exemplary career in pop publishing, we present:

To Be a Rock and Not to Roll –
A Day Trip into the Strange and Megalithic World of Julian Cope

Head On, Julian Cope's delirious autobiographical whirl through the Liverpool punk scene of the late seventies and early eighties, bears the same happy relation to Iggy Pop's *I Need More* as Billie's 'Honey To The B' did to 'Never Ever' by All Saints (which is that of a respectful younger sibling who still has something distinctive of their own to contribute). From the moment the author puts an end to the bullying which results from his triumphant performance in a school production of *Oliver Twist* by kissing the ring-leader squarely upon the lips, to his band's final dissolution in shame, rancour and financial degradation, a dull moment is not on the agenda.

As well as pushing back previously established boundaries of personal hygiene and sexual licence, and proving once and for all that hallucinogenic drugs should not be treated as a primary food group, *Head On* manages the rare achievement of demystifying the creative process ('it needed a refrain after each verse, so we tried to copy the chorus at the end of The Doors' "Winter-time Love"') in such a way as to make it seem more fun rather than less.

Cope's next volume, *Krautrocksampler* – an impassioned introduction to the esoteric German experimental music which supplies the first 9/16ths of the title – confirmed him as someone deserving to be taken more seriously as a writer than he ever seemed to ask to be as a musician.

His third book did not so much push the outer edge of the envelope as crumple the envelope up into a ball and throw it out of the window. Cope's *The Modern Antiquarian* is a pioneering survey of megalithic Britain, eight years in the making, featuring not only an exhaustive gazzetteer of three hundred places of prehistoric interest – each one visited (and most photographed) by the author – but also a wealth of anecdotal material along the lines of Cope's immortal couplet: '*Atop Knap Hill I eat my snot/for 'tis the only food I've got.*'

An investigation into Britain's pre-Roman remains by the former lead singer of The Teardrop Explodes might seem like the final stage in the colonisation of every sphere of our cultural life by the celebrity dilettante. But *The Modern Antiquarian* should not be bracketed with Alan Titchmarsh's heist movie or Roy Hattersley's guide to DIY colonic irrigation. It is both a work in the finest tradition of pop literature and a Rosetta Stone into the eternal verities of showbusiness. And by bearding the man who wrote it in his lair, it might be possible to tease out connections between rock 'n' roll cultures BC and AD which will be of great interest to us all.

Cope and his family – his glamorous American wife, Dorian, and their oddly well-balanced four- and seven-year-old daughters Albany and Avalon – live in a converted stables, the least ostentatious part of a three-house manor conversion, behind a church in a tiny Wiltshire village, not far from the Avebury stone circle.

The great man's head appears – gurning gleefully – around the wall of his house. The first thing you notice is a halo of wispy blond hair, then Cope bounds into the open and suddenly the pressing concern of the moment is how unnervingly high he wears his track-suit bottoms. His infectious energy – a favoured expostulation is 'I love that kind of righteous poetry' – refracts through a disarming disregard for conventional notions of personal space. One minute he is expounding through the kitchen doorway from outside in the garden, the next he is standing four inches away.

One can imagine the neighbours being slightly trepidatious on his arrival about the possibility of teepees in the garden. 'We're *impossibly* quiet,' Cope whispers, 'like hermits on Skellig rock. The teepees in the garden, unfortunately they do happen, because we have a lot of road-protester friends. We don't have them in the house' – his obvious concern as to how inhospitable this sounds fades into a beaming smile – 'but they don't *want* to be in the house.'

His words are punctuated by a series of staccato barks from the Cope's ancient dog, Jeep. The jovial canine is a pedigree schnauzer, but there is something strange about the way it looks. Julian, it turns out, obliged Dorian to get rid of its whiskers. The man notorious for dressing entirely in flourescent yellow and appearing on album covers wearing nothing but a giant turtle shell apparently objected to them on fashion grounds. So Cope made his wife shave her schnauzer? He feigns outrage: 'There is nothing vulvic about my dog.'

Before he can turn the conversation around to *The Modern Antiquarian*, Cope gets sidetracked into a fantastic story about his drummer, Rooster, who got put under house arrest in Japan after putting a major international hotel out of action for three days with an incendiary device. Inspired by the presence onstage of a posse of straight-laced Japanese policemen, Julian performed wearing a horri-fyingly skimpy thong. In flourescent marker pen he inscribed a W on one butt-cheek and a W on the other. 'When I bent over', he exults, 'I spelt Wow!'. He refuses to let me tape record this anecdote because he 'doesn't want the person who wrote this book to be the person who would tell that sort of story'.

If Julian Cope was entirely committed to a new scholarly image he would not have packaged his book in an outer cover promising

'Britain divided into seven rainbow colours' and 'over fifty poems'. This 'refusal to toe the line' as he terms it underpins a serious mission to redress the balance of what he scathingly terms 'all that Raquel Welch on a pterodactyl stuff', i.e. the misrepresentation of the megalithic (literally 'big stone' though this is in fact somewhat of a misnomer as they did stuff with earth and wood as well, it's just that the stones have survived) era. 'You go to Avebury', Cope says disgustedly, 'and there's t shirts with cavemen on them.'

What would he like people to get out of *The Modern Antiquarian*?

'We're all so paranoid about standing on the edge of time getting ready to jump off, that it's good to know that there was *always* this sort of shit going on. People have been standing on the abyss for thousands of years – even the *Abyss*inians were always freaking out! And people need to know that even if it's only to make them feel a little less lonely.'

One of the most invigorating things about Cope's book is that rather than the expected idealised vision of smiling stone circle builders in harmony with their environment, it creates an image of people 'just as stubborn and obsessive and over-achieving as ourselves'. Rather than these remains embodying an understanding between man and nature which we have now lost, he seems to be saying that our lostness began at this point – the moment we attained sufficient separation from the land to feel the need (and have the time and tools) to celebrate our affinity for it.

Cope nods vigorously: 'It's so easy to jump into this stupid new age thing [assumes crazed hippie voice, fractionally different to his own]; "Oh man, the bronze age . . ." Ha! Ha! It's like, the bronze age was *bollocks*!'

The section of the book which will give rise to the most furrowed brows is probably Cope's 'Etymosophy'. What is the difference between an etymosophy and the more conventional field of linguistic enquiry – etymology?

'When it's an 'ology, there's less chance of it working – when its an 'osophy, that's a *belief* system, *Sophia* gets involved . . .'

Sensing that he might be losing us here, Cope embarks on an epic voyage of clarification. 'Look, if you take the God lug, he was full of light – lug coming, literally, from the moon. As the bronze age progressed, people began to "lug" stuff around. In the Nordic countries they had a sort of Troggs hairstyle which was called "luggan", then to be "as lug" was to do nothing but it's also to stand up and "slug" you. Etymologists would say, "So here on one side we have the slug people who believe slug is sluggishness and on the other, the slug people who believe in whacking people." They can never make that leap to say, "No, it's the capricious nature of the deity lug that unites it!" '

Well, that's that cleared up, then. But there are a couple of other major themes that need further elucidation. Why, in the words of one of Cope's most memorable chapter headings, 'were the Romans so heavy'?

'I think it was probably because they were pummelled by Carthage for so many years before they became the empire, that when they finally did Carthage in, they had to do it and do it and do it.'

And what was so bad about the Synod of Whitby (the key historical moment in 664 AD when the independent British church 'fell into the hands of Rome')?

'Because it was the death of Celtic Christianity, and that banished the female perspective for ever. Well, it wasn't banished so much as in hiding . . . If you think of Latin, which is the ultimate patriarchal language, because it's the one the pope speaks. Even Latin gives away the fact that the mother comes before the father. If you go to Leicestershire there's a village called Appleby Magna and another one down the road called Appleby Parva. Magna means greater and Parva means smaller [Cope pauses significantly] ma is in front of pa! [said with the utmost seriousness] It's self-evident!'

While the full impact of these revelations is still sinking in, Julian alludes to a poem he has written (as yet unpublished, so he refuses to quote directly from it) called 'Cliff Richard Is A Pagan': 'The day the heavens opened at Wimbledon and he danced around in front of the crowd and sang "The Young Ones" he proved he was a heathen. You can't say "I am not a heathen" if you're dancing on the heath, because that is what it means. Cliff is a pagan for Christ,' Cope declaims proudly, 'but he's still a pagan.'

The Prism/The Souls/The Choir

(The recorded work listed at the end of each section is certainly a representative sample but not necessarily a defining moment.)

Air

'Digital is like your wife: she stays at home to raise the children and make the cook.'

Any list of the cultural turning points of 1998 would have to start with January's first *Top of the Pops* appearance by the French duo Air. Two mild-mannered Parisians in their late twenties – one a former architect, the other a reformed maths teacher – Nicolas Godin and Jean-Benoit Dunckel (J-B to his friends) seem unlikely shock troops for a pop revolution.

But with the release of their album *Moon Safari*, these two soft-spoken young men overturn one of Britain's most cherished delusions. Thanks to Air, it can be no longer be said – even by idiots – that the people of France (with the possible exception of Serge Gainsbourg, but he came from another planet and therefore didn't count) are temperamentally incapable of producing great pop music. As outrageous as it is that the works of such Gallic legends as chanteuse Françoise Hardy, ambient Godfather Erik Satie and hip-hop pioneer Pierre Boulez, should have ever been overlooked in this way, British small-mindedness gives Air something to react against.

Beyond the beguiling suppleness and sheen of the single they are miming to, there was something magnificently insouciant about Nicolas and J-B on television that night: a certain jut to their hips that proclaims 'We are French and we don't care'. Subsequent live appearances (an unexpectedly – and thrillingly – tumultuous show-ing on *Later*; a tour in which they perform 'Sexy Boy' in the style of Tik and Tok) offset their music's easy-listening tendencies with a welcome combative edge.

'La Femme D'Argent', *Moon Safari*'s instrumental opening track, becomes, with its optimistic rolling bass guitar and laid-back hand claps, a kind of signature tune for all that is good and unthreatening about life at the turn of the century. Whether sidling out of the doorways of cafés and restaurants, or insinuating itself into innumerable different dramatic contexts thanks to the herd mentality of the people who arrange the background music for TV trailers, the music of Air seems to have the rare ability to draw strength from its surroundings[34].

'Sexy Boy' seems on first hearing to be a diverting if slightly vacuous piece of bilingual homoerotic intrigue with mild disco-revivalist overtones. And yet after hearing it a few times, and watching the gripping animated video in which a monkey experiments with rocket flight, another story begins to emerge – a story of dry, Darwinian wit and expectations elegantly overturned. Who is that simian space invader, and what is he up to? 'He wants to be fashionable,' J-B explains to the NME, 'and in his dreams he's sexy boy, but in reality he's just a monkey.' I think there's a little bit of that monkey in all of us.

Getting off the Eurostar at the Gare Du Nord and whizzing through the underpasses of Paris in a record company Mercedes with tinted windows, you realise that it would be possible to speak to Air on their home ground without any sense of the country they come from. The funny thing is, the country they come from has very little sense of them either. Given France's somewhat lax record in producing international pop sensations, one would think Air's homeland would be only too keen to take them to its bosom. But if the Legion of Honour is on its way, it is still in the post.

At the end of 1997, one French music magazine voted the emergence of 'La Scène Groove Francaise' (the sudden upsurgence in internationally acclaimed homegrown dance music of which Air, along with friends Daft Punk and Etienne de Crècy, are the demure figureheads) as the year's ninth biggest event, behind such epoch-making happenings as the reformation of Echo and the Bunnymen. In this unsympathetic climate, it's hardly surprising Air are managing to keep their feet on the ground.

'People tell us we are successful,' says ebullient, shaggy-headed Nicolas, showing the way into the small Versailles recording studio

Air hope to buy when they have a bit more money, 'but we have no real evidence for it.'

'Some day,' adds the smaller, quieter, J-B, 'we will go to live where we are popular, just to have a little pleasure when people recognise us.'

When it comes to the esteem in which French pop music is held, things are no different on the other side of the Channel. 'If you go out to have dinner in Paris and say you are a musician,' Nicolas explains, 'people think you play on the subway . . .' Air seem to share this low opinion of their countrymen's efforts. 'For each hundred good English bands,' Nicolas insists, 'there is maybe one good French band. In our own country, I am proud to say, we are considered as foreigners.' Because some of their lyrics are in English, Air don't count as part of the 40 per cent of music played on French radio which the law decrees must be in their mother tongue. 'That's why there is so much bad music here,' J-B complains. 'Record companies have to sign bands who are horrible just because they sing in French.'

Growing up with pop music in your second rather than your first language doesn't have to be a problem. 'As a kid,' Nicolas explains, 'you don't understand the words, and you don't care, because books are more important for that.' Like Kraftwerk and Björk before them, Air mirror the assumed superiority of English-speaking pop back on itself with very entertaining results. Sometimes talking to them feels like being an extra in that Hollywood Old Testament epic where the small army hold up polished shields to reflect sunlight into the eyes of their oncoming attackers and they all run into a ditch.

Asked to explain the difference between analogue recording – the old-fashioned method associated with the nostalgic, almost easy-listening feel of *Moon Safari* – and the more modern digital technique, Nicolas replies with typically satirical reference to national stereotypes (at least, I hope he does, because if he means this, Air have a problem): 'Digital is like your wife,' the Frenchman twinkles, 'she stays at home to raise the children and make the cook. Analogue is like a mistress – it's passionate, but you can't count on it . . . that's why people in my country like to have both.'

Having the best of both worlds is something Air seem to excel at. Their studio is located between deer-infested woodland and a quiet suburban golf-course. It's half an hour from the centre of Paris, but the only disturbance is the gentle babble of birdsong and the soothing swish of the trees. In the room beyond their flickering computer screens – the title of the new tune they're currently working on reads, rather ominously, 'Punk Song' – there lurks a veritable treasure trove of antique keyboards and amplifiers. Air have been collecting them for years. Rare as lizards' teeth in other countries, they're relatively easy to come by in France where people don't tend to know their value. And the mythic brand names – Moog, Vocoder, Korg, Hohner, Marshall, Wurlitzer – are an international language all of their own.

Those curious as to the spiritual origin of *Moon Safari*'s pristine pastoral reveries need look no further than the place it was made in. There is none of the mouldering smell of old takeaway food and drummer's athlete's foot which all too often set the atmosphere in the environments where music is recorded. How can they work in these conditions?

'We are the fresh French,' says Nicolas, smiling, 'You English give us your fashion designers and we give you our DJs.'

Air's enthusiasm for every aspect of the pop process is in sharp contrast with the rather jaded current mood of the Anglophone pop establishment. Their manager is an old friend from their schooldays in Versailles. Eschewing the venality and cynicism usually associated with his profession, he positively brims with excitement about the demands of an imminent world tour. 'For us,' he says excitedly, 'everyday is something new.' He then plunges into a too-rapid-for-lapsed-A-level-students mother tongue conversation with the nattily attired chauffeur. The only word which emerges clearly is 'le remix'.

Before qualifying as an architect, J-B studied classical piano at the Conservatoire de Paris, so talk of the influence on Debussy on the mood – if not the mechanics – of Air's music is less fanciful than it might seem. They do have a traditional pop background as well. Nicolas and J-B first teemed up as teenage members of an unsuccessful indie band called Orange. 'Everybody else went off to do something different,' Nicolas remembers, 'until we were the only ones left.'

Air's debut single 'Modular', first released in 1995, combined J-B's old and new careers in French dance music's first (and last) explicit tribute to Le Corbusier. Asked about the relationship between music and architecture, this elfin father of one was once heard to observe that, 'For me it's the same thing, you are still building shelters.'

If Air's suburban idyll offers a respite from the turbulence of the grim, racially divided estates immortalised in the film *La Haine*, that's because their music – eloquently characterised by the group themselves as being 'like the sci-fi of Jules Verne: starships made of wood' – harks back to a time before their nation's idea of the future lost its innocence.

Moon Safari (Virgin France, 1998)

Marc Almond

'My record company were saying, "Please don't go on TV dressed like that, it'll harm your career."'

Now that more time has passed since A Guy Called Gerald's 'Voodoo Ray' than separates that unforgettable UK acid/techno landmark from The Tavares' 'Don't Take Away The Music' the connections between acid house and northern soul are revealed ever more clearly, like sandstone fossil formations cleaned by the wind [see **Psychedelic Ear**]. Beyond the obvious parallels (industrious northerners take drugs and dance all night to obscure US dance rarities) there lurks the intriguing story of 'the middleman' – a human fulcrum, the original missing link.

Legend tells of a shadowy figure – saucy, camp, diminutive, dressed in the style of a catalogue toreador – slipping through Soho and New York doorways like an evangelistic will o' the wisp. Pixie, degenerate, sex dwarf, humanist, Jacques Brel-nut: Marc Almond, this was your life.

Matthew Collin's *Altered State* recounts Almond's gleeful embrace of Ecstasy while Soft Cell were in New York making their first album *Non Stop Erotic Cabaret* (and brazenly titled remix collection *Non Stop Ecstatic Dancing*) in 1981. Alongside the delightful sensations of chemical abandon procured through their Brooklyn dealer Cindy Ecstasy (who even got to do a breathy rap advertising her wares on the remix of 'Memorabilia', which was commercially released without controversy because as yet no one knew on earth she was talking about) there was also worrying evidence of the drug's dramatic dilution of the critical faculties.

The first time he took it, Almond was listening to The Cure's album

Faith, and under its influence he came to believe that the song 'All Cats Are Grey' was 'the best record he'd ever heard in his entire life'. Fortunately, Ecstasy's influence on his own music was a good deal more positive. The sequence of Soft Cell singles book-ended by the covers of two Northern soul classics – Gloria Jones' 'Tainted Love' and Judy Street's 'What' – marked the ultimate high-water mark of early eighties synth-pop.

Soft Cell didn't have to go looking for stardom – it crept up behind them armed with a rolled-up tabloid. One minute they were scrabbling around on Fine Arts courses at Leeds Polytechnic, Almond supplementing his DJ-ing income with long hours as a cloakroom attendant; the next they were Number One with 'Tainted Love'.

Unlike rival Yorkshire post-punk pop pioneers ABC and The Human League, Soft Cell did not lose their confrontational edge in the first flush of fame. The pleasure they took in 'getting up everybody's noses' was evident from their first appearance on *Top of the Pops*, sandwiched between Aneka and Shakin' Stevens. Despite the director's best efforts to protect the nation's innocence by smearing the camera lens with Vaseline (at least I think that's what it was), the sight of Almond dressed in biker gear, bangles and eyeliner sent shock waves through the nation's living rooms. 'My record company were saying, "Please don't go on TV dressed like that – it'll harm your career,"' Marc remembers fondly. 'Well, it didn't.'

Almost overnight, Almond replaced Marc Bolan and David Bowie, his own teenage heroes, as the inspirational embodiment of dippily deviant glamour. This turn of events had its downside. Anyone who remembers the press persecution Almond suffered as the first of the eighties 'gender benders' could not fail to realise the absurdity of later criticism of him for 'not being political enough' about his gayness.

'People were actually very cruel about it at the time. I'd gone through home and school-life (in Southport, Lancashire) suffering a lot of hurt and abuse, and now I was going through the same thing with the press, so I decided to pull away from it.'

Perhaps it wasn't so surprising that after Soft Cell, Almond's determination not to live off past glories should have bordered on the pathological. 'I've always been the person who's gone out and not played my hit singles,' he admits, casually dressed in tracksuit and trainers in the plush offices of Warner Brothers, the record label which has benificently secured him the services of a forty-piece orchestra for his celebratory career pageant *Twelve Years Of Tears* (see below). 'I've tended to concentrate on obscure B-sides and track three off the forgotten album.'

There are a number of these in the Almond solo canon. He is a prolific writer – 'Left to my own devices I'd probably only make triple albums.' And although he baulks at the suggestion that he ever made records which are not easy to listen to ('Which might those have been, may I ask?' he demands imperiously) many people's ears still wax up protectively at the thought of his 1987 opus *Mother Fist and Her Five Daughters*.

Almond's willingness to be difficult – to drop out of the mainstream while he works on a new direction – might not have gone down well with some of his shorter-suffering record labels, but it has played a vital part in sustaining him as one of the spikiest of British pop icons, and made his periodic returns to centre stage – like 'Something's Gotta Hold Of My Heart', 1988's gloriously overblown number one with Gene Pitney – occasions to remember. And the most memorable occasion of all is the one we are about to get to.

How Many Years of Tears Was That Exactly?

'Welcome to *Twelve Years of Tears*,' Marc Almond the diva proclaims to a suitably ecstatic Royal Albert Hall in May 1992. 'Tears of sorrow, but also tears of joy.' What follows is a brilliantly realised live pop extravaganza: moulding an up and down career – from Soft Cell's pioneering electro sex-angst, through years of bold but sometimes slightly wearing solo eclecticism, to 1991's excellent *Tenement Symphony* – into a single joyous pageant.

The star of the show makes a boxer's entrance, complete with exotic escorts and sequinned robe. This he removes – the first of more costume changes than Diana Ross could shake a sequin at – to reveal a leather biker's outfit, setting the tone for the warm-hearted sado-disco of the opening numbers. Much of the recent material is co-written with old Cell-mate David Ball, and the best of it – 'Meet Me In My Dream', for example – is right up there with the old stuff.

Almond darts compactly about the stage, giving little bows and waving his arms in the occasional baroque flourish. The show changes gear effortlessly, through tortured torch songs at the piano to ancient pop monuments like 'Bedsitter', and on to grand orchestral epics like 'The Days of Pearly Spencer'. Dancers, backing singers, keyboard wizards, percussionists, and coach-loads of grumpy-looking violinists (perhaps angered by the knowledge that Almond himself can't play an instrument – he sings vocal lines into a tape recorder and instructs others as to what musical flesh should clothe his melodic bones) troop on and off stage exactly on cue.

When Almond first turned to the songs of Jacques Brel, the world responded with a nervous cough, but nowadays he can carry off the amyl symphony of 'Jacky' and the florid melodrama of 'If You Go Away' with equal aplomb. Almond's own struggle to get himself taken seriously as a *chanteur*, and the nervous agonies he admits to suffering in live performance, add extra resonance to these songs of dignity in desperation.

And when the eagerly awaited intro to 'Tainted Love' – the opening bars of which had assumed such a nightmarish quality for Almond ('Every club I went to anywhere in the world I'd hear the introduction and think, "Oh my God, not again"') that he hadn't performed the song live for almost ten years – is put deliberately off-sequence, so the crowd's handclaps go out of time, a symbolic reconciliation is achieved between his career's pop and non-pop elements.

Finally, amid the immortal soapy clank of 'Say Hello, Wave Goodbye', ('We're strangers meeting for the first time, OK?') a shower of pink balloons falls from the roof, and Almond leaves the stage to a noisy firework display of bursting rubber and exploded preconceptions. If the whole thing has gone to his head, he hasn't shown it. Well, not much. One of the adoring adults in the front row passes him a teddy bear, which he accepts, kisses, drops, and then flamboyantly stamps on.

Soft Cell: *Singles* (Some Bizarre/Phonogram, 1984)

Badly Drawn Boy

'If you get a gentler, more patient pixie, you might end up with ballad.'

There was one gig that really caught the attention of the swarming hordes of A&R men at 1998's In the City convention in Manchester. The man behind it – mild-mannered twenty-nine-year-old Lancastrian Damon Gough, aka Badly Drawn Boy – had already signed a substantial record deal, and was acclimatising to his newfound status as one of the brightest hopes of a recession-hit British music industry. And yet this hometown showcase was, its perpetrator ruefully admits, 'probably the worst gig anyone in the audience had ever seen'.

'The thing about doing something which can potentially fail at any moment,' Gough observes, 'is that sometimes it will do.'

How could a ninety-minute cabaret of half-finished original songs and karaoke Smiths and Simon & Garfunkel cover versions possibly go wrong?

'I knew it was going to happen – I just hadn't put any effort into preparing it, and usually for my show to be as shoddy as it is takes quite a bit of preparation.'

Damon Gough didn't get where he is today by being over-prepared. On leaving school in the late eighties he started work in a recording studio – 'I was trying to learn engineering but I could never really get my foot in the door. You either bundle in like a bull in a china shop and take everything over or you end up on the sidelines making the brews.' Inspired by visions of a lifetime of tea-making, Gough picked up a guitar and beavered away writing (but not singing) in bands for seven years while earning a crust working for his parents' printing business.

Finally realising that if he wanted anything to happen to his songs he was going to have to sing them himself, he released two EPs, helpfully entitled *1* and *2* on his own Twisted Nerve label. At first motivated purely by curiosity ('I wanted to see what they would sound like on vinyl') the two EPs swiftly sold out their initial 500-copy print runs, and Badly Drawn Boy became the subject of an unlikely bidding war.

Gough's 'works in progress' – from frenetic home-made sixties caper movie recordings to wistful acoustic laments, with the odd flash of *Third Man*-type bazouki and a Sister Sledge cover version thrown in for good measure – eventually secured him the backing of The Verve's intimidating management stable and a high-profile deal with X-L, the same label as The Prodigy.

EP3, his first release for X-L, showed a commendable determination not to yield to new commercial pressures. Gough insists his music is 'more about capturing the essence of a moment than trying to get the perfect intro, middle eight and outro for radio', and he is not kidding. *EP3* contains six tracks (twice as many as the maximum number which can now qualify for the singles chart). Of these no less than three are instrumental interludes – one sounds like a CD sticking (but in a good way), one is actually called 'Interlude', and the third, 'Kerplunk By Candlelight', is a twinkly electronic paean to MB Games romanticism.

Of the three 'proper' songs, one meanders jauntily like the theme to some futuristic Ealing comedy, while the other two firmly establish Badly Drawn Boy's credentials as a major new force in British pop. The lovely lilting two-step of 'I Need A Sign' does nothing to deter those trying to hang an unhelpful 'British Beck' tag around Gough's neck, and 'Meet Me On The Horizon' is a gorgeous neo-folk rhapsody, containing in the line 'We go there just to be there' as near a thing to a perfect statement of the Badly Drawn Boy aesthetic as the world is currently ready for

The next year's eagerly awaited LP has got, Gough insists, 'to be a classic'. He cites the debut albums by Air and The Smiths as inspirational examples of 'records that you put on and you've got to listen to all the way through'. Eighteen months and two more wild and winsome EP's later, and his own debut – arrestingly titled *The*

Hour of Bewilderbeast – is finally complete. Gough's determination that people should listen to the whole thing in one go is such that he was thinking of leaving out the track idents – the marks which tell the CD player which song is which – but that would have been using a sledgehammer to crush an orange.

When this record finishes in the lovely whistling and birdsong whirl of 'Epitaph', you just want to put it on again anyway; to hear the courtly cello and french horn intro at the start of 'The Shining', to hear the water sound effect at the end of 'Fall In A River', to bathe in 'This Song's one minute thirty-two second eternity.

From the first glow of attraction, through the underwater tug of surrendering to a momentum beyond yourself, to the final hope for something to hold on to, the first Badly Drawn Boy album is the complete story of a romance and/or a friendship. The only accurate comparison I can think of for the way its individual songs seem to speak directly out of the whole is the hypnotic voices dropping in and out of the soundtrack in Terrence Malick's poetic war film *The Thin Red Line*.

But first things first.

Like where on earth did that title come from?

'The word bewilderbeast came from this guy who was in the band when we were playing in Japan,' Damon explains. 'He was a bit the worse for wear – a bit bewildered, the way you get. He said, "I feel like a bewilderbeast," and that name just stuck in my head as a picture of what I wanted the album to be about. I wanted this to be *our* hour: not just mine, but everyone who's ever had that underdoggy feeling which anyone who's got a bit of humility feels sometimes, even if they're an achiever.'

If you've ever seen Damon Gough play live, you'll probably know what he means by the line in 'Pissing In The Wind' where he sings 'I chanced a foolish grin and dribbled on my chin'. But if you want to understand what gives *The Hour of Bewilderbeast* the power to summon up the ghosts of Nick Drake and John Lennon[35] without ever being about anything other than the here and now and the thrill of the exact moment we are living in, you have to delve into Badly Drawn Boy's mythical theory of songwriting.

'I go to a tree which has several doors in it,' Damon says gravely. 'Every door has a bell and whichever one you choose to ring, there's a pixie living behind it. They're like little ninja superheroes with detachable capes, and each pixie gives you a different nucleus for a song – a little bit of melody or a couple of lyrics. That nucleus could go anywhere, and how far you choose to extrapolate is up to you . . .'

Would the pixies know how it's supposed to turn out?

'In their heads they probably know the best realisation of what the song could be, but sometimes you can surprise them. They've all got different characters. Sometimes you'll get a snappy little feller who's very impatient, so that will have to be quite a quick song, but if you get a gentler, more patient pixie, you might end up with a ballad. The randomness of everything is an important part of the whole picture . . .'

What would Damon's little helpers think the title of this record meant?

Badly Drawn Boy pauses for a moment: 'I believe they would perceive we humans as bewilderbeasts.'

Patient pixies notwithstanding, Gough once described the business of his songwriting as 'capturing little essences' (as if to back this theory up, he produced as a promotional device an exquisite musical box which plays a fragment of one of the tunes from his very first EP). Shards of pure emotion wrapped up in ramshackle gossamer, his best songs prick at the listener's unconscious for months on end.

From the moment The Fall's Mark E. Smith got into his car outside a chip shop in the mistaken belief that it was a minicab (Gough took the legendary Mancunian curmudgeon where he wanted to go, in return for a promise that his band would record with him) Badly Drawn Boy's career has had the air of a waking dream.

A strange thing happened to him on the train down South from the flat he shares with his girlfriend in Chorlton. 'I saw my arm lift up but I knew it wasn't actually moving,' Gough recalls with a vague shudder. 'All the people in my carriage were in the dream. By the time I finally woke up, we'd been through so much together that it was like they were old friends . . . I was going to ask the person opposite if they'd noticed me behaving strangely,' he smiles, 'but then I thought better of it.'

The Hour of Bewilderbeast (X–L, 2000)

Blixa Bargeld

'What is happened is gone and unrepeatable, but we can save the tracks.'

1982. The Birthday Party at the London Lyceum. It's a compellingly savage and violent spectacle, and what's happening onstage is even worse. The band are visiting their fury on a nation which dragged them half-way across the world with promises of punk-rock fury and then gave them the New Pop. 'I'm not going in there,' says a psychotic-looking mohican, casting an anxious eye at the human maelstrom that Nick Cave, Tracey Pew et al. are whipping up on the dancefloor, 'it looks *dangerous*.'

Even amid the atavistic frenzy, the crowd seem to be in shock. The Birthday Party were preceded on to the stage by kindred spirit Berliners Einstürzende Neubauten, making their UK debut. Metal was bashed, a piano was sawn in half, and a new musical form (not so much the garage as the building-site band) was born amid the clanking and pounding of power-tools and home-made instruments constructed from old air-conditioning ducts. In the unearthly Teutonic yowl of gaunt-cheeked bandleader Blixa Bargeld, the Neubauten idea – that as music is made more and more by machines, it might be possible to make a new music by taking machines apart and hitting them – is somehow made flesh.

1983. A notice outside the ICA auditorium reminds the crowd that what they are about to experience is not a concert by Einstürzende Neubauten but 'a concerto for voice and machines'. Neubauten take their pneumatic drill to the stage, and are set fair for The Birthday Party's old Australian stomping grounds[36] before some of the crowd's unrulier elements decide to get involved in the destructive project and the police are called to quell the ensuing mini-riot.

The most cherished image of a memorable evening is the hulking figure of Neubauten's mighty human talisman FM Einheit, advancing into the crowd in his blacksmith's apron brandishing a fully operational chainsaw. This action – long before the Archaos circus had made such antics a cabaret staple – sends the leather-clad cream of London's counter-culture scurrying to the back of the hall, their faces struggling to convey the message: 'I just want to get a look at this from another perspective.'

Ten years later, the tinkling crockery of a grandiose London hotel lounge provides the ideal backdrop for a meeting with the man famed for orchestrating such powerful destructive forces. Blixa Bargeld is an urbane guerrilla in his black suit with blacker pinstripes, bootlace tie drooping above a high-buttoned waistcoat. 'There are a lot of stones on this record,' he says solemnly[37] of Neubauten's new album *Tabula Rasa* (which comes in the form of a triptych, sandwiched between two singles 'Interim' and 'Malediction', all three wrapped in exquisite reproductions of seventeenth-century still lifes).

There are indeed stones, and sand, and burning oil, but there is also a newfound delicacy to compliment the violence of old. Just as the watered down Neubauten lamely dubbed 'Industrial Rock' is becoming America's new post-grunge overground, the originators of the form have expanded their original all-out attack to make room for a new and icy beauty. Thus confirming themselves as not just a brutal novelty act but the third (oh, all right, the fourth, if you count Faust, who used to make a fair old racket themselves with that industrial threshing machine) in a proud line of German avant-pop originals alongside Kraftwerk and Can.

  BT: What kind of tea would you like?
  BB: Darjeeling, please.

'A lot of what happened in the avant-garde in earlier times has appeared later on in popular music,' Bargeld says, 'but somehow, it stopped. Things like Joseph Beuys are not pop yet, but I think we have taken a bit from [he uses an impressive-sounding German phrase, presumably the name of a renegade European art tendency, which is undecipherable on the tape] which means "saving the tracks": what is happened is gone and unrepeatable, but we can save the tracks.'

Tabula Rasa's climax – the infernal fifteen minutes of 'Headcleaner' – includes one of the most brutally constructive cover versions ever, in which The Beatles' 'All You Need Is Love' is taken apart piece by piece and rebuilt as a tank. This song also wrestles bravely with the German post-war experience and the spectre of Fascism, which is a dirty job, but someone's got to do it.

BT: How different is what Neubauten do in the studio to what a 'normal' band would do?

BB: The first time we went into the studio the engineer told us what everything was and which button we should press to record and then said we could call him if we had any problems – he would be at home. He simply hated what we were doing. The instruments we construct are first of all things. They don't have names, so if we want to talk about them, we can't keep saying, 'Hit this thing!' 'Hit that thing!' So we start naming them, and that is the beginning of the recording process. The title of our single 'Thirsty Animal' came from the name of an instrument.

Just as this process was getting underway for *Tabula Rasa*, the Gulf War broke out. So the names and materials began to take on a martial character. Hence also the stones and sand and oil. The last of these, Bargeld enthuses, 'didn't make a very interesting noise until we lit it, and then the dripping, burning oil made a fantastic sound'. It can be heard at the end of the chillingly beautiful '*Wuste*' (Desert). 'About one month later the oil really was burning in the desert. It was bizarre for us.'

Life imitating art to ghoulish effect is nothing new to Einstürzende Neubauten. In the first months of their existence, when their name – translated as Collapsing New Buildings – had begun to be dropped in their hometown of Berlin, the *Kongresshalle*, the city's highest-profile new building, duly collapsed, its butterfly wings folding in on themselves.

2000. Einstürzende Neubauten celebrate their twentieth anniversary in Berlin with a show that lasts a mighty three and a half hours. Those who are lucky enough to attend proclaim this to be a notable event. Who would have thought that a band called Collapsing New Buildings could prove more enduring than the physical structures whose decline they were created to commemorate?

Tabula Rasa (Mute, 1993)

The Beta Band

'We're handwriting everything instead of getting it typed.'

You know that magical feeling when the music sounds so strange it feels like a secret, and you look onstage to the people who are making it and then offstage into the faces of the audience, and you realise that hundreds of people are getting the secret at the exact same time? That's what it's like seeing the The Beta Band live for the first time.

Three Scotsmen and a lone Englishman – though due to their tendency to swap instruments in mid-song, one might easily suppose them to be an octet – their strange, surging, pagan, deceptively simple music applies a desparately needed shot of life-giving adrenalin to the prone form of the four-piece pop group. Not just slotting into other people's bills but stubbornly filling whole evenings with their own warped and wonderful hybrid of great music, terrible poetry, and alarming home-made videos, The Beta Band were the most exciting new British band to emerge since Arab Strap.

Imagine how The Beatles would have sounded if Ringo had written all their best songs. Imagine one of the legendary late seventies New York block parties where hip-hop was invented, reconvened on top of a Scottish mountain. Imagine if, instead of spending hours trying to hone down the perfect three-minute pop nugget, four self-absorbed ex-art students decided to play their instruments for three hours straight just to see what the resulting mess sounded like. The Beta Band don't need to imagine these things: this is their reality.

Part art-school rhumba, part dub reverie, part pastoral idyll, their music resists all attempts at classification. 'We all come from the countryside initially,' explains turntable wizard John Maclean on the telephone from the tour hotel in Liverpool, 'and musically we like to think that we inhabit our own village.' The band's first three four-track EPs – *Champion Versions*, *The Patty Patty Sound* and *Los Amigos Del Beta Bandidos* (later collected together, to stop mad people paying over the odds for them, on a single disc which the band insisted was 'not really an album') – marked out that village as a very desirable place to live, but it was onstage that the band was hardest to resist.

'When we first started to play gigs,' Maclean continues, 'the idea was to make it like a 1989 House club, but everyone was just standing and staring and not dancing. They've started to move around a bit now though.' Inspired by a stage covered in ferns, a band wearing thrift-shop karate suits, and video backdrops including a bizarre ritual on the side of a Scottish mountain, and a fast-forward odyssey through a selection of record sleeves so eclectic as to be almost hallucinatory ('The scary part is,' Maclean says, 'that was only two of our record collections'), there really is no other choice.

But while their forerunners in what might casually be termed British pop's nouveau psychedelic strain – people like Spiritualized and Primal Scream – seem to be merely shuffling the cards of their musical heritage, The Beta Band are playing with a whole new deck. If rock history is a hotel, they have checked out and gone for a walk along the clifftops in bare feet. But don't tell them face to face that's what you think they're doing. In fact don't try to tell them anything, or they will look at you with the paranoid, wounded expression of a small child who thinks you are about to take away its chocolate biscuit.

Before The Beta Band started to make it big, the secret NUJ list of the world's most obnoxious interviewees contained four names. Jazzie B, Chris Penn, Ricki Lake and Will Oldham of the Palace Brothers. Trying to talk to our heroes in drummer Robin's attic flat – located conveniently near to Highgate's suicide bridge, for those journalists who may want to end it all on the way home – it's as if the four resolute non-communicators listed above have decided to form a group. There's nothing intrinsically unfriendly about The Beta Band – without a tape recorder in front of them there is a strong chance that they would be agreeable and interesting people – but the inclusiveness and warmth of their music is in inverse proportion to their desire to talk about it.

In a perhaps understandable reaction to the discredited Oasis/ Embrace school of 'We're the best band in the world' self-promotional overkill, The Beta Band regard name, rank and serial number as frankness beyond the call of duty. They once refused to do an interview with *The Face* on the grounds that they 'weren't really a band', but getting an initial foot in the door is only the first step.

Beta Band techniques for frustrating friendly attempts at interrogation begin with standard Beatles-inspired obfuscation (asked to say their names on tape for voice identification purposes, they start off by pretending to be the Beach Boys – 'Brian, Dennis, Carl, Mike' – and then run the gamut of names which aren't actually their names until the joke is lying in the gutter begging for mercy). They move on through vague disdain (a valiant attempt to start a discussion about the problems caused by noisy oystercatchers to coastal birdsong recordists ends in total humiliation) to downright hostility if the name of another group is mentioned.

Do they think you have to be secretive about something in order for it to be powerful?

'No,' says Gerry Rafferty-influenced vocalist Steve Mason, 'I just think people waste too much time talking about music that happened thirty years ago instead of trying to do something fresh.'

But other bands – Primal Scream or Spiritualized, for example – would be very happy to be identified as coming from, say, a psychedelic tradition.

'But if we're being described with reference to a genre that's thirty years old, we have failed in our quest to make brand new music . . .' Mason insists. 'I don't even know what psychedelic means.'

It comes from the greek 'delios' meaning to make apparent and 'psyche' meaning, well, the psyche. It was originally used with reference to drugs that were supposed to have this effect, and then to music that was supposed to complement, intensify or echo such revelations.

'But surely all music is about coming to a deeper understanding of oneself?'

Oh. He might have a point there.

'The reason we don't say very much,' interjects jumpy Portsmouthian bassist Richard Greentree, in the grip of a momentary merciful impulse, 'is that if we had to think hard, really hard, about what our influences are or why we're doing what we're doing, it would take all the fun out of it. Those sort of questions should be in the back of your head, not the front of it.'

That seems fair enough. So is there anything The Beta Band wouldn't find it painful to discuss?

Greentree pauses. 'Talking about what we actually do – what instruments we used and how different making the third EP was to making the first – that would be acceptable.'

OK then, how was making the third EP different to making the first?

Richard [excitedly, as if somehow vindicated]: 'It was just a really new approach to recording for us. The first EP, which I didn't play on, was basically just translating demos into the studio, so it probably felt pretty clinical. *Patty Patty Sound* was quite live and recorded as much as possible in one take, all playing at the same time. The third EP was done closed-miked, with fewer instruments and more attention paid to getting individual sounds exactly right and then overlaying them all together.'

But these are exactly the kind of mundane everyday details from which the music of The Beta Band seems so joyously capable of transporting us. What an irony – that the only things The Beta Band are willing to tell us should be exactly the sort of things we really don't need to know. And that's the exact opposite of the way their music works! '"Its about waking up in the morning and reaching for a guitar," they told *Melody Maker*, in a rare moment of *glasnost*. 'Or a glockenspiel, or a gong.'

A year or so later, The Beta Band are putting the finishing touches to the artwork for their debut album in the same East London design studio that gave Oasis and The Verve their public faces. There are tiny bits of paper strewn all over the room ('We're handwriting everything instead of getting it typed,' explains MacLean), and the air is heady with the scent of Pritt-stick. It would not be an exaggeration to say that from the moment they graduated to picking up actual instruments from playing the pots and pans in their west London bedsit, The Beta Band's whole career has been heady with the scent of Pritt-stick.

The first song on their album pays tribute to this spirit of cottage industry with a cod-rap history of the band's career so far. 'Miles gave us an album deal, we said yes and went for a meal,' Steve Mason intones in an unconvincing American accent, laying bare the mechanics of The Beta Band's rise to prominence in enough detail to satisfy even the most diehard fan, and to make impartial observers fear for their sanity.

'Are you asking us to explain why we're rubbish?' demands the combative Mason, shocked at the suggestion that such wilful self-indulgence might be a deliberate act of provocation.

'We thought of it more as a present to everyone who buys the record,' insists mild-mannered drummer Robin Jones.

'Like a shoehorn to lever people into the album,' elaborates Richard Greentree.

Once firmly levered in, the listener can look forward to extravagant minor-key orchestral interludes, a strangely moving adaptation of Bonnie Tyler's 'Total Eclipse Of The Heart', and a hybrid of ancient folk vocals and sparse electronic beats that is as captivating as it is unique. Why the dramatic move away from the more unified, natural sound which won The Beta Band's early singles universal acclaim?

'We've kind've done organic,' Mason explains. 'We're trying to move into the twentieth century as quickly as possible,' Greentree splutters: 'just in time for it to end.'

With its speeded-up voices, sampled orchestras, incessant birdsong and a festival of wonky handclaps, *The Beta Band* is a gateway to a private universe which anyone can visit. The band might have broken with the traditions of pop hyperbole by using their *NME* front cover to announce that their album was rubbish, but it's best to take anything this lot say with at least a pillar of salt. 'I'm at ninety degrees to the rest of the world,' sings Steve Mason. To be honest, the correct angle is probably more like a hundred and eighty.

Three EPs (Regal, 1998)

John Cale

'It built up over time into this roaring noise that sounded like you had a B52 in your living room.'

It's Sunday morning, but not like in the song. There are three things you notice about John Cale on first encountering him in the flesh. How absurdly tanned and fit he looks, when he ought to look like a walking cadaver. How the high-shaven sides of his impeccably dandified haircut heighten the impact of slightly pointed ears. And how his face calls to mind an elongated Dustin Hoffman. These impressions are compounded by being crammed with him into a hotel service lift which is really only big enough for one person.

Exasperated by a brief moment of inactivity in the lobby of the Portobello Hotel, Cale has – on first sight of an approaching interviewer – leapt up out of his lounge chair and dashed into the lift. Sudden close proximity to him is unnerving. After all, this man did once decapitate a chicken onstage, albeit a dead one. And he frightens people for other reasons, too. His solo records are often austere to the point of well, austerity, and his unmatched punk and art-rock pedigree is marbled with forbidding classical and avant-garde bloodlines (a teen prodigy, he was performing improvised pieces on the BBC at the time of Bill Haley and Elvis). The manner in which these different traditions come together in his work is often confusing, even to him.

'If I have to choose between rock 'n roll or classical, I always get into trouble,' Cale admits – out of the lift now, seated nervily at a rickety table, which he occasionally rattles for emphasis. 'It's always better if I forget about it and try to write songs that live and breathe, and then think about categories afterwards.'

Long years in America have given a strange twist to the deadpan Welsh lilt immortalised on his narration of The Velvet Underground's 'The Gift'. Cale first moved across the Atlantic in 1963, under the patronage of Aaron Copland, to study classical composition. There he took up with avant-garde luminary LaMonte Young, with whose Theatre of Eternal Music Ensemble he worked on gruelling experiments in forty-minute sustained notes.

BT: Was this was an introductory course in The Fall's Three R's (Repetition, Repetition, Repetition) or an attempt to get to something stranger?

JC: On the one hand, we didn't know what we were doing – we were just pushing and pushing. But whatever it was that we didn't know what we were doing, we worked very hard at it. Usually we got together for dinner, then we played solidly for an hour and a half, just sustaining notes and taping it . . . Slowly, as things evolved, it went on from me bowing the viola: I sanded the bridge down so that I could play three strings at once, put guitar strings on it and used a cello bow. It built up over time into this roaring noise that sounded like you had a B52 in your living room . . . People would come up and ask 'Who's that playing trumpet?' or 'Who's that playing flute?' But it was all these harmonics that were flying around.

Andy Warhol's duplicated dollar bills, which were beginning to cause a stir in uptown art markets around this time, were widely thought to be derivative of Young's work. But Cale didn't think so. 'It was a totally different, visual sensibility,' he says, 'which came from advertising.' Accordingly, the young Welshman forsook the rigours of downtown to hang around with the stars at Warhol's Factory. ('On the one hand,' he insists, 'it was deprivation therapy, but on the other it was very rich.')

He still isn't quite sure how the Velvet Underground 'got from point A to point B'. He was part of the band for only three years, but the themes of dissonance and iteration that his viola and keyboards brought out in their work were not going to go away. And Cale would play a useful supervisory role in the development of that legacy; producing the recorded debuts of such vital Velvety inheritors as Iggy

Pop's Stooges, Jonathan Richman and Patti Smith. His reason for working with these people was, he says rather grimly, that he 'knew they were not going to go away'. Surprisingly, given how strongly he left his mark on them, Cale insists that 'the feeling of being a benign figure watching over it all gives you a certain sense of impotence'.

'I don't think,' he comforts himself on reflection, 'that Patti would say I was a benign figure. There was a certain amount of aggravation involved with *Horses*. It was a literary event that you had to preserve – make sure that after the record was done, yes you had a rock 'n' roll record for her pleasure but not *just* another rock 'n' roll record, so all those years of poetry writing would not have gone in vain.'

Did his early experiences with Andy Warhol help establish a model for his own collaborative endeavours?

'I saw Andy as very helpful,' Cale remembers. 'He was mischievous, but there was no master plan. I don't think he had a vicious bone in his body.'

In 1990, John Cale collaborated with Brian Eno, his only rival in the catalyst and polymath stakes. The resulting album, *Wrong Way Up*, was neither's best work, but it did throw up an intriguing clash of characters.

JC: He definitely was interested in being in full control of the whole project. I had to keep an eye on him – watch when his hand was on the erase button. He would get rid of things without telling me. I'd say, 'Let me hear that,' and he'd say, 'It's not there any more . . . well, it wasn't any good, was it?' And I'd swear at him. It was funny. His studios are in a lovely part of Suffolk, and the birds were singing, and there were these two old curmudgeons in this room, two old eccentrics mumbling and cursing at each other.

Cale's 1993 live album, *Fragments of a Rainy Season*, imposed a fascinatingly deceptive uniformity on the body of his solo career. The material it draws on covers an imposing span of moods and textures – from the lush, pastoral, elegiac feel of the gorgeous (and unjustly neglected) Welsh rhapsody 'Paris 1919', to the terrifyingly sparse 'Music For A New Society' – but on all but two of the twenty songs,

Cale accompanies himself at the piano; setting out his stall as a post-apocalypse Randy Newman.

'When you do something alone with a piano,' he shakes his head vigorously and grimaces, as if this is a worrying thing to contemplate, 'you've got a direct line to the audience.' Cale's hilariously funereal version of 'Heartbreak Hotel' gets this point across especially clearly.

Watching him onstage at Glastonbury with the reformed Velvet Underground at around the same time, it is hard not to see the funny side of the original anti-hippies' choice of venue. A short while before it happened, this reunion seemed no less unlikely than all four Doors or the Jimi Hendrix Experience getting back together, and if ever there was a band that was not meant to be heard under an open sky in surroundings of outstanding natural beauty, The Velvet Underground are that band. And yet when Lou Reed endeavours to perform 'Rock and Roll' in the style of John Cougar Mellencamp, Cale hits the mulletted reprobate with a voodoo hex that turns his guitar off.

Annexing 'Waiting for the Man' with a clanking keyboard and inspired monotone, Aaron Copland's star pupil somehow manages to create a real feeling of claustrophobia. And that, in this setting, is a notable achievement.

Paris 1919 (Island, 1973)

Captain Beefheart

'I sound partially interrupted by chewing on sunflower seeds.'

Don Van Vliet lives in the small and beautifully named town of Trinidad in Northern California, up by the Oregon border, 135 feet from the ocean. He paints there. He is a painter of note – *Stand Up to Be Discontinued* – the second British exhibition of his work, arrived in Brighton in the autumn of 1994 to confound anyone who doubted this – but he used to be a painter of notes.

Until the early eighties (and forever more in the minds of those whose psychic foundations have been shifted by him), Don Van Vliet was Captain Beefheart. It would not be an exaggeration to call Beefheart the most mythical figure in all popular music. Except that his music was never what you would call popular. 'For my whole life they've repeated to me that I'm a genius,' he observed ruefully, around the time he formally swapped his harmonica for a paintbrush. 'But in the meantime they've also taught the public that my music is too difficult to listen to.'

Just because you're paranoid, it doesn't mean they're not after you. Decades of critical histrionics have built up an aura of difficulty around the music of Captain Beefheart, and the wrong kind of difficulty at that. It's not listening to it that is difficult, it's *not* listening to it. Tumbleweeds of eccentric poetry on desert guitar winds; howling harmonica; nimble marimba; and a voice that can freeze-dry your soul one minute and tickle your ventricles the next. A voice that's got so much grain you could make a loaf out of it. A voice that growls, 'I love you, you big dummy. Ha ha ha ha. Quit asking why.'

The strict separation between Beefheart the shaman/showman and

Van Vliet the reclusive artist – he's described it as 'having a second life' – was largely a matter of tactics. Both the Captain and his wife Jan (an enigmatic and influential presence who crops up in old interviews, sitting on a sofa, reading a copy of *Madame Bovary*) realised that he would never be taken seriously as a painter so long as he was still making music. In fact, Beefheart was always a poet and a painter as much as a music-maker. His pictures adorned several of his album covers, and themes and words from his songs still reappear in his pictures. In any case, as he once wisely observed, 'Talking about different art-forms is like counting raindrops: there are rivers and streams and oceans, but it's all the same substance.'

Don Van Vliet makes a much better living from his paintings than he ever did from his records. And his decision to turn his back on his musical persona has had unrecognised beneficial consequences, wrapping the extraordinary Beefheart oeuvre in cling-film and preserving it unspoilt. Not for the Captain the grisly indignity of toilet-bound drug death or mortgage-motivated reunion tour. He is still alive and he is doing something else.

Meanwhile, his music awaits discovery by successive generations, and his life resists all attempts at demystification. Captain Beefheart went without sleep for a year and a half. His ears are three-and-a-half inches long. He once sold a vacuum cleaner to Aldous Huxley. Even if none of these stories turned out to be true, the allure of a life lived as myth would not be undermined.

Beefheart was born in 1941, in Glendale, California, and christened Don Vliet (the Van came later, it had transmission problems). Not deeply enamoured of formal education – 'If you want to be a different fish, you've got to jump out of the school'– he seems to have acquired most of his early learning in Los Angeles' Griffith Park Zoo. Here he met the celebrated Portuguese sculptor Augustinio Rodriguez, who was so impressed with his precocious talents that the child prodigy ended up on daytime TV sculpting 'images of nature' while the older master looked on. At the early age of thirteen, Vliet Jr won a scholarship to study art in Europe, but his parents – convinced, their son later claimed, that to be an artist was not a manly occupation – decided to move him out of art's way, with them, to the desert. This strategy proved felicitously unsuccessful.

At high school in the small, hot town of Lancaster, Don Vliet met the young Frank Zappa, with whom he shared a love for the then esoteric pleasures of West Coast r'n'b. By the early sixties, Don and Frank were collaborating on various ludicrously ambitious film and opera projects in the small town of Cucamonga. From one of these – *Captain Beefheart Meets the Grunt People* – Don took his new name. They also recorded demos together as a band called The Soots, but these proved too much for the record companies of the day to cope with.

Zappa went to LA to form his Mothers of Invention, and Don ranged off in search of 'desert musicians'. His first Magic Band – the first of the shifting agglomerations of extraordinary musicians via whom the sounds in his head would get out into the world – was a spring-heeled electric blues outfit, with Beefheart's Howlin' Wolf growl and punchy harmonica-playing much to the fore. They released a couple of singles on A & M Records, but Jerry Moss (the M to Herb Alpert's A) thought their music 'too negative' to be album-worthy, adding that one song in particular, 'Electricity', 'wouldn't be good for my daughter'.

When the song finally came out, Beefheart's unearthly drawn-out howl having broken a $1200 studio microphone in the recording process, you could hear what Moss meant. The 1967 album *Safe As Milk* was to be the first of many triumphant Beefheartian re-emergences from semi-retirement; his sound palette now expanded to pinks and oranges as well as the blues, his unique ecological sensibility already firmly established (the title was not, as widely supposed, a drug reference, but a warning of the dangers of Strontium 90 in breast milk).

Unfortunately, the pattern of Beefheart's dealings with the music business was already set, too. The band had to pull out of playing the Monterey Pop Festival (which helped make stars of Jimi Hendrix and The Who among others), because their then lead guitarist, a certain Ry Cooder, didn't think they were ready. Their next album, *Mirror Man*, recorded around the same time as *Safe As Milk*, was not released until three or four years later, while its successor, *Strictly Personal* (1968), did come out straightaway, but only after manager

Bob Krasnow had done his best to ruin it by adding absurd 'far-out' hippie phasing effects while Beefheart was away on tour in Britain.

Zappa, who by now had his own record company, offered Beefheart the chance to make a record without such interference. Beefheart grabbed it with both hands, and the result was *Trout Mask Replica* (1969), a revolutionary twenty-eight-part song-cycle which still sounds like both the most modern and the most primitive music ever made.

The whole thing – apocalyptic blues, avant-garde hoe-downs, sung and spoken poems, impossibly intricate instrumentals – was, Beefheart claimed, composed at the piano in eight and a half hours. ('Why did it take so long?' *Rolling Stone* journalist Langdon Winner asked jokingly. Beefheart replied that he 'hadn't played piano before and had to work out the fingering'.)

It is clear that the Captain was not an easy man to work for. Various members of the Trout-era Magic Band – Beefheart's 'cousin', the Mascara Snake, drummer John 'Drumbo' French, bassist Rockette Morton, guitarists Antennae Jimmy Semens and the outlandishly tall Zoot Horn Rollo – have expressed dissatisfaction with the amount of credit they received. Last year, part-time record-shop manager Bill Harkleroad (formerly Zoot Horn Rollo – Beefheart owns the copyright to all stage names) described him as 'Manson-esque . . . People don't like to be used as paint.' Van Vliet shot back: 'If they're going to be used by me, that is the only way they're going to be used.'

Beefheart cares about trees, though. *While Trout Mask Replica* was being rehearsed at his house, Beefheart pestered the record company to pay for a tree-surgeon to calm surrounding oaks and cedars, in case they might be frightened and fall over. Straight Records refused, but Beefheart sent them the bill anyway.

Over the next three albums, the Magic Band's fiendishly complex web of sound unravelled into progressively more recognisable shapes. *Lick My Decals Off, Baby* (1970) was perhaps the most life-enhancingly libidinous record of all time, with the recently married Captain proclaiming 'I Wanna Find Me a Woman to Hold My Big Toe Till I Have to Go'. Beefheart threatened – or was that promised? – in *The Spotlight Kid* (1971) to 'grow fins, and go back in the water again'. All the time, the beat was getting less jagged, but the spirit was just as free. *Clear Spot* (1972) was Beefheart's most accessible and in some ways most magical record yet. As well as the lovely 'My Head Is My Only House Unless It Rains', it contained, in the immortal 'Big Eyed Beans From Venus', the nearest thing there is to an archetypal Captain Beefheart moment: 'Mr Zoot Horn Rollo – hit that long, lunar note, and let it float.' It was not a hit.

In revenge, Captain Beefheart sold out. The sleeve of *Unconditionally Guaranteed* (1974) pictures him wishfully clutching wads of bank-notes. Twenty years on, this sounds like an underrated pop record. At the time it was, to put it mildly, a let-down. The disgruntled Magic Band swanned off to form the ill-fated Mallard (a dead duck), leaving Beefheart to make the deplorable *Bluejeans and Moonbeams* with a load of session musicians. He later urged anyone who bought either of these records to return to the shop and try to get their money back.

The Captain was down, but not out. After recharging his batteries by hooking up with Frank Zappa again, he formed a new Magic Band, built around guitarist Jeff Tepper, and eventually released *Shiny Beast (Bat Chain Puller)* in 1978. This was a sumptuous return to his best, with a seductive new Latin shuffle. The wired and abrasive *Doc at the Radar Station* (1980) followed, to show those ungrateful punks and new-wavers who was boss. *Ice Cream for Crow* (1982) was, in retrospect, a suitably restless and open-ended swan song, but it had at least one prophetic moment in 'The Past Sure Is Tense'.

Since then, the Captain has retreated behind a veil of painterly swank, with a little help from friends like crockery specialist Julian Schnabel and German expressionist A.R. Penck (who, with the phrase 'Re-achieving naivety', came as close as anyone to pinning down what it is that both Van Vliet and Beefheart are up to). When he had his first British exhibition at the prestigious Waddington Galleries in Cork Street, London, in 1986, fans of his music gathered in a mixture of pleasure and puzzlement.

They did the same thing at his next one eight years later, some of them even venturing the time-honoured opinion that – in view of the increasingly sombre tone of Van Vliet's work, and the decreasing number of funny animals in it – they preferred his early stuff. Fans of his paintings meanwhile muttered about Van Gogh and Franz Kline and scrabbled through their pockets for the five figures' worth of loose change required to buy one.

A lot of people, myself included, get the same joy from the best of Beefheart's paintings as they do from his music. But what Don Van Vliet does in art already has what the catalogues call a 'distinguished aesthetic history' – which is not, of course, something to be ashamed of. And what he did in music was totally new. This is why people will always tend to be less interested in the development of his technique as a painter than in how he learnt to play the harmonica by holding it out of his parents' window. In one sense this must be frustrating for him; in another, it leaves him free to paint in peace.

At Michael Werner, his New York gallery, they said that their man preferred not to talk on the phone, because he was likely to ramble on for hours and then not be able to concentrate on his painting. A brief exchange of faxes was agreed upon as the best solution. It proved – at least in terms of the unyielding pithiness of the responses Van Vliet dictated for his wife Jan to type up – cruelly successful. He asked for the answers to be printed verbatim.

BT: What are the distinctive characteristics of your speaking voice, and what are you wearing?

DVV: I'm wearing black accordion baggy type pants that are held up by black Oxfords. I am wearing a buffalo plaid shirt, red and black squares. I sound partially interrupted by chewing on sunflower seeds – beautiful, sunflower – black and white.

BT: Is there anything particular on your mind today?

DVV: The thought of diagnosing your question and then sifting through what I think about it.

BT: The idea I have of where you live is of a very isolated place – is that right? Please describe it.

DVV: A painted birdcage above a hacksaw ocean with lovely redwood stalks with zillions of raindrops, falling.

BT: Did the pressure of people being interested in you make you move there, or would you have lived somewhere like that anyway?

DVV: I would have lived somewhere like this anyway, but a prod of the feet of humans made me do it sooner.

BT: Does living where you do make you feel cut off from the world, or more able to see it clearly?

DVV: Cut off just enough to feel well tailored.

BT: Do you have a working routine, and if so, what is it?

DVV: Life

BT: Is it possible to work too hard, and would you if you could?

DVV: Answering your question as asked – I would not like calluses, I would rather have the hands of a fine painter.

BT: What was the first picture you can remember painting, and how do you feel about it now?

DVV: It probably doesn't even remember me.

BT: Who are the other painters who have given you the most pleasure and inspiration?

DVV: Inspiration is a crutch word.

BT: Someone told me you had had some trouble with an allergy to paint. Is that true?

DVV: I hope not.

BT: Do you find it more satisfying to express yourself in paint than in sound? What are the most striking differences between the two forms of endeavour?

DVV: One you can physically drown in, being paint. The other you can mentally drown in. I prefer swimming in paint.

BT: Do you still make music for your own pleasure, and do you have any interest in your musical legacy?

DVV: I'm not doing music now and it's personal. Legacy sounds more like the fitting of a boot and I hope they don't fit me with any bootlegs or stupid compilation albums.

BT: Do you consider yourself to have a special way with words?

DVV: Funny you should ask, you seem to be of good hearing.

BT: Are there any animals for which you have a particular fondness, and what do you especially like about them?

DVV: The inhuman quality of animals.

BT: Is man the best or the worst part of nature? If you ever go to a place where there are a lot of people, do they make you feel hopeful or frightened?

DVV: They make me miss animals.

BT: If you could listen to a song or look at one picture, which would it be?

DVV: Art is close as you can get to perfection without getting caught up in the wink.

Beef Encounters

1. Gary Lucas

Lucas first saw Captain Beefheart play at a New York club in 1971. Their acquaintance was years old before he plucked up the courage to reveal that he played the guitar. Then Lucas's wife became Beefheart's manager, and he was given an instrumental to play on *Doc at the Radar Station*. By 1982 Lucas was a full-time member of the Magic Band. It was at this point that Beefheart decided he didn't want to make records.

> The first time I saw him perform, I was just transfixed. To me it was the pinnacle: so complex and yet so beautiful and effortless and fun-loving. And Beefheart himself was a magical personality: he had a very refreshing iconoclastic attitude – like an early punk – and his comments to the audience used to crack me up. I remember him yelling at people who were sitting down: 'Get up, get up, I'm older than you.'
>
> He had a very unusual way of putting music together. He didn't write it down. He'd either send you tapes of him playing it on the piano, or put tapes together of him singing the parts, or whistling. You'd spend hours, weeks, trying to translate the stuff on to the guitar – I'd learn five seconds a day, about two bars. Then he would give vocal instructions, he'd whisper in my ear 'play like you died', or 'play like you're balancing a tray of red jujubes'. You would do whatever he told you to, there was no improvisation allowed, and sometimes he would pick on each person in turn to intimidate. It was unpleasant – like going to school and he was the professor – but if you loved the music enough, you put up with it.

2. John Peel

Peel drove Beefheart around on his first UK tour, and has been playing his records on the radio ever since.

> The first time I saw him was at the Whiskey A Go Go. I was working for a

radio station in California, and Beefheart was supporting Them. He came over to London when *Safe As Milk* came out, and I actually burst into tears onstage – I was so excited at being able to say, 'Put your hands together, ladies and gentlemen, for Captain Beefheart and the Magic Band.'

At this time he had some strange saxophone he'd been given by Ornette Coleman – a shahnai I think it was called. A lot of his numbers consisted of a great deal of rather tuneless blowing through that. A lot of the audience were understandably fairly alienated by this and would leave. But somebody like that is so manifestly ahead of you in the game, it seems impertinent not to enjoy it.

On that first tour I actually hired a car and drove him to all his gigs. There was one which was legendary at a place called Frank Freeman's Dancing School in Kidderminster. That was not some kind of groovy hippie name: it actually was a dancing school, run by Frank Freeman. He and his wife used to make sandwiches for the bands, and they'd sit and chat as though receiving you in their drawing room. They were really sweet and Beefheart responded to this. I found a tape of that show a couple of months ago and it's stupendous stuff.

He is an extraordinarily productive man. If you spend time with him, his conversations can seem rather impenetrable, but this is just because his thought-processes are not those of anybody else you're likely to meet. A lot of his verbal jokes are quite innocent – you'll think to yourself, 'Why did he say that?' Then a few days later you'll see what he meant.

3. Craig Scanlon

Scanlon, guitarist and co-writer in Salford soul institution The Fall, has never met Beefheart, but his band would not have sounded the same without him.

The first record I got of his was *Trout Mask Replica*. The parental reaction was very satisfying: 'What is that rubbish?' At first I thought what the rest of the band still say if I put it on in the tour bus – it sounds like five people playing different songs at once. But there are so many different layers to it; a lot of really beautiful stuff's going on. People think it's improvised, but it isn't, it's very carefully structured.

Beefheart has influenced my guitar-playing – just in a liberating way; I wouldn't dare try to copy him. We were asked to play on a tribute album, but there's no point. It's a shame he stopped making music. I went to one of his exhibitions. It looked like he was painting Bambi decomposing, but then I suppose that's the kind of thing he was doing with his music.

Clear Spot (Reprise, 1972)

The Chemical Brothers

'For us, I suppose the way the thing sounds is *the song.'*

In the well-lit far corner of a Notting Hill pub, Chemical Brothers Tom Rowlands and Ed Simons are making genial conversation. This is the point at which the trouble normally starts. At least for those people who find the unearthly clanking majesty of The Chemical Brothers' music to be compromised rather than intensified by the everyday humanity of its makers.

If you need a visual image to complement this music's sudden twists and turns, its vertiginous leaps of faith and gut-wrenching physical switchbacks, better stick with the pictures they've already given you. Like the mild-mannered duo whipping a crowd of sharp-eared Argentinians into a righteous delirium via satellite on *Top of the Pops*, or the video for 'Let Forever Be', their second collaboration with Noel Gallagher, wherein fifteen different versions of the same young woman morph and twist through the day in a Busby Berkeley psychedelic kaleidoscope.

The Chemical Brothers' videos are weird – strange tableaux of exuberant physicality and mental disorientation that all seem to be part of the same audacious artistic plan but actually aren't. One of the things that makes them work so well is that the brothers don't tend to be in them. They get out of a car in the one for 'Hey Boy, Hey Girl' and an x-ray pulse shows us their skeletons; otherwise it's all girls with two different personalities making their way through night-clubs, or gymnasts diligently completing their floor routines. Strange as it may seem to say it, there is something about the quality of Tom and Ed's nonappearance that is entirely captivating.

'I like the ones that have a big moment in them,' says Ed, the shorter-haired one without the lemon-tinted spectacles. 'Our records often have a big moment, a sort of turning point, and it's nice when the videos reflect that . . . like in "Setting Sun", where the girl looks in the mirror and sees her dark side, and the music you hear when she does that is quite a scary, dirty sound.'

In the video for 'Let Forever Be', there are, by Tom's reckoning, 'about a hundred' of these big moments. Ed describes them a bit later as 'times when you see that through sensation and imagination you can transcend your normal everyday existence'. This is as near to a perfect summation of the effect The Chemical Brothers music is aiming at as we are likely to get.

But what is the nature of that transformative kick? You might think it had something to do with drugs. The Chemical Brothers' name (arrived at in some haste when LA-based Beastie Boys and Beck production team The Dust Brothers gave them three hours to come up with another one, instead of using theirs as a 'tribute') would seem to back up this contention, but that would be putting the horse *after* the cart. If you are decadent enough to know anyone who has listened to this group while under the influence of narcotics, they will tell you that it's actually the drugs that struggle to echo the impact of the sound, not *vice versa*.

As the opening words of the first track on their third (and, so far, best) album *Surrender* put it, this is 'music that triggers some kind of response'. 'We always liked the whole hip-hop idea of putting things together that weren't supposed to fit,' Tom explains. 'But twenty years after the fact, the initial idea of doing something radical to Kraftwerk has rather lost its shock value. That's why we wanted to do something more integrated: to make powerful music that affected people, but without relying on things like heavy breaks and acid lines that had maybe a become formula.'

'When we made *Surrender*,' Ed joins in, 'we wanted it to be a record that was completely individual to us. One of the consequences of DJs making and playing their own records is that people tend to see it as a kind of Meccano. Records almost take themselves apart in your mind – a bit of techno here, a respectful nod to seventies funk there – and you reach a point where the description becomes the music, whereas a lot of the things that are most exciting to listen to come from people being *disrespectful* of the past. If you think of something like Joy Division or New Order, it comes out of nowhere.'

One possible response to *Surrender*'s undoubted genius – in simultaneously managing to be the perfect embodiment of everything The Chemical Brothers ever set out to do, and also to take them to another level – would have been to acknowledge the fact that it stood head and shoulders above any other British pop record released in its year by giving it the Mercury Prize. But that would have been too simple.

Heaven forfend that such a complex and multi-faceted beast as an awards jury should fall into so obvious a trap. Better leave *Surrender* to languish in obscurity with also-rans like *Parklife* and *OK Computer*, rather than elevate it to the pantheon of the immortals: M People's *Elegant Slumming* and the debut album by Gomez.

The Chemical Brothers are commendably phlegmatic about their Mercury snubbing – a couple of days before the ceremony they are still cheefully (if misguidedly) telling anyone who will listen to 'put a tenner on *Faithless*'. Posterity's healing embrace will be their consolation. *Surrender*'s enduring thrill has been sustained and even enhanced by its authors' decision not to asset-strip it to the advertising industry, in the disappointing way that Massive Attack did with their 1998 landmark *Mezzanine*. 'If you have a whole album licensed to sell different things,' Ed explains, 'the imaginitive process of listening to it as a whole is ruined. You're just thinking, "This is the car advert and that's the film trailer."'

The fact that when 'Out Of Control' (the third single to be taken from *Surrender*) finally comes out, it still feels freshly minted, testifies to the wisdom of this policy. 'Out Of Control' is a thrilling recontextualisation of Giorgio Moroder's primal disco pulse as the perfect framework for the off-kilter lyricism ('Could it be that I'm just losing my touch?/Or maybe you think my moustache is too much?') and deceptively pristine guitar-playing of New Order's Bernard Sumner. The headlong energy rush which results is as exhilarating as anything either party has ever done, and the fact that Bobby Gillespie's backing vocals are barely audible is just the icing on the cake.

With the exception of their more organic involvements with

Mercury Rev's Jonathan Donahue, The Chemical Brothers' way of working with other people is not really a collaboration in the traditional sense. 'The seed of the idea will be ours,' Tom explains. 'We generally don't send people anything until six or seven months down the line when the mood of the thing is already in place ... Then they send us something back, we do what we want with it and hope they like it.' His rather apologetic expression at this point suggests that – in Sumner's case at least – such autocratic methods caused a certain amount of creative tension.

'I always thought of New Order as making quite sparse electronic music,' says Ed, 'but it did become apparent while working with Bernard that he thought of music quite differently to us – for him the song was everything, and for us I suppose the way the thing sounds *is* the song. Each record does have some core idea, but probably not in the way he would express it ... what we're trying to do is make noises and little riffs into hooks which are as powerful as a great chorus.'

How did this generation gap manifest itself when it came to actually working together?

'We sent him something very simple,' Tom remembers, 'then he came back with these really complicated chord changes. He'd spent ages recording hundreds of different guitar parts, and we sort of got rid of them, but even though we got rid of them, they'd still affected the writing of the track up to that point, so their spirit was still there.'

'I love the idea of the imprint of music that's not there any more,' Ed butts in winsomely.

The Chemical Brothers have codified this idea into something they call 'The Turin Shroud Theory of Implied Music'. 'The way our songs are put together,' Tom explains, 'the positioning of sounds, the way things happen – is built on a certain structure, and then that structure is removed, so the reason these sounds happen at the points they do seems sort of random ... There is a reason why they happen in the way that they do, but it's gone. The reason is gone, but the *effect* ...' He is beaming now: 'The effect still remains.'

Surrender (Virgin, 1999)

George Clinton

'I go to Disneyland and they make me cover my head, because Mickey Mouse might get mad.'

George Clinton has learnt some things in five decades of music-making, and one of them is how to make an entrance. As the Clinton party empties out of its limousine, the top-hatted commissionaires in the Mayfair hotel lobby are left scraping their bottom jaws off the carpet. Clinton, the legendary hairdresser turned funkateer, the self-styled 'maggot overlord', has a uniform of his own to wear to work. It is an arresting combination of fluorescent cape, bright green football shirt and multi-coloured hair extensions, matched with a three-cornered pirate's hat and – the finishing touch – a yellow feather boa.

From the snappy West Coast gangsta rap of Dr Dre and Snoop Doggy Dogg to Moloko's sinuous South Yorkshire electro-funk, Clinton's legacy is as omnipresent as his garb is regal. His name is one of three (the others being James Brown and Kraftwerk) on the blueprints of all modern dance music. And a beneficent reissue programme of the innumerable albums made by his psychedelic cornucopia of shifting collaborative incarnations – Funkadelic, Parliament, Bootsy's Rubber Band, the Brides of Funkenstein – is constantly introducing new ears to the original Clintonian brew of sex and sedition.

A quarter of a century on, listening to Funkadelic's early seventies recordings is still a gloriously disorienting experience. Where exactly is the common ground between the psychedelic metal blow-out of 'Maggot Brain' and the uplifting gospel of 'Can You Get To That'? The typically understated sleeve notes to 1974's *Standing on the Verge of Getting It On* perhaps put it best: 'On the eighth day the cosmic strumpet of Mother Nature was spawned to envelope this Third Planet in Funkacidal vibrations. And she birthed Apostles Ra, Hendrix, Stone and Clinton to preserve all funkiness of man unto eternity.'

In the flesh, Clinton's handshake has a regal limpness to it. Within the frame of crazy hair and pirate's hat, the thin rectangular frame of his spectacles gives his bright eyes an unexpectedly studious aspect. Inside his hotel suite, his entourage has ordered a medieval banquet. 'It's like the seventies in there!' the press officer proclaims, admiration mingling with alarm as the not-far-short-of-four-figure bill for trolley-loads of fish and salads and pies and potatoes will be on his credit card. It's not hard to see why Clinton has had more record companies than George Michael has had hot dinners.

How would he characterise his relations with the music industry over the years?

'They always gave us strange looks,' Clinton responds between mouthfuls. 'But I couldn't analyse them, because I was looking at them strange too.'

Could their strange looks have actually been a reflection of his own?

'Probably.' The munching intensifies. 'Things have got a little different lately,' he continues in upbeat mode. 'I still look at them like this [mimes astonishment at unsuitability of corporate apparel] – "What've you got on?" But now they know I'm supposed to look the way I do.'

So there's no problem with his new label Sony yet?

'It hasn't got to that point,' he chuckles. 'I'm still spending their money.'

In the title of his 1996 album *T.A.P.O.A.F.O.M.* (that's The Awesome Power Of A Fully Operational Mothership to you) there is a tacit recognition that not all of Clinton's recent releases have been quite up to scratch. From the exact science of 'Mathematics' ('any per cent of you is as good as the whole pie') to the historical accuracy of 'Funky King' (with its irresistibly tasteless hook-line: 'When I do it, I be sticking to it, like hotgrits on Al Green'), this one sounds pretty carefully polished. Clinton is unequivocal: 'We buffed it.'

T.A.P.O.A.F.O.M. invokes the name of one of Clinton's biggest

successes, *Mothership Connection* (1975): the potent and hallucinatory cocktail of politics and porn, social allegory and sci-fi that
established his P-Funk musical dynasty as a genre in its own right. So
why did he decide to relaunch the Mothership?

'We're going to need a vehicle to get where we have to go ... I
loaned the spaceship out and it's taken a while to get it back.'

Clinton's backing vocalist Gary Cooper, sitting next to him, takes
up the story in a crazy helium voice. 'I'll bring your spaceship back
... in the next millennium!'

For a man who has been associated with Clinton for almost thirty
years – 'I was fourteen when I met him, I'll be forty-three this year' –
Cooper looks remarkably healthy. 'I don't have a fixed income,' he
maintains cheerfully, 'but I have a fixed outcome.'

Clinton's relations with an extended family of extravagantly
talented sidemen – such celebrated P-Funk alumni as Bootsy Collins
and Bernie Worrell are among those returning on *T.A.P.O.A.F.O.M.* –
recalls that of the great jazz-band leaders.

He defines his role as somewhere 'between referee and traffic cop'.

How about dictator?

'The music dictates itself.'

Onstage with the P-Funk All Stars in 1990 – on one of the special
occasions a threatened UK concert appearance actually materialises –
Clinton makes the following observation: 'We are just biological
speculations ... I believe in God, but law and order must prevail.'
The gravity of this important announcement is only enhanced by the
fact that at the time he makes it he appears to be wearing half a zebra.

Life in the fast lane takes its toll, however. In mid-conversation,
sitting perfectly upright, Clinton's eyes close. This has happened a
couple of times already, but this time he's out like a light. His band
rouse him from his slumber with shouts of 'Animation!' This word
reminds him of something. 'Animation is a reality,' he observes. 'I go
to Disneyland and they make me cover my head, because Mickey
Mouse might get mad.' Like many of Clinton's nuttier utterances, this
one turns out to have an unexpected basis in reality. On a recent visit
to Disneyland, his flamboyant aspect caused him to be charged with
the heinous crime of 'character obstruction', and he was forced to
cover his head on pain of expulsion.

There could only be one winner in this battle between the shocktroops of corporate leisure and the man who has done more than any other American this century (with the possible exception of Frank Zappa, but you can't dance to him) to fuse the libido and the intellect.

George Clinton showed Mickey a half-hour's respect and then took his hat off. 'Someone came up to me and said, "Didn't I tell you to keep your head covered?" I told him, "I thought y'all had changed shift." '

Maggot Brain (Nine, 1971, reissued on Westbound)

Missy Elliott

'When I finish here today, I'll probably go to a mall.'

Missy 'Misdemeanor' Elliott is an infamously snappy dresser, so when she emerges from a discreet recess in her LA hotel room wearing nothing more elaborate than track-suit bottoms and a t-shirt with a cartoon dog on it, there's a moment of disappointment. Admittedly, the tracksuit bottoms are of the designer variety – the Sean John label run by her fellow rap mogul Sean 'Puffy' Combs ('It would make him very happy to know I was doing his advertising,' Missy notes crisply, as if pondering a lost percentage) – but still, she seems a little casual.

And then you notice the diamonds. Round her neck, on her finger, and most effulgently of all, marching in well-ordered ranks across the wide open spaces of a bracelet that looks like it could single-wristedly redeem President Clinton's budget deficit. It's one thing to wear your heart on your sleeve, it's quite another to wear your pension there.

When Missy 'Misdemeanor' Elliot first barrelled on to the hip-hop scene – taking the MTV awards by storm in the autumn of 1997 – a pension was the last thing on the minds of most of her peers. The violent deaths of ghetto superstars Tupac Shakur and Biggie Smalls had given rap's materialist *bragadoccio* a queasily fatal look: eat drink and be merry, for tomorrow we get shot. In this overheated climate Missy's felonius sobriquet has turned out to be somewhat of a red herring. Far from committing what we British prefer to call misdemeanours, she never seems to have put a foot wrong.

Her success is measured not only in personal terms – the millions of records sold, the countless hit songs written for herself and others.

It's in the general atmosphere of the hip-hop community that Missy Elliott's impact can be seen at its most dramatic. Where a few years back, all was dreary machismo – blustering death threats and lumpen gangster beats – now the US Top Ten bulges at the seams with women and men singing together in an atmosphere of hyperactive musical innovation. Others have played their part in this unlikely turnaround, but Missy has been its key player.

So how did a short, rotund twenty-seven-year-old woman from Portsmouth, Virginia come to save rap from itself? First she gave conspicuous consumption back its innocence, replacing drive-bys with picnics. From her first single with its gleeful rhetorical flourish 'Beep! beep! Who got the keys to the jeep?' the pleasure Missy has taken in the fruits of her success has been entirely infectious.

Embracing rap's materialism, she has thrown off its surliness – replacing destructive feuding with co-operation and enlightened self-interest. An encounter with Missy is a far cry from the litany of hard stares and scary bouncers that made up the old-school rap interview ritual. A lone bodyguard sits among the cheery record company posse outside her room in the hotel corridor. Admittedly, he is the size of a Californian Redwood, but intimidation does not seem to be on his agenda. At a brief hiatus in the conversation his head whips round anxiously – 'Why's everybody looking at me?'

Inside the room, the hotel walls resound with Elliott's infectious Woody Woodpeckerish laugh. In her courtly Virginian drawl she remembers singing to her dolls as a child, with a hairbrush for a microphone, in a bid to emulate British teenypop sensations Five Star. That celebrated outfit were just one of many – alongside Michael Jackson and Diana Ross – to whom she used to write impassioned letters.

What sort of things did she write?

'Things like, "Come and get me from class. I know I'm a nobody and you're a big star, but I've got songs that I think are good and you've got to let me write them for you."' Missy laughs. 'This was in eleventh grade in high school – I wasn't a little kid. I just knew I had to get involved in the music business. I couldn't be wasting my mother's money going to college.'

Missy's parents split up messily when she was fourteen. She is close to her mother but doesn't see much of her dad. ('I've still got love for him,' she says. 'I just don't talk to him.') Her most important professional relationship – with Tim 'Timbaland' Moseley, the shadowy co-conspirator she describes as 'a musical genius', whose syncopated beats incorporating adventurous samples from crickets and birdsong have redrawn the sonic map of American radio – was forged in her late teens. At that time Moseley was hooked up with a group called SBI (the initials stood, rather nattily, for Surrounded By Idiots), working on a primitive Casio keyboard – 'little handclaps and whistles and stuff' – but Missy knew she had to work with him.

Her letter-writing activities stood them in good stead. After hassling lubricious swingbeat bigwigs Jodeci at a local gig, a scorched-earth postal campaign secured Missy and Moseley a deal with the band's off-shoot label Devante Swing as a group called Sista. Unfortunately, the big break turned out to be a false dawn when the company went bankrupt and the album they'd recorded never came out. 'You could release it now and people would think we just did it,' says Missy.

She did not go away from this experience empty-handed. 'It made me realise you should never put everything in the hands of your manager or your accountant or your lawyer. You have to be at them all the time – "OK, there's five dollars missing from my account, where did that go?" If they see that you're not questioning things, they can slip stuff past you.' When she eventually emerged as a solo artist, it would be on her own label – The Gold Mind Inc – with a corporate giant (Elektra) carrying all the risk. But before that could happen she had to rebuild her confidence.

Constructing her career like a hip-hop song from cunningly chosen samples, Missy wrote and appeared on numerous hit singles for the likes of New Edition, MC Lyte and SWV, her infectiously guttural vocal style earning her the title 'the hee-haw girl'. Her appearance at the 1997 MTV awards with her friend Lil' Kim and peers Lisa 'Left Eye' Lopes and Da Brat simultaneously ushered in a new era of mutual assistance and confirmed Missy as the leader of the pack. Everyone else had to dress up as scantily clad Egyptian princesses but she was, well, just Missy. She laughs. 'I'm *always* just Missy.'

Talking about oneself in the third person is usually a sign of celebrity dementia. When Elliott talks about 'givin' 'em Missy' it is a mark of how shrewdly she has constructed her own persona. Nelson George has described the way black female American singers are traditionally viewed as 'creations or adjuncts' of male performers, but Missy Elliott is nobody's adjunct. 'No one has given me tracks or written my lyrics or switched me round to make me Missy,' she says firmly. 'I pretty much made myself.'

In her first video, she appeared not as the booty-shaking fly-girl of hip-hop convention (Missy, by her own admission, 'doesn't make music for sad little men hiding under the covers with their flashlight and their Barbie doll') but as a human bouncy castle. A huge inflatable suit blown up at a car-tyre fitting workshop was just one of a remarkable series of science fiction images that positioned Missy in a territory all of her own, a place described by one perceptive critic as 'midway between Buzz Aldrin and Josephine Baker'.

'People were waiting to see how my hair was going to be and what I was going to be wearing,' she remembers, 'and I felt like since I wasn't the size that people were used to seeing a female artist be, I wanted to do something that could capture people's attention without being a sexual-type thing. Like in school, if everyone else had on Pumas, I had on All Stars. If everyone else was wearing ski jackets that you unzip so the sleeves come off, I would wear a trench coat. I was always doing something so as not to fit into everybody else's category.'

So which was the teenage-style innovation that Missy was most proud of?

'I used to have this hairdo that sat up real high, and I did like a V at the front of my head and put these lines in . . . [she senses this is not sounding quite as impressive as she remembers it] well, *I* thought it was hot. At school it's almost like you're crazy, but then when you become a star it's cool with everyone. You go out wearing a blue sock and a green sock and an earring hanging down to your ankle and next day there will be twenty people trying to copy you.'

Missy is keenly aware of her responsibilities as a fashion leader. 'When I finish here today,' she says, 'I'll probably go to a mall.'

What would a Missy Elliott trip to the mall involve?

'I'll probably go to a jewellery store and get something.' She looks demurely at her wrist. 'Or sneakers – I'm a sneaker fanatic . . . I don't think anyone in the world has more sneakers than me.'

A woman from *Rolling Stone* came to look around Missy's house in New Jersey recently and, on seeing over four hundred pairs of trainers in her main footwear storage area, remarked that Missy had even more sneakers than Will Smith, whose closet she had also recently been privy to. Missy was delighted. 'I know he has way more money than me,' she insists, her usually impeccable business sense deserting her for a moment, as she fails to realise that that's probably because she's spent all her cash on shoes.

How many times would she wear a favourite pair?

'Twice'.

Wouldn't it be better to have the courage of her convictions and never wear anything more than once?

'But there's some that are so hot . . . I got this pair of red and grey Nike Air ahead of time that I loved so much I just *had* to put them on again.'

Missy Elliott's impassioned consumerism is no idle sideline, it is vital evidence of her participation in the American dream at the very highest level.

As proof that she is 'coming back hard and saying whatever', the first single from Missy Elliott's second album goes by the combatative title of 'She's A Bitch'. 'I was going to call the whole album that,' Missy admits, 'but I wanted it to get into K-Mart . . . When a guy acts in a certain manner it's thought of as healthy aggression, but when a female acts in the same way she's called a bitch: all it really means is a female knowing what she wants.'

Presumably it's all about turning a negative into a positive – to use the word in a different way until its meaning changes?

'Exactly. The same way as back in the day it was like, "Don't you dare say 'nigga': that's the slave word." Now it means your homeboy – [fondly] *my nigga*. Some people have it down as kind of a dumbfounded word, but when [chart-topping hardcore rapper] DMX says "I love my niggas", he ain't saying, "This is an expression of fondness for all my illiterate friends," he's embracing the word: if that's what you're going to call us, then tell all my niggas I love my niggas. A word is just a word – it's the meaning you put behind it that matters.'

It's not what you say it's the way that you say it. Timbaland's sulphurous beats and skittering strings overlain with Missy's deliciously incendiary mutter make 'She's A Bitch' a suitably potent follow-up to 'I Want You Back', her number-one single with Spice Girl Mel G (née B). And *Da Real World* album which follows hammers home her advantage with awesome finality.

Beneath the capacious umbrella of Missy's controlling presence gather a formidable array of voices – from the smooth r'n'b of Destiny's Child to the helium craziness of Bustah Rhymes, from rougher than rough reggae diva Lady Saw, to Eminem – the instant megastar white rapper who Missy, shrewd as ever, had signed up to do a track on her album 'while he was still cheap'. The latter plainly made a good impression – 'When he was in the studio,' Missy says approvingly, 'he wasn't trying to act like he was black.' It's not so much the list of people who feature on this record that counts as how hard they're all trying. With Missy cracking the whip, you can't afford to be found wanting.

The New Yorker said that Missy Elliott has 'taken what little she's been given in life and transformed it into something complex and outrageous' but that seems a rather condescending way of looking at someone who can, in her own words, 'pretty much do it all'.

Supa Dupa Fly (Elektra/Gold Mind, 1997)

Eminem

'I'm still young, I don't want to do anything immature.'

The atmosphere of ersatz serenity that is supposed to prevail in newly refurbished West End hotel lobbies was never going to withstand the arrival of Eminem. It's not that the twenty-five-year-old Detroit rapper means to cause trouble. It's just that his very existence seems to divide opinion, or, as he puts it himself, with characteristic eloquence, 'God sent me to piss the world off.'

There is nothing especially offensive about his appearance. In fact, as Eminem emerges from the hotel lift, his shining eyes and *retroussé* snout give him the appealing air of a newborn marsupial. His road manager politely asks the receptionist if he can sit in a quiet corner of the restaurant to do an interview. It is one minute past twelve. The restaurant is formally open but completely empty. *The maître d'* is called. He looks at Eminem. He does not see the most extraordinary pop success story of 1999, a man who has come from nowhere to sell four million copies of his debut album and who could buy and sell this whole paltry establishment in the blink of a baby blue eye. He sees dyed blond hair plastered down on a pasty white forehead. He sees tattoos.

As we are ushered hurriedly into the crowded bar, a fresh difficulty becomes apparent. Eminem – real name Marshall Bruce Mathers III – is virtually unconscious. Swaying gently from side to side – the breeze from the lobby doorway gently ruffling the artificial fibres of his sportswear – he apologises politely for his debilitated condition. In a welcome departure from traditional euphemistic practice, someone in the Eminem camp admits that the rapper 'took something he shouldn't have' in the course of the previous night's riotous appearance at a hip-hop club in King's Cross.

Such a forthright admission might seem shocking to those unfamiliar with Eminem's work, but anything less than full disclosure would have been a disappointment from the man whose lurching, syncopated signature tune 'My Name Is' is probably the most outrageous litany of unfettered calumny ever to go multi-platinum. In the course of introducing the world to his demonic alter ego, Slim Shady, Eminem finds the time to rap about drunk-driving, expectoration, sexual abuse by teachers, a vicious assault on former *Baywatch* star Pamela Anderson-Lee, teenage suicide, reckless drug consumption and the impregnation of the Spice Girls. On a more personal note, he also accuses his mother of taking more drugs than he does (even before today's unsteady entrance, the general consensus was that this would be a considerable achievement), and of being too flat-chested to breastfeed him properly.

Even on *The Jerry Springer Show* – the previous high-water mark of American moral turpitude – it is taboo to disrespect your mother. Small wonder that Eminem's *Top of the Pops* debut earlier in 1999 elicited enough complaints to fill a special edition of *Right To Reply*, and a subsequent appearance – promoting his second British single 'Guilty Conscience' (a Socratic dialogue in which Eminem appears to advocate armed robbery, the seduction of a minor and the murder of an unfaithful spouse) – was broadcast only in the midnight repeat. Small wonder that American music industry bible *Billboard* devoted a whole page of crisis editorial to decrying his pernicious influence on the youth of today.

But the Eminem story does more than just restore the faith of those who feared that pop had lost its power to divide the generations. It is at once an unlikely romance, a strange new twist on the American dream, and – last, but not least – an aesthetic triumph, since in swapping the self-aggrandisement which is rap's traditional stock in trade for a self-loathing whose eloquence and wit are utterly compulsive, he has not only taken an upbringing of grinding poverty and violence and made it painfully funny, but also effected the most successful translation of alienation into art since Dostoevsky imagined the murder of his landlady.

Like his similarly heavily tattooed rap hero Tupac Shakur, Eminem's body tells a story. His wrists bear the legend 'slit me'. His upper arm carries a sombre tribute to the beloved uncle – his grandmother's youngest child, only a few months older than he was – who was Eminem's constant companion until he killed himself at the age of nineteen. His stomach is inscribed with the name of his long-term girlfriend Kim, also the mother of his beloved three-year-old daughter Hailie, and the touching inscription 'Rot in flames'.

Presumably this spur of the moment break-up gesture took a bit of explaining when they got back together a short while afterwards?

'That's how I am,' says Eminem – his tour manager has bought him a Coke now and the caffeine is beginning to work its magic. 'If I think something, I'll say it. Maybe I'll regret it afterwards and maybe I won't.'

Another lowpoint in the same turbulent relationship inspired ''97 Bonnie and Clyde', one of the most controversial songs on Eminem's album *The 200 Slim Shady LP*. In it the rapper describes in gruesome detail taking his girlfriend's dead body down to the pier in the back of his car, dumping her in the water and heading for the Mexican border with their bewildered and newly motherless daughter in tow.

The chilling effect of the song's baby-talk monologue – 'Dada made a nice bed for Mommy at the bottom of the lake' – is enhanced by the happily gurgling contributions of Eminem's daughter on backing vocals. He had spirited her off to the studio claiming to be taking her to fast-food emporium Chuck E. Cheese. 'When I went in to record that song,' Eminem explains, 'my daughter's mother was trying to keep her from me, and this was just a way for me to get back at her. It's better to say something like that on a record,' he adds, somewhat gratuitously, 'than to actually go out and do it.'

It is testament to the success of Eminem's unconventional methods of diplomacy that he and Kim are now reunited and preparing to move Hailie to a new house 'way out in the suburbs, away from everything'. Given that he never knew his own father ('If you see my dad', he observes matter-of-factly in 'My Name Is', 'tell him that I slit his throat in this dream that I had'), Eminem's devotion to his progeny is heart-warming evidence of the enduring nature of family feelings. Not for nothing does this man take his name from a sweet.

'When my daughter was born,' he says – and with the intensity of the memory, his deathly pallor is suffused with something very like a flush – 'I was so scared I wouldn't be able to raise her and support her as a father should . . . Her first two Christmases we had nothing, but this last Christmas, when she turned three [Hailie was born on Christmas Day, though not actually in a stable], she had so many fucking presents under the tree, she kept opening them saying, "This one's for me too?"' Eminem pauses contentedly. 'My daughter wasn't born with a silver spoon in her mouth, but she's got one now.'

In the sort of wide-screen irony for which American showbusiness is deservedly celebrated, *The Slim Shady LP*'s grippingly authentic litany of blue-collar woes – 'I'm tired of committing so many sins . . . tired of using plastic silverware . . . tired of being white trash . . . tired of wearing the same damn *Nike Air* hat' – has earned its author unimaginable riches. When Eminem performed at 1999's MTV video awards, the lavish stage set was based on the trailer park he was still formally living in a few months previously.

How he will cope with the sudden change in his fortunes remains to be seen. For the meantime, apart from the new house, he's put his money where he can't get at it – 'I'm still young,' he says, 'I don't want to do anything immature' – and professes no interest in the conspicuous consumption with which other rappers are wont to celebrate their accession to the big time. Except where his daughter is concerned, obviously. When he gets home from promotional trips, he takes Hailie to the store and tries to buy her everything she sets her eyes upon. 'She says, "Daddy, you don't have to get me something everywhere we go," but I can't stop myself from spoiling her. I don't know whether it's good or bad. I'll find out when she's a teenager.'

When Eminem was a teenager, a high-school bully hit him so hard he had a cerebral haemorrhage which kept him in a coma for five days. The name of that bully, D'Angelo Bailey, is just one of the innumerable fragments of personal detail that make *The Slim Shady LP* a jigsaw puzzle of its author's psyche. 'My album,' says Eminem, tiring slightly, 'is so autobiographical that there shouldn't really be any more questions to answer. It's just the story of a white kid who grew up in a black neighbourhood who had a pretty shitty life – not the worst life in the world, but still a fairly shitty life.'

Just how shitty a life it actually was remains an issue of legal disputation, as Eminem's mother Debbie Mathers-Briggs has just sued him for $10 million. The defamation suit, described in an official statement by Eminem's manager and lawyer Paul Rosenberg as 'the result of a lifelong strained relationship', will make the sort of legal history more usually associated with *Ally McBeal*, not least because one of the observations it deems actionable is Eminem's description of his mother as 'lawsuit happy'. 'She's always been out to get me,' he shakes his head sadly, 'and now she knows I have money, she won't leave me alone. I know that's not a nice thing to say about your mother, but unfortunately it's true.'

Before he got his record deal, Eminem worked for three years as a chef at a suburban family restaurant called Gilbert's Lodge. He was sacked for not wearing the correct work apparel shortly before Christmas of 1996. 'I go back there now and pull up in a limo, just for the spite of it,' he says vengefully, 'hop out, go to the bar, drop a couple of hundred dollars for a tip and throw it in their faces.' He assumes the sneering voice of a former workmate, '"Well Marshall, we thought you'd be blowing up by now . . ."' They took me for a joke, but now the joke's on them.'

As with many an Eminem diatribe, there is more to this one than meets the ear. 'When I go back in that restaurant, it's not to flaunt,' he continues, contradicting himself. It turns out that he pops in to Gilbert's Lodge regularly, not just every once in a while, like you'd imagine. 'I go back to try to be cool with people and see how they're doing,' he insists. 'I went in there the other night to see my old manager' – he mimes extending a hand – '"What's up, how you doing?" But he couldn't look me in the eye.' Eminem pauses. 'It's funny,' he says, sounding less convinced with every moment that passes. 'It's very funny.'

In some strange way, Eminem's rapid elevation from the bottom to the top of the food chain seems to have entailed losses as well as gains. To someone with the imagination to see it, there might even be a downside to the mysterious increase in attractiveness to the opposite sex which is contingent upon newfound celebrity. 'That actually makes me feel kind of sick.' He pauses. 'Some girl will be telling me how fine I am and trying to sit on my lap and I'll be thinking, "If I was just me and I didn't have all of this fame, you wouldn't look at me twice ... you wouldn't look at me *once*."'

'People wonder why my lyrics are so misogynistic and violent towards women,' Eminem continues. 'But my opinion of girls is not very high right now.' The air of old-fashioned formality with which he says this is strangely reminiscent of Elvis Presley. And Eminem's heroically dysfunctional take on rap is undoubtedly the most explosive appropriation of a black musical form by a poor white boy since the king made rock 'n' roll his own in the mid-1950s. Anyone who wanted to find out what had happened to America in the intervening half century could do a lot worse than listen to 'Heartbreak Hotel' and 'My Name Is' back to back.

Ask Eminem what the future holds, and he'll tell you that his next album – already two-thirds complete in the notebooks he fills with his tiny, spidery handwriting – promises to be 'a little more controversial'. 'People already think I'm the antichrist,' he grins winningly, 'so I'm at that point where if everyone's like "you're an asshole", I'm like, "I'll show you what an asshole *really* is."'[38]

The Slim Shady LP (Interscope, 1999)

Brian Eno

*'I don't have a linear argument to offer, just a series of observations
and a way of training yourself to notice things.'*

On the back cover of *A Year With Swollen Appendices*, Brian Eno's
diary of 1995, he supplies a handy guide to some of the things that he
is: 'a mammal, an Anglo-Saxon, an uncle, a celebrity, a masturbator'.
Further insight into the mind of the enigmatic musician, record-
producer and artist is furnished by his diary entry for 26 August:

'Pissed into an empty bottle so I could continue watching *Monty
Python* and suddenly thought, "I've never tasted my own piss", so I
drank a little. It looked just like Orvieto Classico and tasted of nearly
nothing.'

Before this heroically indiscreet volume established him as art-
rock's answer to Sir Alan Clark, bodily functions did not loom large
in the public perception of Brian Eno[39]. But that's all changed now.

'On the beach,' he notes on 15 August, 'watching topless French
ladies with huge wobbling sousaphones of bumfat, wishing I could
hear them fart.'

Didn't his wife Anthea (who runs Eno's business affairs) take
exception to that?

'When I first got the idea of publishing the diary, she had never
read it. I said, "I don't know if I should show you this – I do go a bit
on about ladies' bottoms," and she said, "I don't mind, I've got one
too."'

Eno's own bottom is seated as he speaks. It's a quiet Saturday
morning at his studio in a peaceful Notting Hill backwater. This
beautiful airy room contains just about every possible means of

amusing yourself – tools, musical instruments, computers, recording equipment, endless tapes and discs, a swing.

BT: Isn't it hard getting down to work with all these different toys to play with?

BE: You do have to be driven in some way to stop yourself from just frittering away your time, and I suppose I'm driven by guilt. I was raised a Catholic so I don't have a Protestant work ethic, but I've ended up in this quite privileged position, which so many people would love to be in, and I can't help wondering if I'm making the best of it. One of the things I don't dwell on in the book, because it would sound a bit self-pitying, is that being completely free to choose what to do is actually quite difficult: it can lead you to very depressive crises. If your time is structured you don't have this problem of 'what am I going to do today?'

Realising that this is quite a luxurious problem to have, Eno mocks himself for owning up to it: 'I'm totally misunderstood [assumes whining artist tone] I've been waiting to tell someone about this for ages.

'The most attractive thing about the diary form for me,' he continues, 'is that it gets rid of the idea of separating thought off from the rest of what you do. I kept trying to write a book of [scornfully] "my ideas", and it looked so dull even I couldn't be bothered to read it. Then I realised that this was because I don't have a linear argument to offer, just a series of observations and a way of training yourself to notice things.'

The result of Eno's nightly endeavours is a compelling mishmash of impassioned meditations on the Bosnian situation, whimsical musings on such intimate ephemera as the fact that he rarely gets erections while in Ireland and apparently throwaway aphorisms. Some of these – 'cooking is a way of listening to the radio', for example – are funny and wise. Others ('saying that cultural objects have value is like saying that telephones have conversations') seem to exist solely in the hope of provoking an angry response.

Judging by his diary's accounts of the Eno family dancing to doowop records together, Eno derives a good deal of inspiration from his two young daughters, Irial and Darla (pretty names, which their dad proudly confesses to having made up).

BT: Do you see creativity as a child-like state?
BE: Absolutely. The way children learn is by pretending, imagining what it would be like to be in another situation, which is the essence of culture. There's this crazy supposition that at the age of sixteen or eighteen you should suddenly switch all that off because you now know what you're doing, but the people I find interesting are the ones who carry on playing that game.

One of his daughter's friends from the communal gardens is coming round to learn an instrument later. She and Brian will decide which one when she gets here.

BT: Shouldn't children just be given an instrument and forced to play it on pain of not getting any dinner?
BE [shocked]: A lot of people who are classically trained are socially so inept as a result of having to spend eight hours a day sawing away at a piece of wood for most of their lives. I think it's barbaric, actually. If you think about the things we look at in horror when other societies do them – like making people stretch their lips, or binding their feet – that's child's play compared with putting a kid through learning the violin against their will.

Such indulgent attitudes might have something to do with Eno's being so sought after a collaborator. He seems a very unjudgemental sort of record producer. How else to explain his continual willingness to be associated with James? Or his gentle interest in Naomi Campbell's experiments with the novel?

'I think people who have cultural muscle should always try it out,' Eno insists. 'Something good might happen.'

While his catalytic endeavours – saving Bryan Ferry from himself on the first two Roxy Music albums, helping David Bowie out with his Berlin trilogy – have been justly celebrated and his ambient works (famously embarked upon after being laid up in a hospital bed after being knocked down by a taxi on the Harrow Road) provided the blueprints for many a latterday knob-twiddler, Eno's most neglected achievement is as a vocalist singing his own material.

As it appears on his classic first solo album *Baby's On Fire*, Eno's voice – camp, bitchy, pastoral – seems to encompass many of the good things about English punk rock, four years before it officially happened. The glorious new-wave sneer of 'Baby's On Fire', 'Needles In The Camel's Eye''s adenoidal holler, the hilarious trying on of guises (and painfully acute Bryan Ferry impression) in 'Dead Finks Don't Talk' – where did all this stuff *come* from?

Eno's first band The Maxwell Demons (named in honour of 'an anti-entropy device that could sort hot molecules from cold') was formed at Winchester School of Art in 1968. They were a 'late psychedelic ensemble', inspired by The Fugs, MC5 and especially The Velvet Underground, 'I wanted to capture some of the spaced-outness they had,' Eno remembers, 'and that doowop thing with the slightly sinister undertones. I didn't manage it, but I found that I was making something different which I liked.' He pauses. 'Imitation is a very good way to start, so long as you fail.'

What about his own family background? You'd think Brian Eno could only have been raised by a colony of free-thinking bohemian bee-keepers, but this was not the case. 'My dad was a postman,' he says fondly, 'and my mother was a Belgian immigrant.'

BT: How did they meet?
BE: At the end of the war, when the Germans had left Belgium, they used to billet English soldiers with Flemish households, and while my dad was staying there he fell in love with this picture of a young girl, who turned out to be the family's daughter. She'd been in a German forced labour camp, building Heinkel bombers. When the war ended it took her ages to come back, she only weighed five stone and she had a one-year-old-daughter – the father had disappeared from the camp and was never seen again – but my dad was waiting for her. They got married a couple of years later, and she's lived in Woodbridge in Suffolk ever since.

That's a lovely story.
'It's very romantic, isn't it?' Eno grins.
And any last remaining pretensions he might have to cold-fish

status are finally dispelled when conversation turns to the 'very peculiar and eccentric' uncle he credits with a key role in his creative development. Though the man died in 1992 (four years after his own father) Eno's normally calm and measured demeanour gives way to obvious emotional agitation as soon he starts talking about him.

'His life story would really be worth going into,' he enthuses. 'He went to India with the hussars in the 1930s, but fell off his horse shortly after he got there, and was discharged with concussion. Then he spent six years hanging out with yogis and came back to Woodbridge,' Eno laughs, 'a changed man.'

Eno's uncle worked as the town gardener, with a handy sideline in crockery repair, and used to slip his nephew tiny books (Eno demonstrates just how tiny with a simple hand gesture) from the 'Methuen World of Art' series. It was while looking at two particular plates in one of these books, Piet Mondrian's two Boogie-Woogie paintings, *Broadway*[40] and *Victory* that Eno realised he wanted to be an artist.

'What knocked me out about them was something that I've been fascinated by ever since, which is how something so simple can produce such a strong effect. That economy has always been the thing with me. I want to do as little as possible for the maximum pay-off.'

Inquisitive eyes meandering along Eno's video rack come to a screeching halt at the box marked 'Mud-Wrestling'. 'I think people are so sensitive to what is erotic for them,' Eno insists. 'Precisely how much an eyebrow is raised or what word is used; they're probably more specific about that than anything else, other than food.'

Isn't that what makes those things exciting, the fact that people don't think about them?

'I don't think people think about most things,' he replies quietly, 'but I do. I think, in general, thinking is a bloody good idea'.

Here Come The Warm Jets (Island, 1974)

Godspeed You Black Emperor!

'At the end of the day, there's a good chance that we're as full of shit as the next people.'

A sharp, pistol-like report from an overloading monitor causes the already pained-looking sound engineer to wince into his levels meter. Godspeed You Black Emperor! have been soundchecking for most of the afternoon, and the logistical problems of having nine people onstage are starting to look insurmountable. The venue will be closed down if they go over 105 decibels. Unfortunately they are that loud before they've even plugged in to the PA system.

As they launch into the same stately instrumental segment for the umpteenth time in a bid to isolate the source of the overload, the expressions on the face of the musicians – three guitarists, two bass-players, two-woman string section and brace of drummers – veer between stoical and disconsolate. For the observer, it is strange and slightly disorienting to watch the giant melancholic wash of sound created by this unique Montreal mini-orchestra being broken down into its constituent elements. But perhaps it is no bad thing, given the almost mystical levels of reverence generated by their music's awesome, tsunami-like crests and troughs, to know that they are activated by a drummer saying something as mundane as, 'Let's do the speed-up from the solo part.'

At last, the whole thing comes together. Crystalline shards of cello and violin rip through the venue's loudspeakers as 'Moya' (the first track on their *Slow Riot For New Zero Kanada* EP) attains its full complement of glacial majesty. Moments later, three of Godspeed's nine members – Efrim, Nardola, and Aidan (no second names, no pack drill: Canadian social security don't take prisoners) – convene stiffly on the floor outside the toilets. The band are not at ease with the idea of doing interviews, and the atmosphere is more akin to an encounter with a clandestine political cadre.

Lean, paranoid; hair shaved, shaggy or in messianic top-knots, if Godspeed You Black Emperor! were unable to find a place to stay after a gig, you can imagine them getting together to put up a barn. The sense of mission they carry with them is delightfully infectious. There is nothing wilfully masochistic about an austere and largely foodless touring regimen – Nardola speaks wistfully of 'looking for a middle ground between being treated like superstars and being treated like a lump of shit' – that's just the way things have to be if you want to take this many musicians (and their glockenspiel) round Europe on a shoestring.

It's down to the momentum of their music and the excitement of being part of something that is bigger than themselves to carry them through. 'I realised when I first started drumming with this band that I can't change the tempo,' Aidan explains. 'Once it gets going all you can do is hold on.'

Still, it must be upsetting to cart themselves half-way round the world in conditions of considerable material hardship, only to find that the speakers won't turn up loud enough. 'It's a small thing,' says Efrim affably, 'it's not like getting laid off from a job you've done for twenty-five years.'

Elegiac album sleeve notes and live cinema back projections of deserted factory landscapes seem to confirm that the band's spiritual roots lie in the economic decline of Mile End, the run-down Montreal neighbourhood all but one of them call home.

'We're not representing Mile End as a whole,' Efrim maintains, 'but an idealised notion of certain aspects of the place, like the fact that there's a railway track which runs right through it, and next to the railway track there's a lot of abandoned industrial space.' Abandoned industrial space might not sound like everyone's idea of a good time, but there is pleasure as well as pain in Godspeed You Black Emperor!'s apocalyptic pop aesthetic.

'Bleak, uncertain, beautiful' – the words scraped in the run off groove of their mesmerising debut *f#a#oo*, could hardly be more apt. Despite a prevailing mood on the doomy side of mordant – the album opens with a man who might be Ingmar Bergman's depressive uncle intoning the cheering words 'The car is on fire and there is no driver at the wheel . . . the sewers are all muddy with a thousand lonely suicides' – this record still seems to bring joy to all those who hear it. There is something oddly uplifting about the completeness of its desolation.

The vinyl edition also comes with a free gift worthy of Godspeed's fellow devotees of the nomenclatural exclamation mark, Wham! Each sleeve contains coins crushed by trains on the railway track which runs behind the studio where its music was recorded.

The album's unexpected success turned this touching gesture into a full-time job. 'We did the first thousand for ourselves, but the record company are crushing pennies now,' Aidan admits. When *f#a#00* first came out, he thought it would be like all his friends' bands' records, 'with two hundred copies each in every one of our closets'. Efrim was more optimistic, albeit guardedly so: 'I had a belief that if we toured North America and played well live, we could sell records from the stage.'

Such a return to the pilgrim spirit of early hardcore punk is long overdue in what might fairly be termed American rock's post-alternative era. Efrim recounts the disillusionment of 'being into hardcore, and then hardcore becoming this thing called grunge, and suddenly anything interesting that had grown out of it getting recuperated at a really rapid rate, so you would come across something new, and four months later you'd see a rock video with some horrible band of posers doing exactly what you'd been doing in your basement, and you'd feel like an idiot'.

Why?

'Because real communities only form outside the glare of the spotlight . . . the moment something's named by an organ of the media, it's over.'

Given this distinctly non-showbiz mindset, it's small wonder that being the subject of what sick men in over-priced leather jackets like to call a 'buzz' makes Godspeed You Black Emperor! somewhat uneasy. When a barman asks them to sign a CD for him, they have to go and fetch the only member of the band (inevitably, a drummer) who is willing to do it. The autograph-hunter struggles to come to terms with the fact that the rest of them have refused him as a mark of respect.

The heights of eloquence to which this awkward encounter subsequently spurs Efrim suggests the glare of the spotlight might bring out the best in him. 'We're just trying to do the best we can without pulling a Bono or a Michael Stipe and going, "Look at us, we have these special intricate thoughts that are actually just weird variations of liberal humanism,"' he almost snarls. 'Fuck that! We're just fumbling to try to explain what seems obvious to us' – a thoughtful pause – 'Then again, there are eight million deluded rock and pop musicians who think that they're "keeping it real", and at the end of the day there's a good chance that we're as full of shit as the next people.'

Far from the sombre, improving endeavour which might be anticipated, a Godspeed You Black Emperor! live show turns out to be a magical, unnerving, wild and at times downright scary affair. The walls of the room seem to stretch and then contract as the band perform, as if their breathing was pulling all the air out of it.

Some standard issue black and white film back-projections of ballerinas and people standing on top of oil derricks are an unnecessary distraction[41] from music which already conjours up a heady rush of visual images: like the way a glass dish that wasn't heatproof would throb just before it exploded if mistakenly placed in a really high oven, or the last cartwheel of a tumbleweed impaled on a particularly intractable cactus.

String slashes accelerate alarmingly then flatten to a calming plateau. Rhythms sidle from pulse to flurry and back again, and the drummer relieves the gathering tension with a burst of maniacal laughter. If Hank Marvin of The Shadows was a cosmonaut and his life-line broke while effecting a small external repair, this is what the music playing in his head as he plunged into the eternal abyss might sound like.

f#a#00 (Constellation/Kranky, 1998)

Isaac Hayes

'The response was great: ladies were crying, everybody was moved by it.'

'For a black man to stand and wear those chains as a symbol of strength,' said Dionne Warwick, of the immaculate golden shackles Issac Hayes sported at the great WattStax festival of 1972, 'well, some women took it as a sexual thing.'

It's not so much that Hayes' later incarnation as *South Park*'s chef lends a salacious gloss to earlier landmarks in his remarkable career: the salacity was already coming through very nicely. Ditto the scatalogy. (Perhaps Hayes' most requested songwriting anecdote concerns the way 'Hold On, I'm Coming', one of the biggest hits he wrote for Sam & Dave with Stax co-writer David Porter, sprang from the latters visit to the toilet.) All Satan's animators, Matt Parker and Trey Stone, had to do was put them together.

Hayes' career trajectory – from sharecropper's son to *South Park*, via soul, the civil rights movement, *Shaft*, the bankruptcy court and the church of scientology – is illuminated by diamond flashes of exquisite cool. Peter Guralnick's book *Sweet Soul Music* noted Hayes' receipt in september 1973 of a quarterly cheque, *aside* from royalties, of $270,000. Just over three years later Hayes, who had somehow acquired a staff of sixteen, filed for bankruptcy with debts of six to nine million dollars. Hayes' claim for living expenses included enough money to pay for a place to live, utilities, food and transportation, 'the latter sometimes including chauffeured limousines to take his children to school'.

Meeting him in early 1993, the soft-spoken and courtly Hayes has got himself back on track, and seems able to delve back deep into the past without any visible sign of discomfort.

'My first recollection of singing publicly,' Hayes recollects, 'was in church, across the road from where I lived in the country, when I was three years old. I made my public debut singing on an Easter programme with my sister, and my grandmother played piano.' Isaac's sister 'screwed up' a harmony and her precocious sibling told her to stop and sing it again: 'Of course, everybody thought that was cute.'

When his family moved to Memphis, things got more complicated. Held back a year, as was the custom with new arrivals from the country, Hayes was a somewhat forlorn figure until the day he won a talent contest: 'I didn't have a dime in my pocket – in fact, I had holes in my pocket – and all these girls that smelled good of cologne and stuff, they wanted my autograph. I thought, "Hmmm, I want to do this." '

Hayes' showbiz career took a while to get properly started. He toured the churches of Tennessee, Mississippi and Arkansas, singing bass with a gospel group, the Morning Stars, then with a blues band, Calvin Valentine and the Swing Cats, and a doowop vocal ensemble, the Teen Tones. In 1962 he cut an unsuccessful single as Sir Isaac and The Doodads, called 'Laura, We're On Our Last Go-round' which helped get him signed to Stax as a session sax player and keyboard deputy for Booker T. Jones, of 'Green Onions' fame.

Establishing one of the classic soul songwriting partnerships with David Porter, Hayes went on to pen more than two-hundred songs, including the huge hits 'B-A-B-Y' and 'Soul Man', for artists like Carla Thomas and Sam & Dave. It was also at Stax, in 1964, that Hayes, always a fashion leader (on visiting the label Memphis writer Stanley Booth described him as wearing green cuffless pants, Italian sweaters and matching lizard shoes with a Russian-style cap, while carrying a paper sack full of Zebra material from which he was intending to have a suit made), hit upon his much-copied look of bald head and whiskers.

IH: I used to wear my hair in locks the way musicians did then, and I had to sleep with a stocking cap on it to keep it in place. It got to be such a drag that I thought, 'Screw this,' went round the corner to Mr King's barber's shop and asked him to cut it all off . . . people used to

Missy Elliott's diamonds
© Mark Aleski, 1999

Lee 'Scratch' Perry: some of his headgear is missing

© Chris Clunn, 1990

Sun Ra: his headgear is fully intact
© Jean Marc Birraux

Robert Wyatt pursued by a tree
© Guido Harari, 1999

Ozzy Osbourne and his dog. Note impressive jewels (Ozzy's aren't bad either). Moments before posing for this touching picture with his bulldog, Baldrick, Ozzy Osbourne said, "One thing I've learned in this business is never pose for a photo doing something stupid, because it will always come back to haunt you" © David Sandison, 1995

Captain Beefheart and his cat

© Don Van Vliet, courtesy of Galerie Michael Werner Köln and New York, 1989

ABOVE: The Ex in motion
© The Ex

LEFT: Julia Cafritz and Jon
Spencer of Pussy Galore live
at the Harlesden Mean Fiddler.
Simmering gender-based
tension could at any point
escalate into all-out conflict
© Anne Coffey, 1988

ABOVE: The Beta Band dress up as bandits © Michael Spencer Jones, 1998

BELOW: Destiny's Child: Farrah, Kelly, Beyoncé and Michelle, between the first and second culls. Farrah is right to look nervous © Sony Music 2000 / Steven Williams

Eminem's tattoo © James Burns, 1999

laugh at me – 'Look at that bald-headed guy with the beard' – but they stopped soon enough when they started to see my picture in the papers. Another thing too . . . it's *ageless*.

BT: How do you maintain it?

IH: I cut it every two or three days with outlining clippers that cut real low. If I use a razor my hair grows under in bumps.

In those days, the Lorraine Motel – now Memphis' grimmest tourist attraction – was a place musicians liked to hang out. 'A lot of the artists who came to Stax stayed there and, in the summer time, when it got too hot to record, we'd take off, swim in the pool and eat chicken.' If Hayes' then wife had not insisted on taking the car on that fateful day in 1968, Isaac Hayes would have been pulling up at the Lorraine Motel at about the time Martin Luther King was assassinated.

This tragic event subjected the unusually integrated world of Stax to unprecedented racial tensions, right from the moment just after the murder when Hayes and his white colleagues Steve Cropper and Donald 'Duck' Dunn went back to the studio to get his bass, and police pulled a shotgun on the black man but not his white friends. For about a year after King's murder, Hayes found it hard to write – to do anything, even. 'I was bitter. It was like everything was dead – all our hopes were gone. Man, it was a dark time.'

In 1969, however, he released his second solo album, *Hot Buttered Soul*, which proved to be one of the most influential pop records ever. Hayes extended arrangements of classic songs such as 'Walk On By' paved the way for the expansiveness and opulence of disco – and Barry White, in particular; and his extended story-telling prologue to Jim Webb's 'By The Time I Get To Phoenix' was one of the very first rap records.

BT: You played it for the first time in a club with The Bar-Kays, is that right?

IH: Yes it is. When I got up onstage I thought, 'Damn, everybody's talking – how am I gonna get their attention?' I said 'Hang up on the first chord of the song, hang up on this b flat eleventh', and I started talking. I created a situation in my head which was what I thought could have happened to cause this man to leave, and halfway through the talking the crowd was quiet. I thought, 'I got em,' so I kept on talking, and then at the beginning of the song where I sang, 'By the time . . .' wooh, the response was great, ladies were crying, everybody was moved by it.

When the time came to write the Oscar-winning soundtrack to *Shaft*, Hayes – inspired by Quincy Jones' work on films such as *McKenna's Gold* – called upon his formative experience of arriving in Memphis as a child from the deepest Tennessee backwoods to help him approximate the thrill of the sidewalk. 'The country's so quiet that just the noises in the city were exciting to me: the way certain things happened at certain times during the day: the trashman coming for the garbage, or the pospicle man selling ices. And I tried to capture some of that excitement with *Shaft*.'

MGM sent him three pieces of 16mm footage – 'the opening where Shaft comes out of the subway, the montage of his walk through Harlem, and the love scene' – and Hayes built the music around them. Other records that have expanded pop's vocabulary in the way that *Shaft* did can often sound a bit tired. But listening to it all the way through now, it's amazing how it stands up as a complete piece of music.

There's a song on Isaac Hayes' 1971 album *Black Moses* called 'Ike's Rap 2'. It's the first segment of a medley and it only lasts a couple of minutes; there's a gently descending bass and organ figure, some exquisite spiralling strings and a plaintive piano, as a contrite Isaac begs his woman to forgive him for doing her wrong: 'You see, love, I can't sleep, can't even eat.'

This brief musical fragment provided the basis, in sampled form, for whole songs on both Portishead's *Dummy* and Tricky's *Maxinquaye*. This is just the sort of amazing eventuality that the courses on 'handling the ups and downs in life' that Hayes has taken alongside fellow Hollywood scientologists John Travolta, Juliette Lewis and Tom Cruise are designed to help him cope with.

Shaft (Stax, 1971)

Kelis

'I get influenced by Europe too: it's very, like, bourgeois or whatever.'

Striding purposefully down one of the seamiest streets in Soho in spring of the year 2000, twenty-year-old Kelis (pronounced kuh-leece) Rogers is a day-glo Amazon. She wears a small pink t-shirt with 'Harlem' written on it, bejewelled spray-on jeans, and a jacket made from the skin of a blue crocodile. Her volcanic eruption of multi-coloured hair is complemented by bright green sunglasses, eyebrows and – if the rumours are to be believed – pubic hair to match. The funny thing is, she used to dress the same way before she was famous.

Now universally known, if the trail of excited whispers she leaves in her wake is anything to go by, as 'the "I Hate You So Much Right Now" woman', Kelis has imprinted herself upon the global psyche with the force of an unexpected tax demand. Her debut single, formally titled 'Caught Out There', was the one with a musical backdrop resembling a full-scale mortar attack, where the singer repeatedly unleashes a scream containing all the compressed fury and tenderness that anyone who has ever felt themselves wronged in love would have probably liked to express, if only their voice had been loud enough.

Even after three months' blanket radio-play, it was still an extraordinary record. And the designer brutality of the accompanying Hype Williams-directed video – in which the infidelity of Kelis' lover is punished with a series of savage beatings culminating in his death –[42] makes sitting down to talk to her rather an intimidating prospect. The interview room has been heated, at Kelis' own request, to the temperature of a blacksmith's forge. The natural level of her speaking voice is set somewhere between tannoy and TV preacher, and her laugh echoes through a confined space like the boom of a breeding bittern.

Luckily, she's not about to let the excitement of her third global promotional tour in as many months go to her head. 'Madonna goes to Europe for a few weeks then comes back to New York,' Kelis rasps derisively, 'and she's like [assuming a cut glass accent Noel Coward might have been proud of], "Hello . . ."' She shakes her head in mock outrage: 'Bitch, we know where you're from. I understand. I get influenced by Europe too: it's very, like, bourgeois or whatever, but you don't talk like that. I know 'cos I've seen you in movies.'

Kelis' own roots are permanently on show. Not only do her striking features flow from a one-off gene pool (her father, who died in 1998 after suffering a heart attack while scuba-diving, was an African-American pastor and part-time jazz saxophonist; her mother is half Chinese and half Puerto-Rican) but her parents arrived at that distinctive first name by splicing together their own (Kenneth and Iveliss).

Conflict between their strong religious principles and the free-spirited nature of the teenager they had brought into the world was probably inevitable, and Kelis doesn't blame her mother for kicking her out of the house at sixteen. 'I could've gone back if I'd humbled myself,' she acknowledges cheerfully, 'but that's not what I'm good at.'

Kelis' debut album *Kaleidoscope* is the work of an artiste for whom humbling herself is not an option. Where it could so easily have settled for ten retreads of the same vengeful formula or, worse still, a retreat into lipgloss swingbeat, it opts instead to range effortlessly from the slinky r'n'b of the second single 'Good Stuff', through the freakily Madonna-esque 'Mafia', to the playground electro of 'Game Show' and the psychedelic soul of 'Suspended'. The result is the most audacious and multi-faceted pop record of the new century to date.

The woman whose name is on it had already served a lengthy apprenticeship in the Girls Choir of Harlem and an ill-fated all-female pop trio called BLU (Black Ladies United) when a friend of a friend – 'They, like, did nails together' – put her in touch with her current production team. Inspired by 'the click' which took place when she hooked up with innovative Virginia unknowns Chad Hugo and Pharrell Williams (aka The Neptunes), Kelis backed out of a proposed deal with The Wu-Tang Clan and negotiated her own record contract with Virgin instead.

Sitting quietly in the corner of the room is a young Frenchman – a rapper it turns out, signed to Virgin France – who Kelis picked up in Paris, as you or I might acquire our duty free. He struggles vainly to maintain his mystique while she ribs him mercilessly: 'He mutters to himself in French, it's like a hobby,' Kelis guffaws. 'He thinks his presence here is such a big secret.'

Lunch arrives, and Kelis wolfs her quorn burger with extra bacon and onion rings in a manner that suggests her teenage modelling experiences (a packed CV also includes several years as a drama major at the overachievers' high school that inspired *Fame*) have done no lasting damage. The extra bacon has the last laugh though: twelve hours later it sends her home early to Harlem with chronic food poisoning. But Kelis will return. And when she does, we'd better be ready.[43]

Kaleidoscope (Virgin, 2000)

Leila

'When I'm mixing a song, each channel is a band member fighting for supremacy.'

Leila Arab opens the door of the Finchley Road mansion-block flat she shares with her parents and three siblings. She points the way into the bedroom where her amazing debut album *Like Weather* was recorded ('All musics written, recorded and mixed at home by me', it says on the cover, in case anyone was having any doubts) and goes off to make some tea. Inside the room sits her elder sister Roya, overshadowed by homely mountain ranges of vinyl albums and electronic equipment.

Almost Leila's twin in appearance, but with an accent pitched a couple of thousand miles to the east, Roya is one of *Like Weather*'s three lead singers. It was she who 'virtually raised' Leila and her brother Ali when they came to London in 1979, forced into exile by the Iranian revolution. The Arab family[44] arrived in Britain rich – her father's business empire included numerous hotels and newspapers – but they lost everything when the Ayatollah Khomeini confiscated their assets. 'I remember when we were told we were going to have to leave boarding school,' Leila recalls phlegmatically. 'My brother and me were sitting out on the balcony of our Knightsbridge flat crying, "Oh no, we're poor."'

Leila's luck turned while at college in Stoke, when Björk left a message on a friend's answering machine asking if she would join her her live band. 'She'd been asking around for female keyboard players, and someone had mentioned me: I had a bit of a reputation for being able to play keyboards, even though it wasn't really true.'

Adjusting to the rigours of live performance from a standing start turned out to be all too easy. 'You get to a point where you're up onstage at a festival in front of 60,000 people,' Leila says, matter-of-factly, 'and there's no energy, no fear, no nervousness even; you're just thinking, "Oh no, I forgot to do my laundry."' She's far from casual about her own music, though.

While demonstrating the hand-held mixer on which she made her first recordings, Leila talks about her own music with an evangelical fervour worthy of a character in Colin MacInnes' *Absolute Beginners*. 'You listen to the great bands,' she explains, thumbs battering the tiny console with the practised ease of the hardened computer game veteran, 'be it the John Coltrane quartet or The Doors – I'm talking about ensembles that played shit-hot together – there's *dynamics*; the bass gets loud at one point, and then the guitarist tries to get in. That's why I try to treat electronics like real instruments, so when I'm mixing a song, each channel is a band member fighting for supremacy.'

'As a result of growing up as a foreigner in England,' Leila continues, 'I really know what it means *not* to be able to communicate.' Where many makers of electronic music rejoice in its potential for obfuscation, she reaches out to as broad a constituency as possible, combinging eerie dislocated instrumentals with warm and soulful pop, so that even her sparsest soundscapes embody a humanity and a will to make contact which set them apart from some of her peers' more arid constructions.

Disdainful of 'all that "we are robots" stuff', Leila insists that 'it's the humanisation of the future that's intriguing: the future is about being comfortable – it's not about creating this *distance* . . .' This distinctive vision of the balance between human and mechanical endeavour grew out of a teenage obsession with the music of Prince. At the age of thirteen, Leila would come home from school and listen to it for three hours every night: 'There was all this sexuality there, but his appeal was incredibly sexless – he's the kind of person you could imagine being married to and never bothering to ever have sex . . .'

He'd be too busy?

She nods cheerfully, 'Yes, but so would I – so it would be a great marriage.'

Like Weather (Rephlex, 1998)

Lemmy

'Women are my career, music is just a hobby, really.'

Is there any sight and sound in all of pop music more imposing than Lemmy's powerful upturned chin, silhouetted in trademark deathly green spotlight, the wind machine blowing his hair like some nightmare version of the girl in the *Timotei* advert, as the bomber lighting rig swoops precariously over his head, and he bellows, 'It's a bomber! It's a bomber!'?

No, I don't think there is either.

'I wish I'd brought my waders,' complains a fan waiting outside a Hammersmith Odeon toilet that is an underwater version of Dante's Inferno. In the auditorium itself the sweeter confluence of a hundred different shampoos permeates the diverse crowd. Of course some of the people here are lusty, wart-encrusted Vikings covered in bike grease who had sex on the back of their Triumph Nortons on the way here while drinking vomit out of a firebucket, but not *all* of them are. The odd hermit and a smattering of self-confident women in Brownie and Guide uniforms are also in attendance.

From the moment the distant rumble of drums and Lemmy's garnet-paper growl signalled Motorhead's arrival, heads have been motoring alarmingly – at some points revolving at such speeds as to threaten to detach themselves from be-leathered shoulders and go whizzing across the aisles. Tonight's is not the classic power trio line-up, but Phil 'Animal' Taylor is in place behind his drum kit, and twin guitarists Wurzel and Phil Campbell stage a catgut dogfight which 'Fast' Eddie Clarke himself might have been proud of.

And then, of course, there is Lemmy himself. Born the son of a preacher man, with the distinctly unpromising name of Ian Kilminster, he reinvented himself as an paragon of Anglicised rock 'n' roll menace, and an all-round entertainer to rank with such other twentieth-century greats as Max Miller, Sir John Betjeman and Harold Wilson.

Alongside full-throttle versions of old favourites like 'The Ace Of Spades' and 'Killed By Death', Motorhead also showcase Lemmy's underrated skills as a poet and humanist with a new song 'Going to Brazil': a further celebration of the debauched circus of the roadcrew that rivals the immortal 'We Are The Roadcrew' (which had seemed to be his definitive statement on the subject) for acuity and directness.

'Steve, Clem, Hobbsy, John, Crazy Dil and Pappy,' Lemmy growls, with a mastery of complex scansion that would shame many a Shakespearian actor, 'had to travel second class. They ain't too fucking happy.'

Lemmy onstage, at a safe distance, is one thing. Offstage is quite another. A knock on his Liverpool hotel door at the appointed hour in the winter of 1991 is greeted with the splintering of timber and a screech of overstressed hinges, as an apoplectic Lemmy bursts – eyes bulging – into the hotel corridor. An enormous, troll-like creature with strangely prehensile feet, his savage *mien* makes an arresting contrast with a rather skimpy white towelling hotel robe.

He has just spent several hours explaining to a series of Japanese telephone interviewers that the title track of his Motorhead's new album *1916* – a startlingly considered and thoughtful (especially for a man whose pension fund is a valuable and lovingly maintained collection of Nazi memorabilia[45]) anti-war ballad – is not about the Gulf war, and his mood could not be described as pacific. The tour manager, who 'hasn't seen him like this in ages', advises an anxious press officer to phone him from the safety of another room.

An hour later. Lemmy seems calmer. By the side of the four-poster bed he insists on while touring ('Women are my career,' he growls, 'music is just a hobby, really'), there is an open copy of the notorious Charles Manson biography, *Helter Skelter*. It's wonderful how a little light reading can improve the mood.

For one who has dedicated a goodly portion of his life to the fiercest dissolution, Lemmy is in fine shape. A discreet tattoo on his tanned and healthy-looking forearm proclaims 'Born to lose, live to win' and his determination to live by that motto is not open to question. Before founding Motorhead (whom he originally wanted to call Bastard) in 1975, he performed in sixties showbands in Blackpool, worked as a roadie for Jimi Hendrix and got fired from acid-rock primitivists Hawkwind as a consequence of a Canadian drugs bust. Recently relocated to LA, he finds the return to his homeland somewhat problematic.

'People here still ask what I do in the daytime,' Lemmy shakes his head in disgust. 'The English can't imagine that working as an entertainer can be a real job ... In America they know about real entertainment, because they started it.' Lemmy had a proper job once, as a lathe operator in the Hotpoint factory at Llandudno Junction. Does he miss it?

'It's a real sadness in my life: every time I saw a washing machine I used to think, "Maybe one of my parts is in that."'

It would be fair to assume that Lemmy is not a man prone to homseickness: 'I consider myself a citizen of the world,' he proclaims. 'I've certainly been travelling around it for long enough ...'

BT: But isn't there something very English about Motorhead?
L: I suppose we are the inheritors of the Led Zeppelin/Rolling Stones mantle of crazed on-the-roadness, but you outgrow that in the end, because the bill always comes back to haunt you. You can throw all the TVs you want out of the window – and we did in the early days – but you've always got to pay for them in the end.
BT: Would you count that as one of the biggest lessons you've learned?
L: Life on the road is the best education you could have. I am a wise man, because I *wished* to be one. I was always determined to get more out of being in a band than was obviously on offer: after an opposable thumb, the second greatest gift we've all been given is a brain which has the ability to accumulate knowledge. If you can't

gather that into yourself, then you're worth nothing, your life's wasted.

Motorhead: *No Remorse* (Castle, 1986)

Meat Loaf

'If I were to die tomorrow, on my tombstone they could write "He gave it all".'

'Sometimes going all the way is just a start.' These words come up in antique scroll at the start of the video for Meat Loaf's 1993 single, 'I'd Do Anything For Love (But I Won't Do That)', and the production that follows seems – like the career that preceded it – designed to test the strength of the proposition.

Police cars and helicopters chase the bulky but fast-moving form of a daredevil motorcyclist. He may not look that much like Meat Loaf, but we know in our heart of hearts that it is him. At the entrance to a gothic castle, he vanishes into thin air. Inside we see him as a lonely demon, a Klingon in fingerless gloves, conducting a touching *Beauty and the Beast*-style courtship with a young woman, dressed (her, not him) in a bewildering succession of Marks & Spencer shifts. The scene reaches its climax when he turns a magic crankshaft, and the *chaise-longue* on which she has been disporting herself rises, unsupported, into the air. Then the police come and the couple ride off into the desert on a motorbike.

The song follows the classic Meat Loaf recipe. It has endless stirring choruses, and lasts, in its full-length version, a mighty 11 minutes. The best bit – cruelly abridged on the video – starts about three-quarters of the way in. It's a duet with an enigmatic female Tynesider called Mrs Loud, who peppers Meat with tricky questions such as, 'Can you colourise my life, I'm so tired of black and white?' His replies are heartfelt: 'I can do that, I can do that.' But when she predicts he will betray her, he insists, voice quivering with emotion, that he 'won't do that'. This probably seems absurd, and in many ways it is, but it is also very moving.

Meat Loaf is a big man, but he is wonderfully in touch with his feelings. Born Marvin Lee Aday in Dallas, Texas, in 1947, he played football in high school and sang with the excellently named Popcorn Blizzard in late sixties Los Angeles. He moved to New York a few years later to act in musicals, and met writer and producer Jim Steinman while auditioning for a show enticingly described as '*South Pacific* set in Vietnam'.

The creative partnership of Steinman and Meat Loaf – happily rekindled, after a long period of acrimonious separation, with 1993's *Bat Out Of Hell II* – is one of pop's most enduring and magical symbioses. Tricky and Martina, Kruder and Dorfmeister, Chas and Dave . . . all tip their hats to the man mountain and the master of cod-Wagnerian bombast. Those who complain about the lack of 'progress' exhibited by *Bat Out of Hell II* miss the point entirely. No one wanted Linford Christie to switch to 800m. No one asked Georgia O'Keeffe to paint horses.

'Two weeks ago in America,' Meat reports, 'there was an eight-year-old autistic child who had never responded to one thing in her entire life. She was in the kitchen and "Anything for Love" came on the radio. Her grandma and her parents and her elder sister were there – her whole family – and the little girl got up and walked over to the radio and started responding to the music, and everybody began to cry.'

Hearing the glad news, Meat Loaf's record company sent her a complimentary CD. 'And now,' he concludes triumphantly, 'she's responding to the whole album.'

Why does he think the original *Bat Out Of Hell* became a part of so many people's lives?

'Because it gives you a mirror image of yourself,' he observes gnomically. 'You're not borrowing time from me; you're not walking into my life and living my life with me when you listen to it; you're only living your own life.

'In America,' Meat Loaf continues, 'psychologists give people a copy of *Bat Out of Hell* to take home and listen to, and then they ask them what they thought of it, because you can get an image of a person from that, you can find out how they're thinking.'

But wouldn't that be true of a lot of people's music – why should it be more the case with Steinman and Meat Loaf's?

'Because these songs are not written about us,' he explains. 'They're not written about anything that happens in our lives. That's why we use fantasy art on the sleeves; not to represent motorcycles or bats or anything, but to show that what you're stepping into is a fantasy, and that fantasy is about yourself.'

Steinman's genius is to take a cliché and inflate it so dramatically that it takes on strange and beautiful new shapes. 'Objects In The Rear View Mirror May Appear Closer Than They Are' picks up Bruce Springsteen's famed fondness for absurd motoring metaphors and carries it over the central reservation and into the path of oncoming traffic. ('If life is just a highway,' the song concludes, 'then the soul is just a car', neglecting to confirm whether that would make memory a speedbump.)

Meat Loaf's genius is to maintain a persona with broad enough shoulders to carry Steinman's epic pretensions – a sort of rock 'n' roll minotaur, condemned to forever patrol labyrinths of sexual and emotional fervour that most of us escaped in late adolescence. 'I'm a performer,' he insists modestly. 'That's what I do. I think I'm an OK singer, but I don't sing like Aretha Franklin. I would never put myself in her category – she's brilliant. And Lisa Stansfield's great too. I don't even know if I'm as good as Lisa Stansfield. But there's never been a single moment in my career when I have walked on to a stage, a set or a recording studio when I haven't given everything I had to give. People can say what they want about me, but at the end of the day, if I were to die tomorrow, on my tombstone they could write, "He gave it all".'

Meat Loaf's maternal grandfather was a minister in the Church of Christ. Is that close to Southern Baptist?

'Real close. Here's the difference: Baptists have an organ in the church but the Church of Christ doesn't because there's a passage in the Bible that says you sing and make music in your hearts.' He rolls his eyes. 'I love religion.'

Despite a prevailing view that 'showbusiness was the root of all evil', Meat's mother and her three siblings were encouraged to perform as a gospel quartet, The Hukel Sisters, with their engagingly clunky name testifying to Germanic origins.

The other side of the family were 'real redneck hillbillies', Meat Loaf says with a shudder. 'I mean like *Deliverance*.' He left home, allegedly at the point of his drunken father's knife, when he was sixteen, shortly after his beloved mother had died from cancer. 'Her death had a horrible effect on me. I don't remember doing it and I sometimes say I didn't, but people tell me I literally pulled her out of the casket at the church because I didn't want them to take her away ... I know what she looks like from pictures but I have no memory of her: it's like she's headless. I'm a little kid and I can only see feet and shoes and table legs.'

It would be the epitome of crassness to suggest that Meat Loaf might be 'using his pain in his work', but anyone who has ever wondered where his legendary reserves of intensity come from could be forgiven for wondering if this awful formative trauma might have had something to do with it.

Meat is sceptical. 'Sally Field describes herself going into a picture as taking razor blades to her insides and cutting herself – she has to feel the pain. When I heard her I thought, "I wonder what that feels like?" I've been trying to do it, but,' and the suspicion that he might be taking the mickey here is probably jusfitied, 'it kind of *hurts*.'

Bat Out Of Hell (Epic, 1978)

Mercury Rev

'We went to New Orleans at Mardi Gras and saw all these marching bands playing really fast: it sounded like jungle to us.'

Not since Joy Division turned into New Order has a band coped as well as Mercury Rev with losing its lead singer. But given that the departed vocalist in this case – porcine provocateur David Baker – was one of the most annoying men in the history of pop music, perhaps their subsequent elevation from aspiring to actual greatness was not such a big surprise, after all.

Like 1995's initial post-Baker breakthrough *See You On The Other Side, Deserter's Songs* was an album that was still taking people by surprise on fourteenth and fifteenth hearing. If you were looking for a simple way of summing up the difference between the two records, you might say that the first is more like a motorway and the second is more like a ring road.

'We decided to edit ourselves a bit,' explains bequiffed guitar reel and woodwind journeyman Sean 'Grasshopper' Mackiowiak. 'Instead of twenty things going on at once, now there are only ten . . .'

'*Deserter's Songs* is more internalised,' adds whey-faced vocal, guitar, strings and Chamberlin maestro Jonathan Donahue. 'I think the lyrics are a lot deeper embedded emotionally. The record has to do with feeling deserted and at the same time deserting someone – it's like love: sometimes you're leaving and sometimes she's leaving, it's never easy to quite say which.'

On encountering the two Mercury Rev mainstays in a quiet west London pub, it is hard not to be struck by the contrast between their day-to-day demeanour and the celestial aura of their music. Excitedly grabbing a copy of *Loaded* and lasciviously holding up a tacky pin-up of Natasha Henstridge to a toilet window is not the sort of behaviour you expect of warriors of the new space-gospel vanguard.

'How can such obnoxious people make such beautiful music?' an old man reading his paper at the bar asks. Presumably because day-to-day life takes care of the obnoxiousness, leaving Mercury Rev free to explore their more spiritual dimension in music. Keith Moon wasn't any less great a drummer because he liked to wear a Nazi uniform for a laugh, and once you have got over the small problem of their personalities, Donahue and Mackiowiak actually talk a great deal of sense.

'If you hear a Del Shannon record,' says Mackiowiak, 'it might only have four tracks, but there's still this creepy element which makes you feel uneasy – something else is taking place musically beyond what's happening on the surface – and that is the kind of feeling we've always been looking for.'

'We went to New Orleans at Mardi Gras and saw all these marching bands playing really fast,' Donahue enthuses. 'It sounded like jungle to us.' The ability to make these kind of connections is integral to Mercury Rev's music, but ever since their patchily compelling 1991 debut *Yerself Is Steam*, the band's righteous disdain for anything that looks like a pigeonhole has sometimes caused their admirers a certain amount of confusion.

'We've always found it strange that people in Britain have tended to think us as "this really weird rock band from America",' says Donahue, 'because the music we listen to is ten times weirder than the music we make . . . Like, *The Smithsonian Folkways Collection*. What's weirder than that?'

Donahue's definition of rock 'n' roll – 'a large placard that says "inside these doors, anything goes"' – seems as close to definitive as it is possible to get. Mercury Rev's bed and breakfast of the musical imagination has a room for Miles Davis and a room for The Chemical Brothers, and who would want to stay anywhere that didn't? 'American rock 'n' roll was originally built on African music, the European classical tradition, Gospel and Country,' Donahue continues. 'If they hadn't called it rock 'n' roll, they would probably have had to call it "Western Bebop".'

Would it be fair to say that Mercury Rev's musical mission is to reacquaint those diverse original constituents?

'I hope so,' says Donohue modestly.

Accordingly, *Deserter's Songs* presents a marvellous shimmering landscape of bowed saws and Disney horns, shameless 'Silent Night' rewrites and audacious orchestrations that one moment seem to be plunging into the farthest reaches of the stratosphere, the next deep into the darkest inner reaches of the listener's cerebellum. The album somehow seems to run in a loop without ever losing forward momentum.

Its unexpected commercial success launched the band on two neatly contrary trajectories. Their video treatments progressed from the funny *faux* regular guy-hood of the first, ultra low-budget film for 'Goddess on a Hiway' – wherein the band go fishing in the Catskill Mountains – to the bravura oddity of the creepy German expressionist submarine film Anton Corbijn made to accompany 'Holes'.

Meanwhile, live onstage, Mercury Rev's old maverick liquidity crystallised into ever more conventional rock shapes, as they were obliged by public demand to tour with pick-up bands featuring ex-members of Dr Feelgood. In the long run, it will be fascinating to see if these two opposing impulses can ever be reconciled.

Deserter's Songs (V2, 1998)

Orbital

*'The John Craven sample has a lovely, old-fashioned synthesiser quality
to it.'*

It's a grey weekday lunchtime in glamorous East Anglia. Cambridge
town centre is brought to a resentful standstill as a series of huge
pantechnicons disgorge their cargo. Leathery-looking men with loud
laughs and eyes that have not bags but whole sets of matching luggage
under them haul a succession of huge boxes into the municipally
supported music venue. The catering woman struggles upstairs with
crates containing picallili and other old-fashioned delicacies.

The character of individual performers seems to have little impact
on the time-honoured ritual of the rock 'n' roll circus coming to town.
Phil and Paul Hartnoll – the two men cheerfully contemplating ten
years on the road in an unfurnished dressing room illuminated by
brutal strip lights – are electronic harbingers rather than hardened
rock beasts. Phil (three children; gleaming scalp; well-trimmed
goatee) did not sleep a wink on the overnight trip from Wolverhamp-
ton because he worries too much about the tour bus crashing. His
more carefree younger brother Paul (clean-shaven; luxuriant locks
newly trimmed; as yet unreplicated) ponders the desirability of a
stroll along the river before sound-checking.

While exhibiting none of the fratricidal tendencies of the Gallagh-
ers or the creepy telepathy of the movie-making Coens, Orbital have
developed a sibling mythology every bit as lustrous. When they
perform – trademark torchlight spectacles dancing like fireflies,
bodies bobbing beneath like hatchlings in an electric nest – they
exude a heady sense of familial intuition which spreads out to
encompass the whole of their audience.

People on this tour are hearing songs from Orbital's fifth album *The Middle Of Nowhere* for the first time, and yet electric tingles of anticipation and recognition still pass back and forth between stage and auditorium. Not because Orbital are repeating themselves, but because their music still communicates as directly with the crowd as it did when they began translating acid house and clubland communion into a gig-going environment. All that's gone from this transaction is the novelty.

While familiarity has not bred contempt among the populace at large, the critical community has been less understanding. 'Ten years ago,' Paul remembers fondly, 'it was [assumes fascinated voice of 1960s science documentary] "What are these strange computerised sounds?" Now it's, "Oh, more electronic music. That's not very original."

'It's like someone came up with the idea of the lute,' Paul continues. 'At the start everyone says, "That's a funny guitar, I don't like that," but then over the years it becomes more popular and integrated with other ways of making music . . . well, in medieval times it did.' He falters slightly, as the analogy begins to get the better of him. 'At least people no longer presume you only do what we do if you can't play the guitar.'

'Even though,' Phil adds, smiling, 'in our case that is actually true.'

While the date of the Allman Brothers' first heart bypass remains an enduring source of fascination in the tolerant world of rock criticism, Techno is not supposed to have a history. As bizarre as it may seem for a form of music which traces its roots backwards as clearly as any other, entrenched – and frankly outmoded – futuristic rhetoric insists that every year must be year zero. Hence, to critical ears at least, it's a young man's game.

But if all Orbital's music (or anyone else's for that matter) had going for it was that it was new, then there wouldn't be much point in it anyway. The same way *The Middle Of Nowhere* unfolds in all sorts of unexpected and delightful directions – stretching and furling like a shy rattlesnake making its getaway – so the duo's achievements become more interesting with time rather than less.

Early in 1990, when Orbital first appeared on *Top of the Pops* (wearing fashionable No Poll Tax t-shirts), 'dance acts' were not expected to play live or make long-playing records. 'That was never a problem for us.' Paul explains, 'because we'd grown up on New Order and Cabaret Voltaire, who did both.' With their first two *Untitled* albums (aka 'The Green One' and 'The Brown One'), and a burgeoning live reputation taking them from the ground-breaking Midi Circus package tour of 1992 to the main stage at Glastonbury three years later, Orbital nimbly vaulted these – and other – obstacles.

Traditional constraints on electronic music could no more hold them than the M25 motorway they took their name from could contain London's urban sprawl. Whether playing eight minutes of 'Satan' on *Later* – at last, something Jools Holland couldn't play along with – or storming the Royal Albert Hall in 1996, nothing could stand in their way. A particularly treasured memory of the latter event was the sight of red-coated RAH custodians shining torches into the eyes of transported aficionados to try to get them to step down off their seats and stop dancing, only to have these cheerily incorporated into the revellers' interior lightshows.

Orbital's determination to take their music to places it was never meant to go reached new heights with *The Middle Of Nowhere*. As well as its demonically infectious Rolf Harris stylophone intro, and a remix featuring bagpipes from the Edinburgh military tattoo, the album's first single 'Style' boasted a vocal sample from early eighties pop reprobates Dollar – not previously a name to drop in dance underground circles.

'Our parents used to run a pub,' Paul explains, 'and my mum collected the old 7-inch singles from the jukebox man – he'd just have thrown them away otherwise. As a result we've got about a yard of early eighties pop singles to dive into if ever we're stuck for a sample.'

Presumably this goldmine was the source of their most spectacular coup – seguing between the mighty drumbeat-driven choruses of Bon Jovi's 'You Give Love A Bad Name' and Belinda Carlisle's 'Heaven Is A Place On Earth'?

'We wanted a rock moment,' Paul remembers, 'something we could put the white lights on to, and Bon Jovi had taken her to court because they said she ripped them off. It's always really funny to watch the crowd's reactions – some of the serious people get really frustrated.'

When Orbital do things like this, is it to break up the surface of the music or to give people a familiar hook to hang on to?

'It's just a matter of whether it's something that makes us laugh,' Paul explains, turning his attention to the album's greatest sampling coup – track two's cunning relocation of the sinister theme to eighties children's TV current affairs staple *John Craven's Newsround*. 'The John Craven sample has a lovely old-fashioned synthesiser quality to it,' he beams, 'and when I find something like that, it just makes me happy.'

For all its rather ominous title, *The Middle Of Nowhere* is probably Orbital's most felicitous record to date – forsaking the edgily compelling widescreen paranoia of its predecessors *Insides* and *Snivilisation* for a new mood that is upbeat to the point of jauntiness. Where did this new cheerfulness come from?

Phil speaks fondly of his new home in Brighton. Paul points to a change of studio – not some lush Caribbean fleshpot, but 'a fresh room with a window and a bit of a view', a hundred yards down the road from where they used to work in Old Street.

What's the view like, then?

'Just a light well two floors down,' Paul smiles. 'It's not much, but it's a start.'

The Middle Of Nowhere (London/ffrr, 1999)

Ozzy Osbourne

'If you've had one of your limbs amputated, you don't want to sit in a room with a lot of one-legged men talking about it.'

It is the winter of 1980–81. Black Sabbath are playing at the Hammersmith Odeon, for the first time without Ozzy Osbourne – widely regarded as the soul of the band – who has been sacked by guitarist Tony Iommi, but will soon become a superstar in America. The man attempting to take Ozzy's place is called Ronnie James Dio. He is very short, and the level of the billowing clouds of dry ice is set too high for him, so as he stretches his arms up to the roof, only his fingertips are visible. Someone starts to chant 'Ozzy! Ozzy!' and soon the whole venue is joining in, so that you can hardly hear the music. *Spinal Tap* could never quite live up to the hilarious madness of heavy metal reality.

Having first experienced him as a deficit, the sight of Osbourne in 1995 should not come as a shock, but it does. You could probably fit three of his lean, wiry new selves into the bloated Oz-monster of yesteryear. 'When I eventually put the bottle down,' Ozzy explains, 'my addiction switched to exercise.' Once aboard the hotel gym exercise bike, 'the natural endorphins kick in and I could go on for ever.'

His guitarist brought back some bootleg old-look videos from Japan. 'I couldn't believe them,' Ozzy shakes his head. 'I looked like Elvis!'

In fact, he looked worse than Elvis; he looked like Larry Hagman in drag. Ozzy Osbourne now feels, and looks 'fitter – both physically and mentally' than he did when 'Paranoid' first came out, a quarter of a century before.

As he sips Diet-Cokes and nibbles at the odd strawberry, his wife and manager Sharon, and school-uniformed son Sam, sit in the hotel bedroom next door, watching *True Lies* on video. Without the redoubtable Mrs Osbourne[46], Ozzy freely admits he would probably be 'dead, or in prison'. As it is, the only legacy of decades of alcoholism and drug dependency is a tendency to foam at the mouth slightly at moments of peak conversational intensity.

'What Sharon would do to try to stop me drinking,' Ozzy remembers, 'was take my clothes. So if I wanted to get a drink I'd have to dress up in hers.' This gambit shaped one of the defining moments in Osbourne lore – generally referred to as the Alamo Incident. 'I was alone in my hotel room in San Antonio and I wanted the hair of the dog, so I put one of her dresses on. I'm walking around the town with this green evening gown on, slurping from a bottle of Courvoisier, drunk as an idiot, and I want to take a piss, so I see this old wall and I think, "This'll do", but unfortunately it's the Alamo.'

Charged not only with being drunk in public but also with the rather more serious offence of 'Urinating on a shrine', it would be fair to say that Ozzy was not flavour of the month in Texas at this point. Soon afterwards he went into a coffee shop 'full of normal, straight-laced people' with his bodyguard, a Vietnam veteran, and another terrible thing happened.

'Someone in a suit and tie started screaming, "Put Jesus in front of you." And all the other people in the restaurant turned out to be with him, so they all joined in. Then this Rambo guy who's with me goes into kill mode and starts throwing them all through the window. I had to crawl out of there literally on my hands and knees.'

Being widely viewed in the US as Satan's emissary certainly has its funny side, but the implication of Osbourne's song 'Suicide Solution' in a number of teenage suicides was no laughing matter. At pains to explain that the song was about alcoholism rather than suicide – 'It's "solution" meaning a liquid' – Ozzy is understandably bewildered by the priorities of those who sought to drag him through the US courts over it.

'I don't know about you,' he says, 'but if I went home tonight and found my kid lying face down in the bath with a suicide note saying "Goodbye Dad, I'm off" and a New Kids on the Block album was playing on his stereo, the last thing on my mind would be suing the group – I'd be grief-stricken.'

It was the authentically sombre character of Black Sabbath's music – Osbourne's haunted bellow emerging from the dank grind of Iommi's guitar – that gave it such enduring power, but the Satanic trappings they dressed it in were pure showbiz. 'When we came out of seeing *The Exorcist* we all had to all stay in one room together,' Ozzy laughs. 'That's how black magic we were.' These were emissaries from Aston, not Beelzebub.

Ozzy's mum and dad both worked in the West Midlands motor industry (his dad did night shifts; his mum at Lucas coil wiring), and his own last 'proper' job – before consigning himself to full-time rock 'n' roll dissolution – was testing car horns.

'If you're in a room with ten guys tuning car horns all day,' Ozzy explains, somewhat unnecessarily, 'you'll come home like a lunatic.' While the quality of compressed psychosis in classic Sabbath recordings like 'NIB' or 'Into The Void' has not only carried through to the present day but also spawned a thousand imitators, from Nirvana to Cradle of Filth, Ozzy professes bemusement at the band's high critical standing. 'We never used to like it if we got a good review,' he remembers. 'It upset us.

'Frank Zappa – who was a very techno guy – invited us to a restaurant once where he was having a party. He said, "The song 'Supernaut' is my favourite track of all time." I couldn't believe it. I thought, "This guy's taking the piss: there's got to be a camera here somewhere . . ."' Ozzy struggles to get a handle on what it is about his band's music that has made it last so well: 'We never consciously knew what we were doing: we were just four innocent guys – very awkward and very unorthodox – who played what we were feeling, trying to make ourselves feel good.'

On the subject of feeling good, how was the miraculous cure of his alcoholism effected (Ozzy notes that the desire to drink has now 'totally gone': apparently he 'never liked the taste anyway')?

Ozzy went to a few AA meetings but 'didn't feel very comfortable' with them. 'If you've had one of your limbs amputated,' he explains, 'you don't want to sit in a room with a lot of one-legged men talking about it.' At the bottom of his own drink problem were almost pathological levels of anxiety.

'If I didn't wake up in the morning worrying,' he explains, 'I'd worry because I didn't have a worry, then it would escalate into this great monster sitting on my shoulder.' An addiction therapist put him on Prozac – 'You still get the feelings of insecurity, but it sort of nips them in the bud' – and this, together with the odd dash of Valium and a healthy measure of newfound self-awareness, saw him through.

'My therapist said, "You're like a man in front of two doorways. You open one and there's a guy standing behind it with a baseball bat who smacks you round the head. Every time you open that door he smacks you, then one day you walk through the other door and nobody's there and you're feeling weird that you didn't get a smack, so you go back through the first door, because it's what your used to."'

As the man who once had to be immobilised with rabies shots after biting the head off a dead bat expounds on the evils of the British quarantine system ('People talk about cruelty to animals, but you want to go down there, man, it's sick. And it's a thousand quid a month for six months'[47]), Ozzy's words are punctuated by the jangle of enough gold jewellery to make Puff Daddy jealous. As so often, his starry trappings have an earthly explanation. The rings and chains are 'guilty gifts' from Sharon.

'When she does some damage on the credit card, I always get a bangle,' Ozzy grins. I compliment him on a particularly fine gold finger-protector which looks like a fleeing caterpillar with a diamond cross in its back. 'Here,' Ozzy says, offering it across the table, 'try it on, it's cool.' Funnily enough, he is not wrong.

Black Sabbath: We Sold Our Souls For Rock 'n' Roll *(NEMS/Warners, 1975)*

Lee Perry

'I am a gnome, I don't know anything about religion.'

Finding himself with a moment to spare in his record company boardroom, Lee 'Scratch' Perry stalks an unwary pot-plant. With cat-like grace he pounces, snaps off a foot-long frond and places it in the front of the strange crown of shining mirrors, badges and religious emblems which he wears on his head. This crown is not just a mark of Perry's regal standing in the history of pop music, it is also an abiding source of amusement.

Whenever he's not stamping his feet or imperiously plucking a hair from his right nostril, he gets up and slowly revolves his head to reflect spots of light on to the walls or into the eyes of whoever is trying to talk to him. In a lesser being, such behaviour might be a little disconcerting, but this diminutive giant has been walking the line between madness and genius for so long it's become second nature.

Born in Kendal, Jamaica in 1936, Lee (*né* Rainford Hugh) Perry took up with Clement 'Sir Coxone' Dodd's Downbeat sound system in the mid-1950s and, together with ex-boxer Prince Buster, joined in its battles for territorial supremacy. 'Everybody wanted power,' Perry remembers, 'but they never could get power off Scratch – he played a trick on them; he scratched them, the cat scratched them in the dark.'

From supervising auditions at Studio One, Perry moved on to producing and performing his own records, cutting numerous ska sides throughout the 1960s. But it was his work with Bob Marley, and on countless classic reggae recordings throughout the next decade, which confirmed him as one of the most influential individuals – not just in the development of Jamaican music – but in the history of pop as a whole. From crossover landmarks like Junior Murvin's 'Police &

Thieves', through the wild invention and awesome technical accomplishments of his four-track dub recordings, Perry's legacy of sonic invention and straight-up weirdness is unchallenged to this day.

At a party in a horrible squat on Homerton High Street, Hackney, in the mid-nineteen eighties, the DJ scratches a record with the house cat's paw in tribute to Perry's maverick spirit. A gang of glue-punks are lying semi-comatose on the floor, banging their Special Brew cans in time to the soundtrack of a grainy pirate video of *A Clockwork Orange*. By about five in the morning they are all mercifully unconscious and you can see the sky beginning to lighten through the big hole in the roof. Someone puts on The Upsetter's version of Hayes and Porter's 'Soul Man', and suddenly every crazy statement Lee Perry has ever made seems to make sense, even that thing about Lufthansa being the best airline in the world because the Germans are the master race.

Sitting attentively by Lee Perry's side at Island Records' offices in 1990 is his youthful (and, reputedly, hugely rich) Swiss girlfriend Mirreille Campbell-Ruegg, formerly married to Perry's fellow roots eminence Mikey Dread. Mirreille has recently inspired Perry to relocate to Zurich. 'Where else should I choose to live? It is positively clear that Switzerland must be the richest country in the universe,' he explains, 'because I am there to make sure that it happens. I was in London and they didn't want me, so I went to Zurich and took all England's riches.'

Mirreille's explanation for the move is rather more prosaic: 'Lee needs somebody to take care of him – to give him cigarettes and to make sure he puts on his clothes.' Either way, the Swiss air plainly agrees with him, as it has persuaded him to make his 1990 album *From My Secret Laboratory* with two of the many people – Island records boss Chris Blackwell, whom he had famously accused of participating in voodoo rituals, and producer Adrian Sherwood, who was at the controls for 1987's deliciously apocalyptic *Time Boom De Devil Dead* – he had sworn never to work with again.

BT: Why did you accuse Chris Blackwell of 'drinking the blood of a voodoo chicken'?

LP: Because he deserved it. I had a good plan with Bob Marley. It was a

master plan, and Chris Blackwell spoilt it. He came and took away Bob
Marley and messed up my life so I got mad. I am Chicken Scratch and it
was my blood he was drinking, but in every man, however wicked, there's
a good spot, so forgiveness is compulsory: I forgave Chris Blackwell
because he is stupid.

BT: What made you want to work with Adrian Sherwood again?

LP: It is not my pleasure to work with Adrian Sherwood. I never wanted
to work with him – he wants to work with me.

BT: Why does he want to work with you?

LP: I don't know, there must be a reason. [Craftily] Maybe it's because he
wants to get famous. I don't fight against his ideas, but if he feels like
his ideas are the best he can keep them. If I need an idea, I will stand
upon my head and put my two feet up in the air and meditate with the
earth. When I come up from the earth, I will have new ideas.

BT: Does this always work?

LP: It must work if I turn myself upside down; I'm a Pisces, so when I
want ideas, I have to get close to the water and get them.

It is possible that Perry's aquatic birthsign played a role in his ill-
starred descision to build a pond in the middle of his legendary Black
Ark studio. 'The only creator in the universe is water,' he explains.
'Because only water can create life. I wanted the creator in my studio
. . . The turtles were crawling all over the place.'

Sensing general bemusement, Perry warms to his theme: 'The
elements sent me to do what I am doing. The air, the water, the fire,
the earth, the wind, the lightning and the earthquake – they sent me.
They couldn't find anybody else to fit the post; nobody else was
stupid enough to do it.

'If you want to know who I'm working with,' he continues with a
conspiratorial wink, 'I'm working with the UFOs.'

'Only for the good ones,' interjects his supportive Swiss companion. 'Tell him where they come from,' she continues. '. . . Playden!'

'Where's that?' I demand naively (I now know it to be a small
village just outside Rye).

'Those who know it, they will know,' concludes Mirreille darkly.

'Playden,' Perry eulcidates, 'means play records from the den
where they are kept. It's a secret place. The records fly magically

through the sky, and you will see the tail of the smoke, and the jet itself sometimes, if you're lucky.'

BT: Do you consider yourself to be a religious person?
LP: I am a gnome. I don't know anything about religion . . .
BT: But why do you have a card with the holy ghost on it on your head?
LP: Because I am a gnome and I depend on ghosts to protect me.

Amongst the other symbols of power which adorn Lee's crown is a badge with 'Buckingham Palace' written on it.

BT: Why do you wear that?
LP: Because I would love to meet the queen – to tell the queen that I am the king and I have come to take over. She knows who I am; she's had nightmares about me. I will come from under the earth into the royal bedroom. I will say, 'Here I am, I appear out of the thin air . . . observe I am here.'
BT: How will she reply?
LP: She will say 'AAAH' and she will drop on the floor, and they will come and pick her up.

The queen is not the only powerful British woman to catch Perry's eye. 'Margaret Thatcher,' he exclaims, *a propos* of nothing. 'I love her till I can't love her no more . . . I love her till I wish her to have a heart attack.' The BBC too, Perry alleges, are 'in his pocket', and to prove it he produces from some deep trousery recess a cassette tape bearing the legend 'lernen English mit BBC'.

'In the beginning was the word,' Perry announces: 'The word which we speak represents God himself and is immortal, and if anybody don't like it they can kill me, but they can't kill the word. Because behold I make everything new, and I make myself new as well, so I give unto myself a new name: Mr Aswell Perry.'

The Upsetter Boxed Set (Trojan, 1985)

Pet Shop Boys

'Let's just state the obvious over a gorgeous over-produced backing track.'

There is no more embarrassing chapter in the big book of Pop Interview Ritual than the one in which you're forced to listen attentively to music you have never heard before in the presence of the person who made it. As I sit in a Notting Hill studio in 1996, while Neil Tennant plays the new, as-yet-untitled Pet Shop Boys album, he kindly obviates the necessity to smile weakly or tap an unconvincing foot by singing along himself, quite lustily, in a slightly stronger Geordie accent than his TV appearances have led me to expect.

The music has a lush, Latin feel: it's the Pet Shop Boys' 'La Isla Bonita' album. Depending on which way you look at it, the duo's decision to employ so many of the samba rhythms they'd come across on a South American tour in 1994 was either a very Paul Simon thing to do, or the perfect starting point for a heartfelt tribute to disco's Latin roots. Whichever way you look at it, *Bilingual* turns out to be one of Neil and Chris' less successful albums, both commercially and artistically: a victim of its own prescience, it jumps onboard the Latin bandwagon three years too early.

'When Chris and I used to make demos a long time ago,' Tennant explains, 'we used to have this di-di-doo-di-di-di-di-doo-doo noise. We just thought of it as a New York disco thing, but someone in the studio said, "I like those Latin bits."' In the early eighties, when the Pet Shop Boys first started working together, they had very definite ideas about what they wanted to do. 'We thought, "No one else is doing gay disco, no one else is doing New York hip-hop with white vocals . . ." When "Blue Monday" by New Order came out, I more or less burst into tears.'

Before their remixed 'West End Girls' finally went to Number One in January 1986, the Pet Shop Boys thought they'd missed the boat. Fortunately the good ship Anglo-Electro-Disco proved to be a roomy vessel. 'I remember being interviewed by this guy in America,' Tennant bristles, 'who said, "Groups like you and New Order make this great music and then just whine over the top." He presented it as if it was a choice, as opposed to singing like Jocelyn Brown or Otis Redding. I said, "Unfortunately, that is all we can do."

'What you can't do,' Tennant continues, 'is always what shapes your sound and defines your style. Though having said that,' he twinkles defiantly, 'we are getting better. I realise a lot of people don't like my voice, but to me it expresses quite a lot of emotion – there's a yearning quality to it which I really like.' In fact, the delicate balance of distance and involvement in Neil Tennant's singing on *Behaviour* or *Introspective* confirms him as the post-industrial Ray Davies.

One of the greatest and most widely prevalent misunderstandings about the Pet Shop Boys – that they are somehow not emotionally engaged in what they do – is, Tennant admits, partly their own fault. The duo's joy at finding themselves objects of the act of consumption is reflected in the fastidious care they take over every product that bears their name. And yet, Tennant continues, 'We've always tried to make it look effortless, as if our pop career was something we dashed off in between doing something else much more important.'

So it hasn't been as easy as all that, then?

'It always feels like you're on a bit of a knife-edge, actually. That's why it irritates me when Russian journalists tell me – as they do – "You worked at a magazine and learnt how to make perfect pop records, and then you did it . . ." I want to say, "Go on then, you try."' Fortunately, it is not necessary to have seen all the appalling bands in which successful music journalists have been involved to agree with Tennant's contention that his having once worked at *Smash Hits* is 'kind of irrelevant' to his subsequent pop life.

It's not as if the Pet Shop Boys' story has been one long cunning plan, a career devoid of mistakes. Anyone who has seen their feature film *It Couldn't Happen Here*, or their *Performance* live tour of 1991[48] will tell you that. And the wisdom of 1999's Nik-Kershaw-on-a-bad-hair-day wigs was also somewhat open to question.

The widespread over-emphasis on Tennant's media-hound antecedents is actually the product of critical frustration. From 'Che Guevara and Debussy to a disco beat' ('Left To My Own Devices') to 'You've both made such a little go a very long way' ('Yesterday When I Was Mad'), Tennant has written his own reviews in a sufficiently witty and trenchant manner as to render further interpretation superfluous.

In parallel with their own meticulous and impulsive career, the Pet Shop Boys have sustained a stylish critical commentary on the rest of pop music. 'We always have an opinion on where it's at,' Tennant insists, amid learned discourses on whether the new Boyzone single is as good as the last one (it isn't) and the chances of Kylie making it as a 'mature artist' (not good). 'I think a lot of pop stars do – we are only unusual in expressing it publicly.'

The Pet Shop Boys' distinctive vision of 'where it's at' has shaped a remarkable and generous history of collaborations. From remixing Blur's 'Girls and Boys' so it sounded like a proper disco record, to adding a chorus and a backbeat to David Bowie's hilarious Babylon Zoo tribute 'Hello Spaceboy', to writing a couple of long overdue hit singles for Liza Minelli, there seems to be no limit to their promiscuity.

'I'm Not Scared' – the Pet Shop Boys' song for Patsy Kensit – was on *TOTP 2* a few weeks before this interview and it sounded fantastic. Needless to say, Tennant saw it too. 'I thought, "Fucking hell! [he winces at the thought of how that cheery profanity will look in print] There's a bit in French: how embarrassing."' He smiles fondly. 'Patsy has a great quality, which is that she'll do anything. We felt she deserved to be a star but wasn't making the right kind of records.'

Why did they make her sing 'Take these dogs away from me' – was that a kind of test?

Tennant laughs. 'She's being threatened by her man and she's not gonna take it,' he explains. 'The dogs are his gangstery pals . . . also it's a line from Betjeman.'

There are a few of those in the Tennant/Lowe songbook – the

touching funeral-lament 'Your Funny Uncle' springs to mind. Some people like to see Tennant as an inheritor of the literary tradition of Oscar Wilde and Joe Orton – how does the man himself feel?

'I don't really see myself that way. The only specific literary influence I've had in terms of songwriting is *The Waste Land* by T.S. Eliot. That would be a great rap record: all the different voices in it – going into German, the conversation on top of the bus – that's what I was trying to do with "West End Girls", really.'

When Neil Tennant met Chris Lowe in a King's Road electronics shop in 1982, he'd been writing songs for years. 'I'd already had my career – which, of course, wasn't really a career – in my bedroom as a singer/songwriter. Chris absolutely loathes the entire concept of that kind of music: his hatred and detestation for it is quite beyond belief.' Heeding Lowe's imprecations to make his words 'more sexy, more current', Tennant 'completely changed' the way he wrote.

An act of will wasn't enough though: the technology had to be there too. 'When the Fairlight 2 was invented,' Tennant says nostalgically, 'the Pet Shop Boys started to exist. Every single sound on our first record apart from my voice was played on anemulator: bass sample, string quartet sample, the "aah aah ooh" from James Brown, the drums from David Bowie's "Let's Dance".' Chris Lowe insists the drums were from Michael Jackson's 'Billie Jean': make of that what you will.

It was no accident that 'Opportunities (Let's Make Lots of Money)' could have been a punk song. The Pet Shop Boys were the first pop stars to sound (and look) as if they had no roots in any music before The Sex Pistols. 'It was meant to be an attitude thing,' Tennant insists. 'Let's just state the obvious over a gorgeous over-produced backing track.'

As a description of the Pet Shop Boys' career, 'stating the obvious over a gorgeous over-produced backing track' just about puts it in a nutshell. Tennant once said 'a pop song should always try to say something that hasn't been said before'. Isn't that rather a lofty ambition?

'It's the most difficult thing you can do, but you've got to try, because when someone manages it – and I think we have a few times – it's the best thing ever.'

In 1995, Tennant gave an interview to the gay magazine *Attitude* in which for the first time he was explicit about his sexuality. The article's assertion that the Pet Shop Boys' brilliant 1993 album *Very* was 'an album about what it means to be gay in the 1990s' (yes, but that wasn't all it was) was the perfect illustration of why he hadn't done this before.

'It's great to be ambivalent in pop music,' Tennant insists, somewhat regretfully. 'It's much more fun to have everyone reading things into what you do, because then you can do something blatantly obvious and pretend you haven't. Now it's all sort of normal and healthy, it's a bit boring, really. It makes me feel like telling everybody I'm straight. I told Ian McKellen that I was sick of being gay and I was going to get a girlfriend and he said, "Don't tell anybody."'

Tennant pauses. 'Actually, part of me – I can say this now I've "come out" – thinks it's all a bit of a cliché anyway: we've invented this thing called homosexuality and now everybody is conditioned into having a way of life which is either gay or straight. I mean, fifty years ago, I'd have been married with three children and having affairs with men on the side and, frankly, I'd probably be happier.'

But isn't the great thing about the Pet Shop Boys the way they've left that kind of thing behind? The gay gene in pop music has so often been seen as something to be hidden away, whereas the Pet Shop Boys have managed to appeal simultaneously to gay and heterosexual audiences without being dishonest.

'What we do is more about a gay ideal than the way things actually are. That ties in with a certain kind of romanticism that we both have: it's a mythic thing, really, rather than being totally truthful.' But it is truthful in that pop's gay iconography is at least partly one of deceit, and the Pet Shop Boys have never been deceitful.

'Chris and I always complain that we're not really icons,' Tennant says ruefully. 'These are our two complaints: 1) We're not icons; 2) We've never written a rock classic.'

But hasn't the whole idea of being an icon ceased to mean anything in the wake of Athena and the eighties?

'Jarvis is an icon though, isn't he? When you see the Chris Evans programme and that horrible cut-out of Jarvis is standing behind him, you think, [jealously] "God, he's such an icon." He represents – and this is what you do when you represent – either what he is or what people want him to be.'

Chris Lowe opted to prove just how ill-founded his reputation for elusiveness is by not turning up for this interview. When the mighty Parlophone arm-twisting mechanism compels him to ring up three days later, it transpires that he had decided to go back to his hometown of Blackpool for the weekend.

BT: Do you like it there?

CL: I really look forward to going back to Blackpool. It can't be denied that when you arrive there, everyone is having a laugh: it's just a lot of legless people enjoying themselves, there's no pretence – no one's standing around being aloof.

BT: But that's what everyone thinks you like doing!

CL: I don't mind that – there being a difference. In fact, it's better that way. I prefer people saying, 'You're not a bit like we thought – you're quite nice, really,' to 'I used to like you, till I met you.'

BT: How do you feel about being left out of this interview – do you trust Neil to give a fair account of you?

CL: I'm quite happy about it. I think Neil quite likes giving interviews and he normally does a pretty good job – he's got a much better memory than me.

BT: Are you like money and youth – most poignantly experienced as an absence?

CL: [Unconvincingly] I'm sorry, there's a funny crackle on this line, could you repeat the question?

BT: Do you prefer to be a shadowy figure, lurking enigmatically in the background?

CL: Yes, I do actually.

Discography (Parlophone, 1991)

Poly Styrene

'It's something to do with punk rock.'

A mix-up in the photographer's schedule means an irate aspiring fashion model is kept waiting on a Battersea Park bench while Poly Styrene has her picture taken. 'What would they want to take a picture of you for?' she demands rudely, looking askance at Ms Styrene's lack of the requisite height and emaciation. 'It's something to do with punk rock,' says the sari-clad Poly, magnanimously.

Indeed it is. Marion Elliott's demure and beautific 1991 incarnation might seem a long way from the gleefully worldly figure whose *Top of the Pops* appearances in dental braces and bin-liner dress were an inspiration to all self-respecting late seventies adolescents (germ-free and or otherwise), but the distance between the two is not so great as it appears.

In their brief one-album-and-a-handful-of-singles lifespan, Poly's X-Ray Spex embodied so much of the best of what punk was about, that for them to hang around to write jeans adverts or become curmudgeons as so many of their peer group did would have been a needless betrayal. On tour in Doncaster in late 1979, Poly saw a UFO ('This sort of energy, this bright bright luminous pink, and it had a disc shape. It was faster than the speed of light') and had a nervous breakdown – subsequently finding much needed solace in the Hare Krishna movement.

Far from being a betrayal of the voice which proclaimed 'Some people say that little girls should be seen and not heard, but I say, "Oh Bondage, up yours!"', Poly's solitary spiritual quest seems, in some strange way, to be a fulfilment of such prophetic statements of defiance. Which is why the prospect of her appearance at 'The Day

The World Turned Day-Glo' – a grim-looking punk revival night at the Brixton Academy with Sham 69, The Lurkers, The UK Subs, Chelsea and 999 – is rather a disturbing one.

The band's other original members are scattered to the four winds – PA to the managing director of Virgin films, an Australian TV producer, a roadie in America, and an employee of the Abbey National building society. None of them will feature in the reunion. 'I wrote to them all and none of them wrote back,' she says forlornly, 'so there's nothing I can do really.'

She's not sure whether to do 'Bondage': 'A lot of people have put the wrong connotation on that song: they think it's all about whips and leather, but it was the bondage of Babylon that I was interested in.'

Is she not a little apprehensive about playing new material like 'Dog In Sweden' (a song about India's president Nehru being reincarnated as a dog in Sweden) to a crowd of superannuated glue-punks?

'In 1979 I played the whole of my solo album *Translucence*, which is a totally soft new age kind of thing, to a really heavy hardcore punk audience in Paris, and I didn't care about that, so I'm not frightened.'

Does she think anyone will spit at her?

'I hope not. That spitting business all started because Paul Simenon from The Clash used to spit onstage; not at the audience, just on the stage. It wasn't nice but it was just his street credibility boy thing. Then journalists wrote about fans worshipping their punk idols by spitting at them and that started it all off. Eventually we built up our own following, and if anybody spat some kid would get up and say, "Don't spit at Poly, because she doesn't like it."'

If Poly is walking down King's Road and someone with a pink mohican asks her for 50p, does she give it to them?

'I don't have 50ps on me that often, being a poor starving artist, but I usually tell them they can get a free meal at the Hare Kirshna temple in Soho Street every day at one o'clock. Sometimes I carry food around with me and just give it to them. I don't want to give them money because they'll just save it up to buy drugs with and kill themselves.'

A lot of people got lost in the yawning gap between what punk promised and what it delivered, but the life-affirming clatter of *Germ-Free Adolescence* is an enduring imprecation to bridge it – to savour and reject commodification in the same blissful instant. The prospect of that Brixton Academy show is just too scary. Finding your walkman, heading for the high street, and listening to 'Warrior In Woolworths' in Woolworths, though, that is quite another matter.

X-Ray Spex: *Germ-Free Adolescence* (Virgin, 1978)

Sir Cliff Richard

'I thought being someone different was good.'

'A chip on your shoulder, an H-bomb in your pants – it's you against the world, baby, and the world loves you for hating it.' There are many rock 'n' roll legends to whom it's easy to imagine these words being addressed, but Sir Cliff Richard is probably not the first to spring to mind.

How did Cliff Richard, the first authentic British rock 'n' roller, and smouldering screen prodigy of *Espresso Bongo* (in which masterwork – see **Film** – the above words were addressed to him by Laurence Harvey's supercool Svengali) become the oft-lampooned national institution of four decades on? It is usually seen as some kind of crazy fluke that the man without whom there would have been not only no Beatles in the form that we know them, but also no David Bowie and even – heaven forbid – no Damon Albarn, ended up leading 1996's Wimbledon centre-court crowd in an a cappella chorus of 'Summer Holiday'. In fact, the development of Cliff's career has followed its own impeccable logic – as ripe with racial, religious and sexual ambiguity as any professor of cultural studies could wish it to be.

To spill on to the street outside Manchester's Palace Theatre after a performance of *Heathcliff* and hear passers-by whispering fearfully, 'Cliff Richard fans – woahh, scary,' is to understand the thrill experienced by the football hooligan and Michael Heseltine's hairdresser: the thrill of being utterly outside the confines of respectable society. And yet *Heathcliff* is to the objective eye a very entertaining production. How could any show in which Cliff Richard savagely beats up his wife while calling her a 'pitiful, slavish, mean-minded bitch' in an accent pitched midway between Barnsley and Tokyo possibly be anything else?

You would think it was the job of the critic to encourage performers to take chances, but the reaction of the theatre-reviewing establishment to *Heathcliff* has not borne this out. The reason for the mauling given to Cliff's bold attempt to bring Emily Brontë's hero to life in song is not hard to divine: the show's inevitable success is a cruel reminder of the futility of all critical endeavour. And so it proves, as all the vitriol expended upon it has not stopped Heathcliff grossing an imposing £10 million in its first six months, leaving Sir Cliff Richard – not for the first time in his 56 years – laughing all the way to the bank.

A first attempt to meet him in his rooms at the gloriously camp new Victoria and Albert Hotel in Manchester – opposite the Granada Studios Tour, with appropriately TV-themed accommodation (Cliff is in the Sherlock Holmes room, which his personal assistant, Roger, describes as 'very masculine') – is frustrated by an untimely bout of the flu. 'Cliff,' Roger proclaims ominously, 'has cancelled tennis.'

Is there any chance that he might be well enough to talk tomorrow?

'I don't think you understand, Cliff *never* cancels tennis.'

A few weeks later – at the David Lloyd sports centre in Raynes Park, south London – Cliff Richard is sufficiently recovered to have been making up his tennis deficiency. Resplendent in neatly pressed sportswear, the photographer has sat him in front of a very glittery gold curtain which, his personal assistant points out, looks like something from *Priscilla, Queen of the Desert*. But Cliff sits in front of it without a word of complaint. He is one of those people who is so famous it seems impertinent to look him in the eye, but his voice is better modulated than the flutey gush of a thousand bad impersonations and, from the onset, he is unexpectedly willing to engage in meaningful discussion.

All of the interviews he's done for *Heathcliff* have mentioned what a great impression *Wuthering Heights* made on him when he first read it as a child. But at no point does anybody seem to have asked him why. Presumably, one reason the story of a dark-skinned outsider might have appealed to the young Harry Webb was that the hero's situation resembled his own at the time: his family having just left

India (where he had spent the first eight years of his life) at the time the country gained its independence, for an England that was unknown to him. 'I certainly had a good tanned skin when we came back,' he admits, 'and I remember getting in fights all the time – I used to get called an "Indibum", and all that business. People would say, "Are you going home to your tepee now?"' He laughs with understandably little mirth. 'I suppose that is part of what drew me to Heathcliff.'

Cliff's father worked for the railway in India but for all the trauma that gripped the sub-continent in the forties, his childhood memories have an idyllic feel to them. 'I remember there was an aunt about a mile away and she was the only one who'd let us eat with our fingers. I also remember flying kites – diamond-shaped kites with tiny triangular tails – and going to my grandparents' house in Lucknow: the train stopped against the buffers and that was it, there was nowhere else to go. They had about ten dogs, and I've never minded dogs barking since, because there was no other security, but you'd be in bed and you'd hear them barking, Woof! Woof!' Cliff essays a passable hound, 'and you'd think: "I'm safe."'

Was it frightening to have to leave all that behind and come to England?

'It was very exciting, actually, because I'd been brought up by my parents, aunts and uncles who were always talking about "when we go back". India wasn't ours: I may have been born there, but I was British, and we'd always been told we were going home, so it wasn't like going to a strange place. We were excited ... we were going home to Blighty.'

All the exotic influences with which the first few years of Harry Webb's life were coloured could not prepare his teenage self for the impact of Elvis Aaron Presley. Like so many of his British contemporaries – Marty Wilde, Vince Eager, Robb Storm – before he could call himself a performer, he felt obliged to change his name in tribute to the new and thrilling reality of Chuck and Buddy and Jerry Lee. 'Harry Roger Webb just didn't cut it – it didn't sound like Elvis.'

How did he come to settle on Cliff Richard?

'I just liked it – it felt like a rock'n'roll name. We [Cliff and his first real band, the Drifters, who became the Shadows in 1959] wrote dozens of possibilities on labels to see what they looked like: first, it was Russ Clifford, then we changed it to Cliff Russord, and the final one was Cliff Richards with an "s". But Ian Samwell, the guy who wrote "Move It", said, "Why not take the 's' off? Then you've got two Christian names, which is unusual and people are bound to call you Cliff Richards in interviews and that way you get to correct them and mention your name twice."

'I think we did a lot to pave the way for bands like The Beatles,' Cliff insists, not unreasonably. 'When you think about it, if we hadn't been here, The Beatles could have been us. I remember John Lennon saying, "Cliff and the Shadows had it sewn up," so they went away to Germany and found the next step, which was even bigger than us, but that's always the way. We invent football and tennis and everyone else plays them better than we do, but that's part of the evolution. We might be the lower rungs of the ladder, but without those lower rungs you couldn't get to the top.'

This seems a very modest view to take of one's own role in things.

'I know a lot of people think I'm a no-no as a musical entity, but when they're writing text books, I will have to be in there. People will hate it, but I will have to be in there.'

The pages of those text books which have already been written are littered with the names of singers – Elvis, Jerry Lee Lewis, Aretha Franklin – who have wavered between the Devil's music and the Lord's songs with no subsequent loss of critical credibility. It was Ray Charles' cunning blend of the sanctified and the secular that gave birth to soul music[49]. And yet Cliff Richard's Christianity (first embraced, after brief flirtations with Judaism and Jehovah's Witness-ing, in the spiritual crisis that followed the early death of his strict disciplinarian father in 1961) has somehow been seen as irredeemable. Does he himself have any idea as to why this might be?

'You have to remember that America is, or was, a very religious country, where people were brought up to express their feelings by singing in church, but that's not so much part of our culture. I also think there's something very intimidating about someone who's singing something you know they actually believe.' Cliff pauses. 'But that's other people's hang-up, not mine: they should be strong enough in their non-belief to recognise what's good artistically. I can play records that have sentiments I don't particularly like, but if the sound of them is good, I can put up with the sentiment.'

Could he give us an example of the sort of thing he means?

'It's like that song "Cocaine". I heard it in a restaurant in New Zealand and I just had to go out and buy the album [*Troubadour* by J. J. Cale]. I love the music and it's a fantastic song, but it doesn't turn me on to cocaine.'

'Well, only at the weekends,' I jest impetuously.

The room is suddenly very quiet. Local shopkeepers roll down their shutters and young children are ushered into storm-proofed cellars. How will Sir Cliff respond to this lapse into jocularity? After a very long pico-second, he laughs, trees blossom, and birds feel safe in their nests again.

He is roused to considerable ire, though, by another suggestion – the idea that perhaps the 'fantastic talents' of which, he says, the music industry has been deprived over the years by drinking and drugs, might not have expressed themselves in the same way without the Dionysian indulgences that eventually destroyed them.

'But if we excuse people from doing it, they'll continue,' he insists. 'I've watched my sisters' kids growing up [Cliff has three sisters]. They stick their fingers in the jam. Mum says, "Don't do that, you'll get it on your clothes and spoil it for other people." They look at her straight in the eyes and do it again. When that happens, you smack their wrist and say, "Don't do that," and they learn not to – they want to do it, but they learn not to, and do you know why? Because it *does* spoil the jam.

'When we have adults behaving like children,' Cliff continues sternly, 'then society becomes the parents. They're looking society in the eye and saying, "I'm going to have my jam," and what we really ought to be doing is taking their hypodermic needles and smacking them across the bums and saying, "Don't be such silly people. You have a fantastic life without this crap." I've watched people doing it and thought, "This is like putting my hand in the fire just to see if it does really burn," and I think, "No, it does burn and I'm not going to put my hand in it."'

Accordingly, he gives short shrift to rock rebels from The Rolling Stones (who, he claims rather intriguingly, were 'notorious for throwing porridge out the windows') to Oasis. 'It's just a shame that part of what gives them their kick is their self-destructive impulse,' he says of the mercurial Mancunians, 'because it means their fans will eventually be denied the source of that pleasure.'

But isn't knowing that it can't last a vital part of the pleasure of the whole thing? It's like a sunset, it's not supposed to last for ever.

Cliff shakes his head: 'That's too complicated for me. The thing with a sunset is, you know it's going to come again the same time the next day.'

Presumably he is aware that his vision of longevity as the ultimate rock'n'roll virtue makes him something of a renegade figure?

'But I am a renegade figure,' he proclaims, only half laughing. 'It seems to me that I'm the only radical rock star there's ever been – because I don't follow the trends that all these other berks go through: I don't drug it up. I don't curse and spit blood at the audience. But all the others did, so in some respects I am the only radical one and I like that. I like being out on my own. And I thought that would have been applauded – I thought being someone different was good.'

At the heart of Cliff Richard's difference is, of course, his enduring bachelorhood, with its intriguing corollary of sexual abstinence. 'To be honest with you,' he notes sanguinely, 'I never thought I would be single all my life, but I don't go around worrying about it like I did when I was twenty-five. I used to worry about it a lot when the Shadows all got married – they all got divorced as well, but that's not the point. The point is that people who are single shouldn't have to be second-class citizens – we needn't be embarrassed or feel guilty about it, we all have a role to play. If you look at the New Testament, Saint Paul never got married and one of the reasons he didn't was because he had given his whole life to what he was doing.'

There is nothing monastic, though, about the mood of the audience at *Heathcliff*. When the star of the show reappears in the second half dressed in a kimono, the crowd emits an audible grunt of desire. Cliff Richard's sexual attractiveness to the women who go to see him is traditionally portrayed in comic terms – as if their pleasure was somehow worth less than anyone else's. The fact is, his avowed celibacy makes him more rather than less suitable as a subject of erotic intrigue. The sensual bond between Cliff and his female fan base is the canny elder sister of the adolescent girl's traditional yen for the androgynous teen idol.

'I'm quite happy with the fact that my audience is predominantly female,' he says. 'I am predominantly male, after all.'

Does he mind the idea of sexual gratification being derived from his performance?

'My decision to be single and celibate is something I've decided based on my faith, and, of course, it shouldn't damage the fact that I might have an appeal for somebody. Male–female attraction is a normal thing that happens regularly and it's part of life that women in the audience might have some kind of fantasy about you.'

Would it upset him to feel that he was attracting the same feelings from men in his audience?

'It wouldn't upset me, but I don't know that I've tended to have that affect on men – I don't think they stay away from my concerts because of that, do they? They're not worried about what affect I might have on them. It's just that they're usually quite a macho group of people who might think I'm gay, and somehow they'll be seen as wimps if they come to my concerts.'

Everyone always wants to believe that Cliff Richard is sitting on a dark secret: that his companionable domestic circumstances – he shares a house in Weybridge with his guru and publicity manager Bill Lantham and Bill's girlfriend Jill – are a cover for orgies that would make Caligula blush. No one seems to realise that he is a far more intriguing figure if taken at face value: not as some kind of plaster saint, but as someone doing his best to lead a life that accords with his principles.

One of the most plausible explanations advanced for his celibacy has been that it resulted from feelings of guilt that his father's fatal illness coincided with the public unravelling of Cliff's illicit entanglement with the wife of The Shadows' bass player. 'I've always been the first person to say if you want perfection do not look to me,' Cliff insists. 'I've been there and done it all.'

Not quite all, surely?

'Well, I haven't killed anybody, but I don't know if there are too many other commandments I haven't broken. The last thing a

Christian should say is that they aren't a sinner: if you're not a sinner, you don't need redemption.'

Is that what he's enjoyed so much about *Heathcliff* – the chance to be a sinner in public?

'It's incredibly satisfying. I go out there and for two and a half hours, I can scream and beat my wife and viciously pump my stepfather's face into the table. These are ugly things, but there is something liberating about it, because suddenly I'm not Cliff Richard for a while.'

It must be quite a relief not to be Cliff Richard every now and then . . . ?

'It is' – as Harry Webb laughs the afternoon sun glints off the gold curtain momentarily to give his bearded face the aspect of a Greek Orthodox icon – 'It really is.'

Wired For Sound (EMI single, 1981)

Bernard Sumner

'Sometimes he calls out for a word with six syllables meaning vague disquiet.'

What does it mean to hear the transcendent beauty of Joy Division's 'Atmosphere' as the soundtrack to a TV bank ad? Thankfully, not much. Like the strongest faith, that band's music is impervious to blasphemy.

Whether busily chewing gum on *Top of the Pops* in 1983, as the glinting start/stops of 'Blue Monday' drill into the bedrock of conventional song structure, or valiantly struggling to maintain his concentration live from the set of Baywatch ten years later, the face of Bernard Sumner never gave too much away about what New Order were up to; and how they got to where they ended up from where they started is one of the enduring mysteries of British pop music. 'We had this strange moralistic profile,' Sumner remembers in 1991, 'when we really didn't have any morals at all.'

The misapprehensions began with Joy Division who were, under the guiding hand of their producer Martin Hannett, a 'party in the studio' type of band. That is not how they tend to be remembered. 'The music was pretty cheerful,' Sumner insists, with a fondly disrespectful nod to Joy Division's singer and writer Ian Curtis, whose suicide in 1980 forced him into the spotlight. 'It was just that twat's lyrics.'

Drummer Stephen Morris roots New Order's famed elusiveness in the traumatic circumstances of their birth. Curtis' suicide, which put an end to their previous incarnation, also brought down upon them an avalanche of purple prose. Under the pressure of 'everyone telling us what a depressing person Ian must have been, when they didn't even know him', New Order closed ranks, locked Sumner in a room and made him write the lyrics when everything else was finished. 'Sometimes,' Morris notes fondly, 'he calls out for a word with six syllables meaning "vague disquiet".'

A lyricist who 'doesn't want other people to know what he's thinking' might seem like a contradiction in terms, but the celebrated (or oft-bemoaned, depending on your point of view) inscrutability and open-endedness of Sumner's songwriting is in marked contrast to his forthright style of conversation.

Asked in 1996 how he feels about the way his now-defunct band's once-daunting aesthetic integrity has been compromised by their record company's frantic attempts to get a return on a misguided investment, Sumner grins: 'It's out of our hands now: to tell you the honest truth, I don't really give a shit – I'm interested in the future, not the past.'

Having been laid low by stomach problems resulting from an almost religious devotion to Pernod and orange juice, Sumner has been obliged to clean up his act a bit[50]. 'The key words,' he posits demurely, 'are health and daylight. I don't abuse myself with alcohol any more . . . apart from this drink [a Pernod and orange] I've got in my hands now.' As if to hammer this point home, he has another one later.

> **BT:** Why do you speak your mind so much more clearly in person than in song?
>
> **BS:** It's just not in my nature to be too literal. If you watch an action film where you just see all these things going on, and there's no need for any interpretation, you might walk away thinking, 'That was quite fun,' and the next day you'll have completely forgotten it. But if you leave thinking, 'What the fuck was that about?', and you have to spend an hour afterwards working it all out, that's much more stimulating. You're a participant within the creativity of the film, and that's what I try to do with my lyrics. If you take 'Forbidden City' for example [the first single from the 1996 Electronic album *Raise The Pressure*], that's a song about two imaginary characters – a teenage boy growing up with his father in a single-parent family, and his father's a drunkard and abusive, and the young lad hates it and wants to leave but he can't get away because of

the pull of that instinctual father–son relationship.

BT: Would you expect the casual listener to work this out for him or herself?

BS: Not necessarily, no.

Sumner ascribes the introverted quality of his songwriting to being raised as an only child: 'When you grow up without a brother or sister, you tend to see things just through your own eyes. You have friends and everything, but you spend most of your time watching TV or sat in a room making decisions about your life on your own.'

The sense of desolation that was so powerful in Joy Division's music has been rooted in the destruction of Manchester's urban landscape that took place in the course of redevelopment of the sixties and seventies.

BS: The whole area where I grew up has completely gone. When I was a kid I used to have six other members of my family living on the same street, and I remember getting up one morning and ten houses on the street were boarded up. It was a complete ghost town. The council just said, 'Right, you go here, you go there,' and the whole family was split up all over Manchester. I still feel a great sense of loss about that. It really has affected me as a person. I feel like my whole past has been rubbed out.'

BT: Is that one thing the dance music for which you has been such a graceful evangelist over the past ten years or so has offered people – an idea of community?

BS: Absolutely. You've all got one feeling, and that's something people need sometimes. Thatcher was wrong; people don't exist – well, they don't flourish – as individuals. Life's about swapping ideas and communicating with other people. I remember being in The Hacienda in the middle of the acid house thing and the thought crossed my mind that it was almost like being in church.

The pristine character of their music is not cold and alienating, as the group's detractors claim, but liberating, allowing it to embody the dreams and fears of both the people playing it and the people listening to it, with intoxicating clarity. I don't quite know why the biscuit-tin drum clatter of 'Temptation' is still a sound that affects me so profoundly nearly two decades after the song first came out (maybe it's just the association with biscuits).

But when New Order headline Reading in 1993, eyes are not watering solely as a response to the poisonous fumes being released into the atmosphere by the traditional ill-judged bonfires of plastic beer cups. The power of a song like 'True Faith' is miraculously undiminished by Sumner's decision to give Michael Jackson a walk-on part in the lyrics. When the band leave the stage it seems odd that there is no spontaneous mass gesture of affection, but thousands of people shouting 'New Or-der, New Or-der' would probably not be such a good idea anyway.

Bernard Sumner's Prozac Adventure

In 1995, Bernard Sumner took part in a bizarre BBC2 programme in which the tabloid psychiatrist Oliver James – the poor man's Raj Persaud – sought to assess the effects of Prozac on creativity by giving it to (and, in one traumatic case, taking it away from) a series of artistic individuals who suffered from depression.

'He said I suffered from hyper-critical voices,' Sumner remembers sceptically, 'that I had this big eye watching me all the time and I would crumble when it was looking at me . . . but if that was true I wouldn't have been standing there with a camera stuck up my nose while I was trying to write lyrics.'

> **BT:** Why on earth did you agree to do this in the first place?
> **BS:** I was interested in Prozac, because I can be a bit moody – things do get on top of me sometimes – so I was quite keen to find out what it would do to my personality.
> **BT:** What did it do?
> **BS:** It made me a little less deep [a Sumnerian half-smile], but it made my life and how I got on with people a lot easier. My girlfriend was in a state of shock the day I ran out. You don't feel like you're on drugs. You just have all the lows filtered from your personality so you end up floating through life on a little fluffy cloud. It was great being happy all

the time, but I couldn't dig so far down – it was like I got to a certain level and there was a steel plate there.

The song Sumner wrote under the influence didn't make it on to the next album, so would he take Prozac again?

'Yes, probably, but I'd be more inclined to buy it off my mates in Moss Side.'

New Order: *Power, Corruption & Lies* (Factory, 1983)[51]

Paul Weller

'I like it when a drumkit sounds like a drumkit, and a guitar sounds like a guitar.'

In the autumn of 1993, two-year-old Leah Weller is given free run of the freshly delivered LP sleeves in her father's management office. She has no trouble identifying the man with the half-smile and the ear-length bob as 'Daddy'. But those who have lived through the Style Council years might find his second solo album *Wild Wood* a bit more of a surprise. It is Weller's best work in, well, a long time; brimming with lusty guitar, impassioned singing and a clutch of potent and engaging songs.

Sweaty, impassioned renditions of the album's first single 'Sunflower' and the self-explanatory 'Has My Fire Really Gone Out?' on *Later* showed the world what it had been missing in the eleven years since the days when The Jam always seemed to have just gone straight in at Number One.

Did Paul Weller – now a sinewy thirty-five, snappily dressed as ever – really feel his fire had gone out?

'I felt that way for quite a long time – two or three years at least.'

Things certainly looked pretty bad in 1989, when The Style Council de-convened in disarray after a disastrous brush with irony on *Confessions of a Pop Group* left its chairman unable to secure a record deal.

He fought his way back by 'keeping my head down and doing what I was good at': touring with the uncomfortably named Paul Weller Movement. 'I hated doing it, but it really helped me. Sometimes you can find yourself onstage: and I think what people liked about those shows was how many mistakes we made – the fact that we were getting away from that kind of slickness The Style Council had.'

Musically, the new model Weller is a lot less uptight, almost Free on occasion, as if he's discovered that you can be both a mod and a rocker. 'I've definitely become a lot more broad-minded,' Weller grins. 'When I was at school there were battle lines – either you had long hair and an army greatcoat and carried a copy of *The Dark Side of the Moon* under your arm, or you were a skin or suedehead and you listened to strictly soul or rocksteady.'

Looking back, is he amused by the fervour with which such style wars were waged?

'In a way, yes, but those hard distinctions give you an attitude, which is what you need. It's a way of thinking that's particular to Britain, and there are problems with it, but it's also what has made music in this country special, and has done for the last thirty years.'

Weller has always respected tradition – 'I like it when a drumkit sounds like a drumkit and a guitar sounds like a guitar' – and has been fighting off allegations of musical conservatism ever since his refusal to renounce the joys of sixties pop made him a punk heretic.

Cut to the quick by a cruel review for an early Jam gig from well-connected punk scenester Caroline Coon, Weller went to his local pub with a card round his neck bearing the legend 'How can I be a revivalist when I am only 18?' You would have to have a very cold heart not to find this touching, and the way such early exchanges set the tone for both Weller's later relationship with the media and his future fate as a martyr to metropolitan sophistication is – even now – highly intriguing.

The very suburban sensibility which made him such an inspirational figure to a mass audience always marked him out as a second-rater in the ears of critical elites, and knowing this hardened his resolve to stay out of their clutches. But with a little more goodwill on both sides, things could have been so very different.

In Paulo Hewitt's sleeve notes to the woeful 1999 Jam tribute album *Fire & Skill*, there is a strange and touching reminiscence from Paul Weller's old neighbour Steve Carver: 'I remember he used to say, "I'm going up to London with a tape recorder." I'd say "What for?"

and he'd say, "I want to tape London." He used to love London: I think he idolised it, he always thought of it as magical.'

When the love affair between Weller and the big city ended, these pioneering ambient soundscapes were lost for ever. 'These days if people say what I do sounds retro,' Weller says, 'I try to take it as a compliment, because it means I'm finally getting that sound together.'

In the course of a single Royal Albert Hall show around the time of *Wild Wood*'s release, Weller shakes his head up and down in the throes of hard-rocking ecstasy, he plays long guitar solos, he sits down at the piano with his back to the audience, he smiles a lot, he struts about like a rooster with a feather-cut; in short, he does many things he was never expected to do, and does them brilliantly. Weller seems newly light of heart, as if after years of frantic searching he has finally hit upon a musical style to call his own.

What does it matter if Paul Weller has taken fifteen years to make a musical journey that Steve Winwood (swapping the Spencer Davis Group for Traffic) made in one? Winwood did not have so much baggage to carry. He did not come from Woking. He never shopped at Mister Byrite.

Weller's newfound folksiness is a way of shrugging off a burden of expectation. With it comes a certain lyrical vagueness – goodbye Tube stations and street names, hello wild woods, fires and healers – but if this is the price to be paid to have him singing and playing the guitar as well as he does on a serrated 'Sunflower' or a tumbling 'Holy Man', so be it.

He certainly shows no hankering for his old voice-of-a-generation status. 'When I was fourteen or fifteen,' he remembers, 'all I wanted to do was just to be in a pop group and be liked, and I don't think there's anything wrong with that. There are some ideas that I took from punk that made things better – mainly that there was more to being in a band than sex, drugs and rock 'n' roll – but for me at least it went too far. I got elevated on to this ridiculous platform where I was expected to know everything, and I didn't.'

Once the initial novelty has worn off, *Wild Wood*'s brand of tough but tender mod psychedelia is inevitably subject to diminishing returns in the years that follow[52]. But, in refusing to give in to pressure for a Jam reunion ('I'd have to really be down to my last pair of loafers before I'd do that'), Weller shows a good deal more spirit than the vast majority of his punk contemporaries, and if some of the things 'To Be Someone' said might happen, did happen, surely that was testimony to the perspicacity of its author's songwriting, as much as any lapses in his moral fibre?

'Someone asked recently if I thought people had a right to feel let down by me,' Weller said thoughtfully, in 1993, 'and I don't think they do. I think you can only let *yourself* down.'

Wild Wood (Go! Discs, 1993)

Wilco

'We're more like Inuit ivory carvers.'

Wilco's Jeff Tweedy (twinkly, weatherbeaten) and Jay Bennett (burly, dreadlocked) are savouring a momentary pause between engagements. A beleaguered two-man colony of battered denim amid the lurid primary colours of a London radio station foyer, they take the opportunity to bolt a grim meal of toxic fast-food. Someone notes, sympathetically, that there's only a certain amount of that stuff you can eat. Tweedy responds sardonically: 'I guess I would be living proof that that is not the case.'

Gently handsome, in a Johnny-Depp's-older-brother-who-didn't-make-good kind of way, and with a compelling repertoire of facial grimaces, Tweedy has one of those great American voices that creaks and cracks like an old sail in the wind. He speaks in a phlegmy midwestern drawl: pitched somewhere between a croak and a whisper, it's the kind of voice you have to smoke really hard to keep. Listen to him sing on the third Wilco album *Summer Teeth* and that act of sacrifice will seem wholly justified. This is a record whose remarkable poignancy and richness recalls Phil Spector's comment about 'little symphonies for the kids', but with guitars and pianos instead of a forty-eight-piece orchestra.

The dictionary definition of Wilco's name might be 'c20: abbrev. for I will comply', but the music of this Chicago-based quartet somehow combines resignation with defiance, and melancholy with joy. *Summer Teeth* wraps its nuggets of downbeat personal revelation in some of the most jauntily bitter-sweet music imaginable. The magnificently depressing chorus of the single 'Can't Stand It' ('You know it's all beginning to feel like its ending/No love's as random as

God's love/I can't stand it') even conducted a brief flirtation with the UK Top Forty. It's not exactly 'Agadoo doo doo eat the apple shake the tree', but it'll do for the moment.

Washing down his foul meal with healing draughts of herbal tea, Jay Bennett considers the limitations of the pop radio promotional interview. 'You'd think it would be liberating,' he sighs, 'working with just a microphone and a voice: you don't perceive your audience, there's nothing to be intimidated by, the opportunity to have fun in that context is *immense*.' He shakes his head mournfully, 'But the DJs don't take advantage of it.'

'They only want to know how we get on with Billy Bragg,' says Tweedy. 'I mean, like, *who cares?*'

Anyone who thought Wilco were going to be swept off their feet by the flood tide of adulation inundating *Summer Teeth* would be well advised to think again. They may have been told their new record is '1999's *Deserter's Songs*' (i.e., the record that somehow magically translates critical kudos into actual status without losing its mystery) so many times they now prefer to refer to Mercury Rev's 1998 landmark as 'last year's *Summer Teeth*', but they aren't counting their chickens until they're in the oven.

'"This is the one,"' Tweedy says wearily. 'We've been told that so many times. After a while you don't listen any more. Well, you do, but only because it's entertaining . . .' Such world-weariness might seems excessive for a band only on its third album, but Tweedy's earlier experiences in critically lauded but commercially negligible country rock legends Uncle Tupelo have given him a unique perspective on the value of record-company prophesies.

'When we put our first record out,' he remembers, 'we were told we were going to be the next Hootie and the Blowfish.'

Wilco's slightly underwhelming 1994 debut *AM* had its faults, but surely it wasn't that bad?

'I'll take an eleven million record insult,' Bennett snorts derisively. 'If that's your way of insulting me, sure, go ahead – insult me all day.' Wilco's band banter has a bracingly stringent quality. Perhaps it's a reflection of their outsider status – marooned between the blockbusting mediocrity of Hootie, the Dave Matthews band and their ilk, and the arthouse credibility of Smog and Bonnie 'Prince' Billy.

'If that guy likes Mariah Carey as much as he claims,' Tweedy says of the latter, 'he should put his money where his mouth is and get her to sing on his next record.'

'He should get *someone* to sing on his next record,' Bennett concurs cattily. 'Last time I saw him play live he put fifteen hundred people to sleep. It was like some kind of scientific experiment.'

It must be rather intimidating to bare your soul to such a demanding audience. Does Tweedy ever feel vulnerable in front of his band-mates, when he first sings them songs like 'How to Fight Loneliness' or 'When You Wake Up Feeling Old'? As befits a man who willingly confesses to having gone into school in the fourth grade with a copy of Bruce Springsteen's *Born to Run*, claiming that the record was all his own work, the singer knows no shame.

Bennett's feelings are hurt by the very suggestion. 'I don't need to hear Jeff's lyrics to know him as well as I know him,' he insists.

'There's a certain power that comes from it too,' Tweedy maintains. 'Having a conversation with your friends and sharing a part of yourself, and it's not a one-way dialogue. Because you get stuff back from them musically.'

He certainly does. Where 1997's equally gripping *Being There* was a ramshackle bar-band eulogy, *Summer Teeth* spirals and quavers like a great lost girl-group album. Wilco do not like to think too much about how they got from one place to another.

'It's not a good story,' Bennett insists. 'It's not like we started our new record and it sounded just like *Being There*, so we went to the pub and decided to make a sixties soul record.'

But that's *not* a good story.

'No it's not,' Tweedy agrees. 'That's *The Commitments*.'

'We're more like Inuit ivory carvers,' the singer continues, some-what mystifyingly. 'We hold the magnetic tape in our hands and then we let whatever needs to be on it come out.'

This analogy turns out to be less facetious than it initially seems. 'Inuit stone carvers believe there are things captured inside a rock,' Tweedy explains, 'so they start carving without any idea of what they're aiming at, and then they find a bird in there. I think that's a really accurate way to describe the creative process.'

'We took a rock and chiselled away until we found the big tooth,' Bennett enthuses '. . . a giant molar!'

'We've actually got e-mail from people saying, "You guys are supposed to be like Gram Parsons – what the hell is this? It's the worst record I've ever heard in my life." Which in a way is kind of gratifying. Because if people read about us being a country-rock band and then they go out and buy *Summer Teeth*, I can't imagine them *not* being confused.'

'People are confused,' Bennett concludes. 'Just not in the way that we want them to be.'

And what way would that be exactly?

'It would be nice for people to be confused to the extent that they just accepted everything for what it was. [Jay assumes the voice of everyman] "I'm so confused by all this music, I'm just going to listen to it, and decide what I like."'

Summer Teeth (Warners, 1999)

Robert Wyatt

*'I'm not like a twitcher, in the sense that a bird doesn't have to be rare
for me to be interested in it.'*

Robert Wyatt lives on an isolated estuary in the misty North-East of
England, where he sometimes likes to sit in quiet contemplation with
his wife – the Spanish artist and poet Alfreda Benge – watching flocks
of waders go about their business. 'She and I are a group of two,
really,' muses Wyatt tenderly. 'Nearly all of Alfie's poems or lyrics
that I use are written about experiences that I've shared with her.'

BT: The impression people have of your lives is companionable but
isolated. Is that fairly accurate?
RW: Absolutely – we're not part of the flow of things at all. Where we
stay on the coast is next to a little village called Humberston – a plot
development of home-made wooden houses opposite Spurn point.

Whether you were already following the serpentine track of Robert
Wyatt's career (with Soft Machine, Matching Mole and then as a solo
artist) before the fall from a second-floor window which left him in a
wheelchair in 1973, or first came across his uniquely plaintive vocal
style at the turn of the eighties, when he was making Elvis Costello's
'Shipbuilding' or Chic's 'At Last I Am Free' his own, or even
stumbled unprepared into the somnambulist reverie of his bewitching 1998 album *Shleep*, the contemplative spaces his best music
opens up are as wide as any coastal horizon.

After several years of virtual silence (his previous new release was
1991's faintly disappointing *Dondestan*) and, reportedly, intense
depression, the adventurous and even jaunty atmosphere of Wyatt's

most recent release came as a happy shock. With a starry backing ensemble featuring – among others – Brian Eno, Paul Weller, and Phil Manzanera, and several of the songs, notably the exquisite central 'bird trilogy' ('September The 9th', 'Alien', and 'Out Of Season'), featuring lyrics written by Alfie, this record might easily have lacked a unifying tone. But somehow Wyatt's voice holds it all together: fragile and yet extraordinarily resilient, echoing out from supple and dextrous arrangements like a curlew's cry on a winter afternoon.

In fact, combining all the best qualities of his earlier recordings – the happy balance of simplicity and complication, frailty and resilience – with a new sense of purpose, *Shleep* is perhaps the most complete and moving record of his entire career.

The exquisite Eno-flavoured opening 'Heaps Of Sheeps' must be the most tranquil song ever written about insomnia; 'Blues In Bob Minor' – a fairground mirror image of Dylan's 'Subterranean Homesick Blues' – gives Paul Weller the cue for his most free-spirited guitar blowout since the heyday of The Paul Weller Movement; and on the bewitching 'Free Will And Testament', Wyatt's voice takes flight to a higher realm of unhistrionic poignancy.

Meeting Robert and Alfie outside a café in Red Lion Square, they are every bit the romantic couple one would have imagined. She is a quiet but strangely playful presence. He is a bearded seraph.

RW: I've taken a very long time – most of the nineties in fact – to write this bunch of songs. I don't like to rush things. I would say throughout my life I've averaged about a tune a year. But I had a nervous breakdown a couple of years ago, when I stopped being able to co-ordinate anything, so I just held on to the little bits I could come up with – a word here, a chord there . . .

BT: Is it right that working at [ex-Roxy Music bassist] Phil Manzanera's Chertsey hideaway helped you to relax a bit when you finally got into the studio?

RW: Phil's attitude was just what I needed. Normally in the studio I'm just watching the clock and panicking. Every time I make a mistake I think, 'That's forty quid down the drain.' And it's very hard to function like that. I think rock costs are geared to people who have hisses . . . no, mits [laughter] . . . I don't even know what they're called!

Robert Wyatt did have a hit once, with an exquisite cover version of The Monkees 'I'm A Believer', which the BBC tried to stop him playing on *Top of the Pops* for 'fear of offending taste'.

The sense of personal liberation which percolates through *Shleep* as strongly as any of the fierce – not to say doctrinaire – political ideals which have coloured so much of Wyatt's other work, seems to have been rooted in the end of a period of sleepnessness.

'Dreaming is a wonderful thing,' Wyatt told the Internet magazine *Stomp and Stammer*. 'In my dreams, I'm very often not paraplegic. I'm swimming and flying and running and walking, so I really look forward to the next night's adventure. I used to think that sleep was something you did so that you'd have the energy to work the next day. Now I think almost the other way around.'

BT: Your feathered friends seem to have been a great source of inspiration too?

RW: Well, they outnumber us ten to one, and I really love watching them, which isn't always true of people. I'm not like a twitcher, in the sense that a bird doesn't have to be rare for me to be interested in it – I really like the ones that just hang about. I think sparrows, for example, are extremely witty and amusing to watch, though that's very anthropomorphic of me, because I know they're really busy struggling for survival. I suppose the sparrow is very easy to identify with – sitting there on its own when all these swifts and swallows have gone . . .

BT: Was it that kind of sympathy for the underdog that led you to offer Paul Weller a way out of his pub-rock impasse?

RW: Shut it [more laughter]. With some people I'm just like a normal pop fan – judgement is completely suspended – and Paul is one of those. I've always liked the cut of his jib, and having spent so much time struggling around trying to do different things myself, I really identify with some of the adventures that he's had. I am the founder member of the 'The Style Council were a lot better than people seem to realise' club.

BT: But can you understand why people might be surprised by an avant-garde avatar such as yourself teaming up with such an arch populist?

RW: Someone who knows my track record shouldn't be surprised at me working with anybody, really. In any case, we musicians think differently about these things – inside the brotherhood. I left him a note once which said, 'If you need an old voice groaning along for a bit of gravitas on a harmony part . . .' Amazingly enough, he didn't need one. But he left a reply saying, 'If you need a bit of strumming, I'll have a go.'

BT: What's 'Blues In Bob Minor' actually about?

RW: The original vocal was a bit influenced by those adverts – 'Papa!' 'Nicole!' I was just singing 'Oh, Alfie' and I thought it was dead good and minimalist, but when I tried it out on my wife she said I was just being lazy and not bothering to write proper words, so after I'd slammed the door a few times and smashed a couple of plates, I thought, 'I'll stuff it with words.' I was trying to copy the original basically, but I couldn't remember the lyrics, which was a good thing because it meant the song finished up as Robert Wyatt rather than Bob Dylan. Alfie thinks the man himself might object, but if he does we'll just bluff it out and say, 'Borrowing is a vital part of the folk tradition.'

Shleep (Rykodisk, 1998)

Neil Young

'Feedback? I hate feedback . . . no, wait a minute, I love feedback!'

The music of Neil Young is a very private pleasure, with the power to transform a car or a kitchen into a spiritual oasis, so the experience of sharing it with more than a few other people is an unnerving one at first. Especially when there are 28,000 of them crammed into Finsbury Park. Fortunately, the magic and mystery of Neil survives and even expands in the embrace of marauding trios of ecstatic (not to say drunken) Welshmen, who don't just sing along with the words, but with the guitar solos as well.

It's no wonder Young dresses like a lumberjack; he wields his guitar like a woodcutter would a chainsaw, channelling its terrifying destructive potential with extraordinary finesse. 'Feedback? I hate feedback,' proclaims the veteran sonic frontiersman. 'No, wait a minute, I love feedback – I'm having an identity crisis here.'

Some confusion is forgivable under the circumstances. Forged in the interminable crucible of Bob Dylan's thirtieth anniversary concert, Young's unlikely 1993 touring partnership with Booker T & the MGs is (after *Weld*'s feedback orgy and the plaintive caress of *Unplugged*) Neil's third complete back catalogue overhaul in as many years. Its finest moments come when Young plays to the strengths of his remarkable backing band. Booker T lights up 'Only Love Can Break Your Heart' with a celestial organ solo, and there's an unforgettable encore, as back-up guitar hero Steve Cropper lets the new boss loose on '(Sittin' on the) Dock of the Bay'.

Neil looks naked without his guitar, but makes a great fist of the whistling bit with his harmonica. When he sings 'I left my home in

Canada/Headed for the 'Frisco bay' somewhere, far away, Otis Redding doesn't feel so blue.

Young's spectacular early nineties renaissance gave British fans the opportunity to see him play with a lot of different people – as well as the Booker T show, he plays with Pearl Jam at Reading a year or so later, and then there's a gloriously frazzled reunion with Crazy Horse at the Phoenix Festival in 1996. But it's on his own – playing 'Like A Hurricane' at the pump organ – that he always makes the biggest impression.

Outside the room where he is being interviewed around the 1992 release of his sublime country-rock elegy *Harvest Moon*, you can hear Young's voice getting steadily louder as he browbeats someone from *Q* magazine on his pet topic: the inadequacy and soullessness of digital CD sound reproduction.

'Don't believe the advertising about CD sound: it's not alive, it's just a status thing,' Young says sadly. 'With analogue records the moment used to be captured – complete with the flaws, but you could hear it: all the *nuances*. With digital what happened was they removed everything that seemed like a flaw and all you have left is the *semblance* of sound. The big thing about digital is you can reproduce it and it never loses its quality. The only problem is it never had that quality in the first place, so the lack of quality is reproduced over and over again,' he concludes with a flourish, 'perfectly'[53].

The journalist is led away, suitably cowed, and Neil Young gets up to say hello. He is wearing a Harley Davidson t-shirt, jeans, funny white trainers, and a brown leather jacket with inspiringly horrible foot-long hanging fringes. Forty-seven next week and still on the run from the fashion police, his only visible concessions to the crazedness of legend are hefty clumps of beard (he has vowed not to shave until he's through this rare bout of interviews).

He is calm, friendly and chuckles easily, removing his non-designer sunglasses only once to reveal not the unhinged stare you'd expect but the eyes of an elderly mole, blinking in the light of their fifth country in as many days.

With each song on *Harvest Moon* Young confronts the realities of decline and decay and makes something new and beautiful out of them. The album is dedicated to his second wife Pegi, and many of its sweetest moments are love songs, but they seem to go beyond the personal.

'They're songs about hanging on and trying to make things last,' he explains, 'and being able to reach back into the past and take it with you, rather than having to abandon it.'

For a while, in the dark, distant eighties, it looked as if Young's determination not to be a slave to the past could be the end of him. He had finished the previous decade in fine musical fettle, with the rip-roaring *Rust Never Sleeps* marking him out as the only true rock dinosaur to rise to the challenge of punk, but then a series of bizarre genre-hops (the computer concept album *Trans*, the rockabilly set, and the redneck country primer *Old Ways*) exasperated fans as well as his record company of the time.

The David Geffen Company, run by the ex-manager of Crosby, Stills, Nash and Young and ultimate post-hippie capitalist, sued him for 'making unrepresentative music'. (Ironically, Geffen would later become the home of Nirvana and Sonic Youth, righteous heirs of Young's frazzled guitar tradition. Even more ironically, Geffen later sued Beck on similar grounds for *Mutations*, which was his best record so far.)

Young bears no grudges, but is properly unapologetic about this creative recharging. 'People were offended by the fact that I seemed to have no respect for myself, or rather for who they thought I was. They had built up this whole thing around me and I didn't give a shit about it, and I guess that bothered them.'

How does he feel now about his eighties back catalogue?

'I don't even have an opinion on most of what I do. I just do it. When I put it out I think it's great, and after that it either stands the test of time or it doesn't. This test of time is a very complicated equation, because it constantly changes. There are some things that don't stand the test of time a year after they're done, but then in ten years' time they do – how did they beat ten years but not one?'

Young was first inspired to do what he does by the dedication and emotional intensity of Roy Orbison, whom he saw play often in Canada around 1962; and the way he's brought these same qualities to bear on personal tragedies – loss of friends to drugs, on the great tequila-sodden wake *Tonight's the Night*; incomprehension at the birth of a second son with cerebral palsy, on the bewildering *Trans* – is one of the things that has made him such a compelling figure.

His best records always leave you feeling hopeful, rather than bleak. It's not so much a single moment (one song on which the needle goes down or the disc clicks in and your heart lifts, though Young has recorded a hundred such songs), it's more a feeling his music connects you to, almost like he's a *carrier*. It's a feeling, at once melancholy and thrilling, of being completely distanced from the world at the same time as being right in the middle of it. His voice has something to do with it: high, plaintive, a shade threadbare, the sound of a fallen angel. Schools of music don't teach 'holding a note the Neil Young way', which is part of the reason why so many people love his singing.

> **NY:** Some people love my singing, but a lot of people hate it.
> **BT:** What do they think about the way you play the guitar?
> **NY:** I'm technically not a good guitar player. I'm not very fast . . . well, my right hand is pretty fast, but my left is really slow. The whole left-hand side of my body – my eye and everything – is really slow, it's pretty weird.
> **BT:** Is that what makes your playing stand out?
> **NY:** It could be. Some kind of spastic, static thing. If I let it go it's pretty dangerous – I like the sound, though, it's kind of like the sound of destruction.

During the Gulf war, Young was making that sound all across America in front of a peace sign, with a yellow ribbon tied to the mike-stand: a typically double-edged and provocative gesture, cut from the same ambivalent cloth as the opposing quotes from Malcolm X and Martin Luther King with which Spike Lee closed *Do The Right Thing*.

Young's actual politics defy analysis, but are far from the usual rock-star platitudes, boiling down on prolonged inspection to a characterful mash of survivalist humanism.

> **BT:** How did that whole thing 'Young backs Ron' thing come about?

NY: Some journalist was ranting to me about whan an asshole Reagan was and the things he were saying were pretty obvious, so I say, 'Well, what about this . . . not everything he says is wrong . . . everybody has something to add to the fucking picture.'

BT: What was it you felt Reagan had to contribute?

NY: It was basically that I agreed with some of the things he was saying about not being able to count on the government to supply child care: it's better for communities to get together and do it themselves. Find people you know who you can trust your kids with.

It can't have been a coincidence Young came in from the cold just as a new generation of scruffy guitar bands was preparing to board a raft made out of his old furniture and sail into the mainstream. While he had spent the eighties wandering in the rockabilly wilderness, his spiritual children had been cutting their musical teeth on second-hand copies of *Decade*: perhaps the most persuasive argument ever made in favour of long hair and hanging around in the desert with your guitar case.

It was the obvious affinity between Kurt Cobain and Young that made it so cruel when the former quoted lyrics from *Rust Never Sleeps* in his suicide note. Young wrote him an exquisite epitaph in 1994's *Sleeps With Angels*, but his subsequent gentle creative decline to 2000's cheerfully inconsequential *Silver & Gold* was the most eloquent riposte of all to Cobain's awful self-destruction, suggesting as it did that it's actually better to fade away than to burn out.

Decade (Reprise, 1976)

The Spectrum/The Ears/The Chancel

Sample Ear

'There were many rumours in King Arthur's time, but are we hearing them now? It's all about what they left – that golden chalice or that sceptre someone found . . . the artefacts.*'*

LL Cool J

'Instead of the swift and imperceptible flowing of time, you are aware of its nodes, those points where time stands still or from which it leaps ahead. And you slip into the breaks and look around . . .'

Invisible Man by Ralph Ellison

August 1997. KRS-1 (aka South Bronx hip-hop eminence Kris Parker) is the guest of honour on Tim Westwood's Radio 1 rap show. Things are not going well. Westwood has just asked the legendary MC what he thinks are hip-hop's biggest problems at the moment. At first, the responses are everything you'd hope for from a man whose stage-name is an acronym for Knowledge Reigns Supreme Over Nearly Everyone.

'We forgot about hip-hop as a *culture*,' Parker insists. 'We lost the rules and regulations . . . when we were all in the parks practising our skills, we used to battle, but it was all in fun. Lord Finesse would not pull out a gun and shoot Lords of the Underground.'

Then, with the vigorous contrariness for which he is widely renowned[54], Parker suddenly turns his pertinent if somewhat rose-tinted reminiscences of rap's arcadian past into a savage attack on his host's hard-maintained reputation for professional integrity. 'The medium you're coming though,' he informs the DJ who has repeatedly insisted on having 'mad love' for him 'from day one', 'is obviously making you dirty.'

Westwood's crime, it turns out, is working for a station which doesn't play KRS-1's records eighty times a day (this number has not been plucked out of the air for effect, Parker actually uses it, and he doesn't mean the great early albums like *Criminal Minded* or *By All Means Necessary*, he means plodding mid-period guff like *Edutainment*).

Parker 'just had some fish and rice' in Brixton, and has come into the studio with the word off the street fresh on in his lips. 'You in particular though, Tim,' he insists ominously, 'you should pay more attention to the way people feel about you . . . I come from the people, and the people are critiquing you.' The exchange which follows is of sufficient gravity to merit reproduction in full.

> **TW:** I'm gonna break it down like this . . . no disrespect to you, but when did you get into the UK?
> **KP:** *(playing for time)* What do you mean?
> **TW:** When did you arrive – yesterday?
> **KP:** Yes, sure.
> **TW:** So you arrived here yesterday, and you haven't been here for six years . . .
> **KP:** *(defensively)* I've been here.
> **TW:** When was the last time?
> **KP:** I'm *always* here.
> An awkward silence ensues as the awesome bogosity of these words sinks in.
> **KP:** *(admonishing)* You're concentrating on the physical . . .

As utterly spurious as KRS-1's claim to omnipresence is when he makes it, there is also a sense in which it taps into the very essence of hip-hop, which might be said to be *being there* and *not being there* at the same time. *Invisible Man*, Ralph Ellison's great novel of the black American condition, laid out the ground rules for this there-and-yet-not-thereness in the late nineteen forties. Ellison's central character found solace in Louis Armstrong, but the words Ellison wrote about Armstrong's music – quoted at the start of this chapter – now read just as beautifully as a prophesy of hip-hop.

The idea of slipping inside time's breaks and looking around is a perfect summation of what the sampler enables Marley Marl or Prince Paul or The RZA or Ali Shaheed Muhammed to do. And if hip-hop – in becoming arguably the world's most powerful single cultural force – might be said to have made black America *less* invisible, then that is the surely the ultimate tribute to the force of Ellison's vision.

The ancestral connection between hip-hop and jazz made in Ellison's writings is not an isolated fluke. As early as 1923, Jelly Roll Morton was opining, 'You don't need to even think about doing anything else if you ain't got a decent break.' 'Without clean breaks,' the maverick jazzman asserted, and without 'beautiful ideas', in those breaks, 'you might as well give up and go home.'

In the Bronx of the mid-nineteen seventies, when DJ Kool Herc was first assembling his 'merry go-round' of instrumental breaks in the recreation room of 1520 Sedgwick Avenue – picking out the bits of records that dancers liked best and stitching them back together to make a bespoke tapestry – he might have had Jelly Roll's words written on a Post-it note stuck between his turntables, if Post-it notes had been invented then.

In separating these snatches of music from their original homes and forcibly relocating them in new and alien environments, Kool Herc set up an eerie echo of the abduction narrative which writers like Mark Sinker and Mark Dery have delineated in the intellectual heritage of Afro-diasporic futurism.

This tradition of black avant-garde thinking – on which hip-hop was subsequently to draw so extensively – stretches from the science fiction writings of Samuel R. Delaney to the science fiction music of Lee Perry and Sun Ra. It begins with the idea of slavery – and thence black people's presence in America – as a kind of alien abduction, and extrapolates to a perception of the human as a treacherous category.

From this perspective, Kodwo Eshun's book *More Brilliant Than the Sun* celebrates the history of hip-hop as a rejection of the tyranny of the essence – 'the live show, the proper album, the Real Song, the Real Voice, the mature, the musical, the pure, the true' – in favour of unapologetic celebration of the machine, of 'the artificiality that all humans crave'.

But hip-hop had its foundations in social reality as well as science fiction (and what else was the impulse to science fiction in the first place but social reality?). In Brian Cross' painstaking history of LA rap *It's Not About A Salary*[55], maverick jazzman Horace Tapscott and his son-in-law, rapper JMD, address the musical generation gap. 'In school, they used to give you instruments like they'd give you books,' JMD insists, harking back to his father-in-law's epoch. 'Rap started getting bigger because kids didn't have instruments [any more].'

Like many a beguilingly simple formula, this one too contains an implicit slur: if only the educational authorities had been a bit more generous with their saxophones, the whole thing need never have happened.

But if hip-hop was simply a progression from people playing instruments to people not playing instruments, then what was the bridge between one world and the other, and where does someone like Tackhead and Little Axe eminence Skip McDonald fit in?

By the end of the seventies, when he was asked to join the house band of New York's Sugarhill label in the wake of the global success of 'Rappers Delight', McDonald and fellow fretboard virtuoso Doug Wimbish were already seasoned professionals. As well as working as session players they'd also released a couple of albums as Wood, Brass and Steel.

'It was a Brass Construction–Earth, Wind and Fire kind of thing,' McDonald remembers, 'but we tried to put our own twist on it.'

What was that twist, exactly?

'We tried to keep the horn players at the back – they tended to be a bit chubby.'

It's strange now to think of the birth of rap as a commercial entity being a window of opportunity for jobbing musicians, but at the behest of Sugarhill's Sylvia Robinson – an old-school soul entrepreneur hellbent on corrupting rap's turntablist innocence with the cheap wine of Old Skool instrumental virtuosity – McDonald and Wimbish played (along with drummer Keith LeBlanc, a fellow Wood, Brass and Steel veteran) on numerous early hip-hop landmarks including Funky Four + One's immortal 'That's The Joint'.

'There wasn't any sampling at first,' Skip explains, 'everything was played live, but I remember the DMX drum machine coming in, which was very bad news for drummers – I think Grandmaster Flash's "The Message" might have had a few live drums, but the bulk of it was machines. Then on the heels of the DMX came the sequencers, and that was where the guitar player, bass and keyboards started to lose their gigs.'

How the Sampler Kept Music Live

Happily for the instrumentalist fraternity, relief was on hand, albeit from an unlikely quarter. 'Just at the point where it was all drum machines and computers,' McDonald remembers, 'rappers started listening to older grooves – James Brown, Funkadelic – and they started sampling real musicians, so the whole thing came back from someone sitting in their bedroom with a computer to people playing instruments again. You could see it in the new groups that started to happen – all the weird marriages between heavy metal and rap.'

McDonald was not the only one to notice this happening. 'Sampling actually breathed life into old music,' insists 3D of Massive Attack. 'In the eighties, when you started to hear organic basslines and drum breaks reoccurring because people had sampled them, it sounded much more interesting than all the mechanical drum machines and synthetic keyboards that were around at the time. And that turned people back to the original instruments. In that sense machinery has really helped keep music alive,' 3D smiles, 'and anyone who feels differently is mad.'

As Massive Attack evolved from functioning primarily as a sound system, to making their own records, to trying to play them live, to making new records in a new way inspired by the problems which arose when they tried to play the old ones live, their spiritual guide was Horace Andy.

Andy – né Hinds – got his second name from the pioneering Jamaican sound system overlord, Coxone Dodd (who wanted him to seem like he might be related to Marcia Griffiths' partner in harmony, Bob Andy), but his voice came straight from heaven. The 'best of' album *Skylarking* – the first release on Massive Attack's Melankolic label – confirms the scope of his achievements. From the title track's captivating Studio One shuffle to his bosses' ghostly 1994 rearrangement of 'Spying Glass', Andy's enduring quaver illuminates a gorgeous gallery of shifting soundscapes.

The auteurist illusion of a unified career progression would of course have been anathema to the despotically fragmented late sixties–early seventies Jamaican studio culture whose cut and paste aesthetic would inform not only the entire subsequent history of hip-hop but just about everything else that ever happened too. It must make a nice change for Andy, though, having all his work in one place, rather than scattered through a stack of various artists compilations?

'If I were to start again,' Andy affirms, 'I wouldn't sing for so many different producers, but when you're young you love doing it. If they say, "Come and sing a song," you will.'[56]

'Tell 'em what they're gonna do Marley Marl . . .'

If there is a single seeming jump-cut into the future in hip-hop's history after Kool DJ Herc (or Jimmy Savile or John Cage[57] or whichever other pioneering turntable eminence you want to give the credit for it) invented the merry-go-round, then it must be the moment in the early eighties when Marley Marl sampled a drum sound by mistake.

When the New York producer was trying to process a voice via his Emulator E1 sampler, a snare drum went through accidentally. In Kodwo Eshun's beguilingly biopic-esque account, Marley Marl looks at his engineer hearing this – sensing the glorious vistas of instantly available classic drum sounds opening up before him – and says, 'You know what this *means*?'

Eshun explains the significance of this moment by comparing it to the animatronic alchemy of 'motion capture'; the film-makers' technique by which a computer picks up a static visual representation and gives it the gift of movement, synthesising and virtualising the living body, in the same way that scratching – and then sampling – 'destratifies voice and vinyl into new textures'.

The link to animation is well worth clicking on, not only for the instant connection it gives you to electro's cartoon heartland – the speeded-up voices, the childish delight of Tyrone Brunson's 'The Smurf' or the time-honoured hyper-modernist battlecry 'Transformers! Robots in disguise' – but also because when you try to morph this whole machine-age future shock thing from two dimensions into three, something strange and unexpected happens.

The idea that Marley Marl was not so much using the sampler as the sampler was using him ties in elegantly with a whole range of visionary schemes – from techno pioneer Juan Atkins' oft-quoted assertion that he wanted his music 'to sound like computers talking to each other', to Blixa Bargeld's vision of the song that 'sleeps in the machine'. The physical realities of Marley Marl's day-to-day professional existence might seem to bring such flights of metaphorical fancy resolutely down to earth, but life on the ground is always more complex and fascinating than it looks from up above.

On the mini-bus to the 1988 Prestatyn Soul Weekender with Marley Marl's New York hip-hop label Cold Chillin', the atmosphere is more akin to the Stax/Volt revue than some dauntingly abstract cyber vanguard. Crammed in alongside Mr Marl on the single coach making its way to North Wales are Roxanne Shante – the Mary Peters of hip-hop, 'smart, intelligent, tasteful and elegant' in her own ebullient and not inaccurate estimation – Big Daddy Kane, Kool G Rap ('My utensil is a pencil'), and Biz Markie, 'the inhuman orchestra'.

One of the group – it would be nice to be able to say with absolute assurance that it was Marley Marl himself, but sometimes the memory plays tricks – is listening to Billy Joel CDs on his personal stereo. Onstage later that night, Biz Markie makes music with his mouth, his throat and the top of his head, but a vicious squall of microphone feedback creates the overall impression of a man giving himself a number-one crop with a motorised lawnmower. While in one sense the human beatbox technique – of which Markie is the undoubted master – might seem to be living proof of our will to emulate the mechanical, it also represents the triumph of individual human ingenuity over technological limitation (or, to put it more straightforwardly, not having a drum machine).

Similarly, pop's futurist breakthroughs do not exist in isolation, they co-exist and intermingle with established and still developing showbusiness traditions until it becomes impossible to tell where old begins and new ends. As if to ram this point home, gargantuan jazz-funk DJ Steve Walsh – his Rolls-Royce parked unobtrusively outside his chalet – battles to persuade two girls from Cornwall to take off their t-shirts for the benefit of the Prestatyn inhouse TV system. Meanwhile Mark Moore and his S-Express entourage sweep through the crowd – past the nuns and the Max Wall lookalikes – in search of the acid house enclosure. They may be dressed in seventies revival garb, but in their deplorably tight satin hotpant pockets they conceal the blueprints for all our tomorrows.

'If Jimi Hendrix Were Here Tonight, He'd Sound Something Like This.'

A few weeks earlier, at The Stanton/DMC World DJ awards at the Royal Albert Hall, pasty-faced Fulham homeboys invade Run DMC's celebrity paddock, drink their beer and greet every winner with drunken shouts of 'smiley culture'. Until Pete Waterman of Stock, Aitken and Waterman – a surprise and far from crowd-pleasing choice in the best producer category – steps up to the podium through a hail of boos and beercans. Waterman surveys the auditorium with the imposing self-assurance of a man who in ten years' time will unleash Steps on a defenceless world, and proclaims, 'I hope your needles get stuck up your fucking arseholes.'

Public Enemy reclaim the night for hip-hop by barrelling their way through an apparently impromptu 'Rebel Without A Pause', forcing waiting prize-givers and their attendants to take cover beneath the turntables[58]. After Run DMC graciously accept their prize for being the best rap act in the world, there is time for one more special award.

Walter Stanton, inventor and marketer of the stylus which bears his name, has flown in to present James Brown with a large and rather unsightly clock in recognition of his 'services to dance music'. (Either in lieu of royalties or so that he, of all people, will always know what time it is.) An immaculately besuited Brown comes forward, thanks God, executes a dextrous soft-shoe shuffle and a sprightly knee drop, glides off the stage, and trips over the step.

A few years later, onstage in his own right at the Wembley Arena, the Godfather of Soul hits more representative form. Even on one of the world's least atmospheric stages, he still cuts an imperial dash; sporting a splendid purple ensemble with gold cuffs and epaulettes and matching gilded shoes. Yet the crucial elements of his music – a grunt, a guitar-line, the funky drummer's shuffle – have been cut up and relocated so remorselessly by generations of eager samplers that it is rather bewildering to hear them all in the same place at once.

Brown's determination to chop everything up into little pieces suggests that he feels the same way. 'If Jimi Hendrix were here tonight, he would sound something like this,' he proclaims, pointing without warning at an understandably alarmed-looking bassist. Later on, he exhorts his similarly hard-pressed keyboard player and guitarist to impersonate jazz giants Jimmy Smith and Wes Montgomery. This all seems rather odd, until you get to thinking about the way Brown's music was originally recorded – in snatched sessions in the midst of marathon cross-country tours, with the prime minister of the heavy heavy funk improvising lyrics and grunts over a bassline here or a horn riff there (i.e., in a fashion remarkably similar to the way later hip-hop tracks would be constructed).

In his fine book *Ocean of Sound*, David Toop recounts his reaction to the discovery that James Brown's cornerstone of heavy funk authenticity, 'Papa's Got A Brand New Bag', was originally played at snail's pace after a hard day on the tour bus and then speeded up in the studio: 'What a privilege to be so easily deceived.' The image of music Toop takes away from this – 'as a shifting conglomerate of manipulable bits rather than a finished entity' – perfectly encapsulates how a composer and musician might look at things, but doesn't quite cut it for the listener.

Cutting It For the Listener

It is the winter of 1985–86. LL Cool J's *Radio* has just come out. This is the first album on Def Jam – not the first 'proper' hip-hop album, but the beginning of the idea of hip-hop as an albums- rather than 12-

inch-singles-based medium. Listening to it on a tiny portable tape recorder, having sneaked into a formal English landscaped garden after a heavy snowfall, the imprint of footfalls on the pristine white ground mirrors not only the joyous crunch of Cut Creator's beats, but also LL's gloriously crisp delivery of lines like, 'You dance like a fat old lady, not saying that fat old ladies ain't nice.'[59]

When he was twelve years old, a benevolent grandfather tried to divert LL Cool J from his destiny by giving him a guitar. 'I love him,' LL observes fondly, fifteen years later, 'but I broke it.'

Native New Yorkers Bryan Brater and Jarrett Myer – founders of inspirational back to basics hip-hop imprint Rawkus – were both musicians themselves until they 'tired of making three hundred bucks a week eating shit, and hopped over the invisible fence'. 'I was a jazz bass-player,' Brater explains. 'But unless you're Jaco Pastorius or Stanley Clarke, you're not gonna help your moms out that way . . . And I personally,' he adds, somewhat unnecessarily, 'love my mom.'

To fully appreciate the family feeling between pre- and post-hip-hop ideals of musicianship, you have to see and hear it in action. Down a shady pathway, with a high concentration of chemical entrepreneurs and a rather self-conscious police car stationed at the end of it, lurks the tasteful oasis of the 1992 Glastonbury Festival Jazz Stage. From the shelter of this lovely, leafy clearing belts out snaky, sinous hip-hop. Under the starlit sky, be-bop-inflected rappers Digable Planets are little short of a revelation: their two real live horn players are not just there for decoration, but do the work of a big band, summoning up flitting shadows of Miles Davis and Dexter Gordon for the group's three wordsmiths to weave in and out of.

As a warm mist rises out of the valley, Digable Planets are followed onstage by veteran vibesman Roy Ayers, who winds the evening down with a superlative set of much sampled crowd-pleasing favourites including 'Everyone Loves The Sunshine' and the immortal 'We Live In Brooklyn, Baby' – the perfect soundtrack for midnight in Somerset. He's got a fantastic wah-wah attachment for his vibraphone that enables him to make it sound like, well, blocks of wood. As if to celebrate the happy union of ancient and modern, the night sky comes alive with fireworks. In his grave somewhere nearby, King Arthur taps a gentle foot.

The idea of hip-hop being played with 'real' instruments makes a lot of people uneasy, not least because of the eagerness with which this tendency tends to be embraced by those whose general feelings towards the form are not what you would call friendly. Kodwo Eshun argues that those performers who compromise their futuristic integrity by dabbling in old-fashioned wood, brass and steel run the risk of leaving themselves 'trapped in someone else's '72' – surrendering all the hard-won benefits of technological advance for the spurious thrill of historically grounded musicianly authenticity.

For the true hip-hop adventurer, such perils are an invitation rather than a deterrent. Why shouldn't the border country between the real and the artificial be, in the immortal words of one of the standout tracks on De La Soul's brilliant third album *Buhloone Mindstate*, 'Just another area for me to patrol'? (Apart from anything else, jobbing musicians are less likely to take you to court and make you pay them huge amounts of money than the publishing companies who own the copyright to samples.) In that particular case, producer Prince Paul's compellingly dense weave of samples and effects is in no way compromised by some exquisite live horn work from erstwhile James Brown stalwarts Maceo Parker, Fred Wesley and Pee Wee Ellis.

And in mixing and matching tradition and experiment, live and sampled, allowed and not allowed, surely hip-hop's embrace of real instruments has been not a betrayal but a fulfilment of its *bricoleur*'s brief for the piecemeal? Admittedly, when The Fugees play a packed and exuberant Forum in the week 'Killing Me Softly' goes to number one, their live band's endless lumbering Bob Marley cover versions are a bit of a trial. But they redeem themselves with a series of hilarious unprovoked pub-rock assaults on unsuspecting early hip-hop landmarks such as Whodini's 'Magic Wand' and Hashim's 'Al Naafiysh (The Soul)'.

If someone had told those sitting in the back row of Wembley Arena at *UK Fresh '86* with plaid blankets over their knees that the jaunty Lovebug Starski electro doodles they were struggling to hear over the frenzied whistling of ten thousand suburban teenagers would in a decade's time be the subject of old-fashioned musicianly interpolations . . . well, it would be fair to assume that they would have been quite surprised.

But just as it was strangely fitting that a form of music which began with DJs' determination to make good on soul and funk performers' disingenuous promises of a party that would last to the early hours[60] should evolve into such a grippingly cursory live spectacle, so hip-hop's later flirtations with seemingly inappropriate ideals of the organic and the humane also makes a crazy kind of sense. By the same token, if you really want to look at the history of hip-hop from the breakbeat's point of view, you've got to consider what happened to the music that got left behind.

What Happened to the Music That Got Left Behind

The Island is a well-run reconverted bingo hall, cropping out into the Ilford High Road, its shores gently lapped by carbon monoxide tides. Inside is the dancefloor that fashion forgot: stonewashed denim rules, and ultraviolet light blesses everyone with severe dandruff and dark yellow teeth. The Trammps are doing a vocal PA to 'Disco Inferno', and tonight's main attractions, sunstrip legends Kool & the Gang, are horribly delayed. An MC with an alarming resemblance to Gary Bushell urges the crowd to 'keep on drinking'.

Time passes and he explains the reason for the hold-up – 'a few technical problems with the DAT, for those who understand that kind of thing'. This would seem to be letting the cat out of the bag somewhat, but the strange thing is, when Kool & The Gang finally do come on, they aren't actually miming.

The dance routines are just as they should be – so cheesy they can only be fully appreciated with the aid of a stick and some pineapple – but the sound is nowhere. At the door a mountainous bouncer calms a gaggle of distressed nostalgia-seekers. 'Groups always do a lot of songs nobody knows at the beginning to advertise their new album,' he counsels with the wisdom born of experience, 'then they play the good ones at the end.'

And so, happily, it proves. Trainee vocalists give way to old hands and gradually, with 'Joanna' and 'Cherish', Kool & the Gang ease into the mighty back-catalogue preserved for all time on the epic compilation *Twice as Kool*. There are plenty of founder members on stage – Robert 'Kool' Bell on bass, and original drums, trombone and guitar too – and the street-funk roots which were always visible, even beneath the exhilaratingly heinous pop-disco sludge of their commercial heyday, eventually show through. The lustrous and much sampled mid-seventies classic 'Summer Madness' takes its place next to later proto-handbag hits like 'Big Fun' and 'Celebration'. The brass section still takes no prisoners: the horn-lines are so taut you could floss your teeth with them.

What Happened to the Music That Got Left Behind II

Even though he had been rapping to the record's introduction for years, Run DMC's Darryl McDaniels had never heard Aerosmith's 'Walk This Way' past the drumbeat until Rick Rubin tried to persuade him to re-record it in boundary-levelling tandem with the original artists. His reaction on hearing Joe Perry and Steve Tyler all the way through for the first time? 'Hillybilly gibberish *bullshit* – everybody's gonna *laugh* at us.'

Such outrageous disrespect for the intrinsic virtues of vital source material is endemic in writing about hip-hop – as if all value was added by the Midas touch of the DJ or sampler, when what has actually happened is less akin to the transformation of dross into gold than that of bullion into hard currency. But those who are actually making the music (with the dishonourable exception of Mr McDaniels) tend to feel very differently about it.

Hence Massive Attack's Mushroom, talking to someone from *Mojo* about the Pink Floyd of *The Dark Side of the Moon:* 'I wouldn't want to sample them. To me they *are* [my itals] hip-hop.' Or Grandmaster Flash rhapsodising about Kraftwerk's 'Trans Europe Express': 'Leave that shit alone, that shit was cutting itself. Go smoke a cigarette.'[61]

A quarter of a century on, hip-hop's diamonds in the rough get shined up and put on show. For those who've only heard this music in its later applications, listening to *The Breaks Volumes 1–3* – 'original b-boy street funk and block party classics' assembled by DJ's Pogo, Skye and Cutmaster Swift for the estimable reissue label Harmless records – can only be a revelation.

Archaeology fades swiftly into delirium as James Brown's 'Funky Drummer' moves into its ninth minute, Vernon Burch's 'Get Up' showcases the whistling noise from Dee-Lite's 'Groove Is In the Heart', and the song the bells on LL Cool J's 'Rock The Bells' came from (Bob James' 'Take Me To The Mardi Gras') turns out to be a lounge piano cover version of an old Paul Simon number. This must be what Duke Ellington was talking about in 1971 (as quoted in *Exotica* by David Toop) when he envisioned a future where 'no one knows 'exactly who is enjoying the shadow of whom'.

Postscript

Face to Face With Russell Simmons – the Living Embodiment of Hip-hop's Motivating Spirit of Enterprise

Trying to speak to Run DMC in their *Raising Hell* heyday, it is more or less impossible to get a word in edgeways. Not because of any particular garrulousness on the part of Joe 'Run' Simmons or Darryl 'DMC' McDaniels, quite the reverse, in fact. Their manager – Joe's brother, Russell 'Rush' Simmons – sweeps away every forlorn attempt at direct communication with a sturdy broom of entrepreneurial ebullience.

'Tell him how many comments you've got about that, boys . . . Tell him where you live . . . Tell him you love Just Ice . . . I want to say something, and this is the last thing I'm going to say: they sing about crack because it affects them and their friends, and they sing about going to school and church and respecting their parents because it's what they believe in, but when it comes to politics, that's not what they know about.'

Eight years later, arriving at his London hotel at the appointed hour for a second meeting – cutting out the middlemen this time – with Russell Simmons himself, the room is empty. Russell has relocated without telling anyone. Fielding an anxious call as to his exact whereabouts (he is now having lunch on the other side of town with Warren G), Russell picks up his mobile and utters words to the approximate effect of 'where have you been?'. Finally tracked down to his new – still more exclusive – address, Russell announces that we are now going shopping.

In the taxi to Hyper Hyper, there is an unfortunate incident wherein Russell's immaculate trainer gets scuffed by his would-be interviewer's hobnailed boot. Perhaps in deference to the feelings of his demure supermodel companion Veronica Webb, he generously opts to overlook it, briskly outlining his current activites, which include producing three films – Abel Ferrara's vampire heroin movie *The Addiction*, Eddie Murphy's remake of *The Nutty Professor*, and the eagerly awaited rapumentary *The Show* ('the truth or dare of hip hop') – and preparing the launch of America's first nationwide satellite radio station: 'You can't follow me to the hell I'm going to, programming-wise.'

The taxi pulls up on Kensington High Street. Russell and Veronica waltz in to the store, leaving their millionaire playboy freelance journalist associate to pick up the tab. Hence the verb 'to rush'.

Amid the clatter of his and hers platinum Amex cards hitting counters, Russell explains the fundamental difference between East Coast hip-hop – of which, via his astute guidance of Run DMC, LL Cool J and Public Enemy among others, he is the undisputed godfather – and the West Coast variant, into which he has recently made notable inroads. With G-funk dauphin Warren G, US number 1 Montell Jordan and brazen crossover hopefuls The Dove Shack ('The most commercial group I've ever had my hands on,' he insists in a rare lapse of judgement – the Boys II Men of rap') already wearing his colours, Russell is feeling very positive about the West Coast.

'The West Coast is very country,' he observes fondly, 'the accents are all slang and twang, and the records are more pop. They speak slowly so you can hear every word they say – listen to a lot of East Coast rappers, they're underground for a reason.'

Long Beach may be the new hip-hop epicentre, but Russell has no intention of ditching the folks back East who got him where he is today. 'LL Cool J came out when Bambaata came out,' he exaggerates shamelessly, 'but he's still around. When his new record comes out, it'll still sell in the first week, even if it's horrible. We don't sell one album and go away. That's why we've got the Free Slick Rick campaign, and that's why when Flavor Flav gets in trouble, we take him to the rehab personally.'

Forsaking the cramped fashion emporium for the wide open spaces of Hyde Park, Russell turns his attention to Def Jam's imminent tenth birthday. 'Don't say we're doing good for a bunch of niggas,' he advises those whose job it is to commemorate this momentous anniversary. 'That ain't gonna be helpful to me.' Generally – if not in this case – Russell's use of the N word is inclusive rather than exclusive. (Basically it means anyone he likes, including former charges The Beastie Boys, and Def Jam co-founder Rick Rubin – the 'most creative' producer Simmons has ever met 'but let's not suck his dick just yet.')

'My crossover is not from black to white,' he will observe a further few years later, after a prudent realignment of his energies towards the Eastern seaboard has engineered the unlikely US pop chart takeover of Jay-Z, Method Man and DMX, 'it's from cool to uncool.'

A man whose moment seems to have arrived anew just about every day since he first printed flyers proclaiming himself 'the force in college parties' at New York City University in 1978, does Russell Simmons ever rest?

'I'm resting right now. I'm always resting; it's only not resting when you're swinging a sledgehammer.'

Metal Ear

'They had brought this music with them when they were born, these bandmen, in their hearts and their muscles, their blood and their bones.'
Jay Allison Stuart on an early twentieth-century Louisiana funeral band, in *Call Him George*, his biography of New Orleans jazz veteran George Lewis

'The cost of their cheap rebellion is that when they are older they will find that their hearing has been damaged.'
Donald Clarke on the ultimate fate of all heavy metal fans, in *The Rise and Fall of Popular Music*

At some point around the time Nirvana's *Bleach* was first released, the day finally passed when a fashion-conscious public bar could be shocked into silence by someone owning up to an enduring affection for Deep Purple's 'Highway Star'. As the old view of heavy metal as a sonic dumping ground for all that is worthless started to fade, the new one had to face the fact that for some people it was this very air of reprehensibility, of beyond the pale-ness, that made it so attractive.[62]

If an early adolescence marked by voluntary exposure to Rush or UFO at the Hammersmith Odeon no longer qualified as a shameful secret, then what on earth *was* the point of it? Chuck Eddy's inspirational book *Stairway To Hell: The 500 Best Heavy Metal Albums in the Universe* pointed the way to a new understanding, reversing the traditional 'Metal equals everything that is not to be cherished' equation to inspiring effect. For Eddy, who cares enough about the distinction to berate bands with the apparently cast-iron credentials of Judas Priest for being 'false metal', the term in its truest sense embraces everyone from Teena Marie to Miles Davis via The Beastie Boys, The Three Johns and Budgie.

In Eddy's musical scheme, Led Zeppelin are no longer the great defilers, perverting the legacy of honest bluesmen in a welter of thinly veiled aural Fascism, but prophets of righteous unashamedness. And every other band that was ever any good then falls into place behind them, under the unifying banner of having no pretension to redeeming social value. While the wholescale adaptation of this approach would probably lead to serious social problems, it acts as a welcome counterbalance to the critical snobberies to which heavy metal has for so long been subject.

A quarter of a century after punk, the reasons why it was so important not to admit how like a metal band The Sex Pistols sounded are no longer so clear in the mind[63]. There was always something pretty stupid about the idea of a strict punk–metal frontier with The Ramones on one side and Motorhead and AC/DC on the other, but that didn't mean it wasn't there. And the fact that this border lacked a foundation in reason did not make its removal any less traumatic – a point The Scorpions could well have been making about the Berlin Wall with 'Wind Of Change'.

But this particular wind of change came too late to save an earlier generation from impaling itself on the horns of the punk-metal dilemma. If these things matter – which fortunately they don't – the New Wave of British Heavy Metal was more of a proletarian grass roots musical upsurge than punk ever was.

Of the innumerable new metal outfits who downed tools to pick up their axes in the late 1970s only Def Leppard and the enduringly unlovely Iron Maiden (who were actually quite good before Bruce Dickinson joined) made it really big. Those less fortunate had only the doubtful consolation of seeing their sub-genre mini-dramas reenacted in different shades of platinum on America's big screen a few years later.

The influence of NWOBHM on the course of later mainstream American metal is there for all to see in the sleeve notes to '79 Revisited, the celebratory compilation album which was meant to commemorate the phenomenon's tenth anniversary but actually came out, with classic metal precision, in 1990. Here Metallica's Lars Ulrich waxes bizarrely lyrical about a pilgrimage to the Woolwich Odeon to see Diamond Head; who along with the death-defyingly unmanly Girl, bravely paved the way for the later 'Dude Looks Like A Lady' LA glam-metal heresies of Poison and their big-haired ilk.

Nor has there been much in the works of Death/Devil Metal acts such as Slayer and Deicide not prefigured with considerably more charm in the oeuvres of Mantas, Cronos and Abbadon of Venom and Mansfield's notorious Witchfynde.

But metal has impacted not only on itself; community service has also played a part in its rehabilitation.

In a well-judged act of atonement for the outrageous blues larcenies of Iron Butterfly et al., heavy metal famously fulfilled the same sonic lending library function for rap that Kraftwerk did for electro. The fact that that this arrangement turned out to be of mutual benefit may have been an irony, but it was a happy one. If at the same time as easing Run DMC into MTV heavy rotation and thence into millions of white living rooms (in the process paving the way for rap's transformation to an album rather than singles-based medium), 'Walk This Way' coincidentally relaunched Aerosmith's career, well, it's a fine wind that blows everybody a bit of good.

Metal's collisions with other genres are invariably portrayed as accidents, when, in fact, the people crossing the central reservation to get involved in them always had a pretty good idea of what they were after. When Afrika Bambaata used to put Billy Squier's 'The Big Beat' in his record box at hip-hop's Zulu dawn, he wasn't doing it out of charity. When KLF chose Extreme Noise Terror to help them put the wind up BPI bigwigs at the 1992 Brit Awards, it was not just their music that fitted the Ipswich speed metal ensemble for the task, it was their purity of spirit (why would anyone make a sound this horrible unless they absolutely had to?).

Earache Records' Gods of Grind (especially Carcass, poring unflinchingly over autopsy reports) bring an almost medieval sensibility to what are essentially experiments with the outer limits of sound. These people are musicians too – you need talent to play this stuff. It's not like the old days when Ritchie Blackmore would claim

Beethoven as his main creative influence and everyone would laugh at him.

A project like Naked City's Torture Garden, in which John Zorn's death-jazz troupe recruited Japanese metal yelper Yamatsuka Eye to give songs like 'jazz snob eat shit' a bit more oomph, has a significance that goes beyond novelty value. It reflects metal's ability to mean the same thing at vastly disparate points on the planet's surface. The phrase World Music has come to mean just about any sound whose glamour is supposedly enhanced by coming from somewhere else[64], but if any music qualifies as a global language, that music is heavy metal.

As it has simultaneously speeded up and slowed down to the point where cutting-edge lyrics are more or less incomprehensible, broken or non-existent English is no longer a handicap in reaching international markets: the silent majority with a taste for noise speaks grunt 'n' grind Esperanto.

For all the presumed chauvinism of its audience, heavy metal is probably the music wherein where you come from matters least; as is emphasised by the worldwide success of Swiss rockers Krokus (as Alpine band names go, it's just a step away from Kuckoo Klock) and the flamboyant Celtic Frost, whose 'Phallic Tantrum' is one of the great rock songtitles of all time. Sometimes, as, for example, with Sepultura's Brazilian Death Metal or Tankard's tragic German Beer-core, the music's apparent geographical rootlessness gives it added force.

If there is a single image which sums up metal's alarmingly accurate reflection of a strange and twisted world, it is Rob Halford – soft-spoken, out gay, ex-Birmingham theatre apprentice and Harley-riding lead singer of metal demons Judas Priest – defending his craft to an American court. On the last day of the 1990 trial in which alleged subliminal and backward messages on the 1980 Priest album *Stained Class* were being blamed for the suicides of two disturbed American teenagers, Halford played the court some other words he'd found when playing the record backwards. Even the deafest of legal ears could not mistake the disturbing messages therein: 'Hey look, ma, my chair's broken' and 'I asked her for a peppermint'.

'I do feel angry,' said Judas Priest guitarist KK Downing, 'when they talk about the harm our music did those kids – I think it was the best thing they had.' It is not necessary to have enjoyed Judas Priest playing 'Exciter' live, or to have kept a tour programme with a pop-up motorbike in it, to get to grips with the ways in which this statement might be true. There is a book which might be helpful, though. It's called *Running With the Devil*, and it's not so much a rusty bath in its field as a well-constructed barn wherein all future wanderers are advised to lay their bedding rolls.

Author Robert Walser – a professor of music at Dartmouth College who spends his spare time playing in metal bands and making five-page transcriptions of Randy Rhoads guitar solos – makes a series of visionary insights into the apparent contradiction between heavy metal's show of outward force and its fanbase's vulnerable social reality. And this is only the beginning of a new understanding of this most reviled form of musical endeavour which ultimately traces a direct lineage to the blues of the Mississipi Delta.

The relationship between heavy metal and the black musical seams from which its original inspiration was mined is a complex and controversial one, most commonly characterised as travesty. Consider the appalling (or if you're in a sick mood, kind of funny) moment in *Back To The Future* when Michael J. Fox's aimiable suburban teenage metal fan goes back in time and teaches Chuck Berry's cousins how to play rock 'n' roll. (Chuck Berry of all people! The man whose storytelling genius and eye for the main chance would be written out of more rock 'n' roll histories than Elvis has had impersonators!!)

And yet, as Walser suggests, to exclude the blues from the origins of heavy metal is no less insulting than starting a history of North America with the arrival of the Europeans. It's not just a question of, say, Black Sabbath's occult leanings sharing some kind of common ancestry with Robert Johnson's Faustian contract or Howlin Wolf's electrifying 'Evil (Is Going On)'. The traditional critical belief system which views metal as a perverted, racist and horribly over-amplified corruption of the blues' primal innocence is based on a fundamental – and in itself profoundly patronising – misconception.

To find out what this is, it is necessary to go back to the History of the Blues. Frances Davis' book of the same title takes as its starting point the fact 'that only nine years separated Geronimo's surrender from Edison's invention of the phonograph, and the record player came first' and moves on from this and companion insights into the development of the camera, food preservation and cotton-picking technologies, to argue convincingly that far from being the last 'pure' folk art, untainted by science and commerce, the blues was actually the form of entertainment whose development most closely paralleled the emergence of a mass culture.

'We like to imagine that we can "hear" the blues in these photographs,' Davis asserts, considering the precious few remaining pictures of the early blues giants, 'just as we like to imagine that we can "hear" in the oldest country blues the blisters and stooped backs of the men and women singing them,' before going on to remind us (and himself) that 'though the blues had evolved from the shouts and chants of men and women at work in the fields, it was the goal of most blues performers to stay as far away from that sort of work as possible.'

The first jazz and bluesmen and women whose stories are now the stuff of myth were social outcasts as much as they were heroes, as prone to disfavour with the forces of law and order as the gangster rappers or gay heavy metal singers of three-quarters of a century later. Their exploits would be the template for all future musicianly endeavour – black or white –[65] and it is not unreasonable to suggest that in their shared pursuit of better living through showbusiness, Axl Rose and Leadbelly might have more in common than has generally been supposed.

In his book *The Black Culture Industry*, Ellis Cashmore describes the notion of an unbroken continuum stretching from rap back through soul and blues to the negro spiritual – the vision of black music enshrined in quotes like the one with which this chapter begins – as a 'melodramatic construction'. (Then again Socialism, Islam, and the marriage of David and Victoria Beckham might all be described in the same way, and that doesn't mean either that they don't exist or that people should not believe in them.)

Eloquently critical of those who regard all black music as embodying an essential Africanness, Cashmore's position is founded on a series of seeming disjunctions – from the whiteness of the Stax bands who backed soul legends Otis Redding and Aretha Franklin, to the key role played by non-black entrepreneurs such as Atlantic Records' Ahmet Ertegun and Def Jam's Rick Rubin in constructing the radical pro-black images of Ruth Brown or Public Enemy. The fact is that to anyone with more than a passing interest in pop history, such intersections are the rule rather than the exception.

This is not to deny the appalling heritage of racial discrimination and unfairness which shadows – and at some points actively drives – the evolution of pop. Quite the opposite. But in casting doubt on the whole authenticist tradition of music appreciation, Cashmore's book opens up an intriguing Pandora's Box. What do people actually mean when they say that white people can't rap or have soul or sing the blues? Cashmore argues that in attributing to black artists a depth of emotion not accessible to whites, they perpetrate an animalisation not dissimilar to those favoured by self-justifying nineteenth-century colonialists.

So where does this leave the traditional view of heavy metal as blues desecration? One of the most eloquent statements of this position is made by Charles Shaar Murray in *Crosstown Traffic*. This fascinating and learned appreciation of the genius of Jimi Hendrix bemoans the transition from the adult swagger of Muddy Waters' 'I'm A Man' – the Chicago blues giant 'defining his manhood against whites who would seek to rob him of it' – to adenoidal proto-metal cover versions by Manfred Mann or The Yardbirds: 'a bunch of young boys laying claim to an adulthood to which they were less than absolutely certain that they were entitled'.

Now the first of these underlying motivations is certainly grander and more implicitly heroic than the second, but that doesn't mean that the second has no human value. While appreciating that 'the ultimate import of a blues, soul or gospel tune is as likely as not communicated as much through the nuances of rhythmic emphasis or vocal tone and melisma as the overt content of a lyric', Murray refuses to extend the same courtesy to metal.

And yet if r'n'b lyrics could use love and dancing as 'codes for singing about virtually every subject under the sun' why should the same not be true of heavy metal's concern with the number of the beast or the mutating effects of atomic leakage? Just as the thrilling precision of James Brown's Famous Flames or the Stax/Volt soul revue paid implicit tribute to a proud tradition of self-discipline and collective effort, so the awesome crunch of Black Sabbath or Metallica might be heard as a deafening Last Post for the demise of a manufacturing base.

The worlds of hidden experience contained in an exquisite live rendition of Smokey Robinson's 'The Tracks Of My Tears' are plainly very different to those encoded in the disturbing ritual of Angus Young's mid-show strip (the sight of a man in his mid-forties slowly removing his school uniform will certainly disabuse anyone of the notion that there is no place in heavy metal for sexual confusion) but both take place on the same stage, and both offer those present a glimpse of something beyond themselves. (Though, admittedly, in AC/DC's case, most people are going to want things to stay that way.)

It's just before Christmas 1987 at the Leeds Queens Hall (a glorified bus station in the pictureseque Swinegate area) and an all day speed-metal show headlined by Megadeth and Overkill is in full swing. There are about four women and absolutely no black people in the audience, and at points it is hard to avoid the conclusion that just this once, the women and the black people are getting the better side of the bargain. Nuclear Assault ('this is a song called "Radiation Sickness"') are quite fun, though. And the overall effect of the seven-band bill is not dissimilar to being shut in one of those huge laundrette dryers while someone dries a boulder. But in a good way.

Five years later, Kiss are unmasking themselves at Wembley Arena. The curtain draws back to reveal a giant papier mâché sphinx. Its huge jaw slowly drops – mirroring the faces of a delighted crowd, loyally resisting the temptation to shout 'put the masks back on'. Out of its mouth come forth Kiss; arms aloft, perms teased to perfection, a riot of studded gauntlets and straining trousers. In the course of the evening to come, green lasers will shine out of the sphinx's eyes and mouth, mighty jets of flame will singe the front row's eyebrows and Gene Simmons will breathe fire with the aid of a trick sword.

But before these things can happen, the cameras must be satisfied. For the first three numbers Kiss focus all their attention on the photographers in the pit, taking audible requests as to which outrageous pose they should strike next. Later on, at the end of 'Detroit Rock City', a roadie rushes out with a suspiciously inexpensive-looking change of guitar, which Paul Stanley smashes and hurls into the crowd. Well, it would have been a shame to waste a real one.

Next to the truly incendiary spectacle of Jimi Hendrix putting a match to his axe at the Monterey Pop festival, Kiss' laughable but profoundly entertaining charade would seem to epitomise what Jay Allison Lewis (referring to early white jazz musicians) characterised as 'capturing the glow from the fire, but never the fire itself'. Sometimes though, the glow from the fire is all you actually want.

At the end of *Crosstown Traffic*, Charles Shaar Murray bridles at finding a Jimi Hendrix album in the heavy metal rack. But surely it was strangely appropriate that a career devoted to systematically expanding the confines of what a black performer was allowed to be (gleefully subverting, as Murray shrewdly notes 'both the black codes in which he was schooled and the British invasion which had adapted those codes for its own') should culminate in storage between Accept and ZZ Top?

If you appreciate that Hendrix's work is actually the fulcrum upon which the blues–metal see-saw is balanced, it becomes easier to see the latter form not so much as a mutant outgrowth of the former – like an ear grown off a mouse's back in some awful genetic experiment – but as an animating spirit, inspiring the inheritors of Jimi's presiding genius: i.e., everyone from Queen to Run DMC to Sonny Sharrock to Joy Division to Mogwai.

The Mogwai Sanitary Protection Incident

'Heavy Metal fans are scum,' says outspoken Mogwai guitarist Stuart Braithwaite, reflecting on the joy of a trip to Donnington Park *Ozzfest* in 1998.

'That,' objects lanky bass-player Dominic Aitchison 'is a really sweeping statement.'

It's one thing to identify with metal's erstwhile reprobate status, another to project society's disapproval on to its entire support base.

'But there's a difference between being a fan of metal and a metal fan,' insists Braithwaite unconvincingly. 'They'll like Slayer, which is fair enough, but then they'll like Queensryche as well: there's no quality control.' Aware that his diatribe is losing focus, he lashes out at random: 'And I hate people who dress heavy but don't sound heavy . . .'

Mogwai themselves sound heavy but don't dress heavy[66]. Where a few years previously it would have been unthinkable for a band from Glasgow's indie heartland to join in Metal's communion to the extent that they have (albeit leavening the wafer of machine-tooled overkill with the yeast of ambient tranquility), in the late nineties it is hardly even a topic for discussion. What does need to be addressed is the possibility that Mogwai might have lapsed into the kind of appalling decadence for which a previous generation's metal warriors were justly notorious.

'The Mogwai Sanitary Protection Incident' is one of those stories which follow bands around – like Led Zeppelin and the fish or 911 and the pact with Beelzebub – getting repeated in various forms in everything that's written about them. The King James version unfolds along the following lines: trapped in a European tour environment where alcohol was hard to come by, Mogwai briefly soaked tampons in vodka and inserted them into their rectal cavities in order to facilitate the swift and efficient entry of the small available stock of alcohol into their bloodstreams.

'Its terrible,' says Aitchison. 'I can't ever let my mum read anything written about us, because that story always crops up.'

'Sometimes they say it happened in Poland,' is the worldly-wise Braithwaite's more practical objection, 'which would be ridiculous, because alcohol is really cheap there – it only makes sense in Scandinavia.'

In the interests of Dominic's mum's peace of mind, Mogwai would like to put it on record that they never did this strange and deviant deed, merely referred to the practice in an innocent conversation with a journalist, whose own alleged drunkenness caused him to misremember it with the band as participants rather than narrators. They told the story in tandem with another – even more gruesome – about shaven-domed Russian ravers splitting their heads open with razors, covering the wound with masking tape, then putting woolly hats over the top so that when they sweat on the dancefloor the glue goes straight into their brains.

Mogwai would like it to be known that they have never done this either. Even though some of their more brutal music – the giant dinosaur grunt guitar in 'Like Herod' for example, or the mighty vortex of 'Mogwai Fear Satan' – could be said to offer a similar level of cerebral disorientation with a less explicit risk of agonising death. Named after the endearing creature in *Gremlins* which became demonic on contact with water, Mogwai essay a similar blend of impish mischief and sheer destructive potential. Other band's drummers use the rhythmic water-wings known as click-tracks. Their drummer has an actual pacemaker.

From an early London gig, in September 1996 at the Monarch (a horrible little room, like watching a band play inside a kidney) to January 1999's triumphant sold-out appearance in the wide open spaces of the London Astoria, it's the unexpected intensity of their music that sets Mogwai apart from their peers. Their sound is largely instrumental, with moments of exquisite delicacy alternating with huge swathes of noise, to create an overall effect that is simultaneously beautiful and daunting – like walking underwater through a school of whales.

'We were never a muckabout band right from the beginning,' insists the diminutive but abundantly charismatic Braithwaite, 'we always had a serious intent to rock . . . we blew up an amp at our first practice!' The healing power of noise is one thing all four of Mogwai are firmly agreed upon. 'The thing about noise is it confuses your brain,' Stuart continues, 'so if tunes are hidden in it, that makes them more rewarding. There are a lot of bands tighter or more technically proficient than us that don't get the same kind of reaction.'

The tingle which runs through a Mogwai audience in the opening moments of a song people recognise is more than a ripple, it's a susurration. This collective expression of pleasure is more reminiscent of a club than a gig. Only the feeling in the crowd as Underworld launch into 'Born Slippy' live comes close to it, but even that generation-delineating anthem has words for people to latch on to. To elicit the kind of emotional response Mogwai do with music that – excepting the occasional taped spoken word interlude, one guest vocal turn from Arab Strap's Aidan Moffat, and the title track of their album *Come On Die Young*, on which Stuart makes a suitably adenoidal singing debut – has no truck with the human voice, is a considerable achievement.

'In two or three years, we'll be a much better band than we are now,' Braithwaite insists. Concerned about technical shortcomings, Stuart wants to learn to play the guitar moving more of the fingers on his strumming hand. 'I want to bring in all five', he insists. Mogwai once asked a member of Chemikal Underground label-mates The Delgados how many fingers he used. 'He said, "Five." We said, "Really?" He said, "Aye."' Stuart impersonates strumming an invisible guitar with whole hand rather than the delicate finger-picking his boast had implied, then bursts out laughing. 'That's scene one in the indie *Spinal Tap*.'

Six Landmarks of NWOBHM

Def Leppard's *Rocks Off* EP Released on their own Bludgeon Riffola records and featuring the blueprint of the immortal 'Wasted' – the best Manic Street Preachers song the New York Dolls never wrote – this paved the way for a marvellously speedy swap of Sheffield grit for stadium swirl.

Saxon's '747 Strangers In The Night' Biff Byford's Bradford tea-drinkers attained an unfeasible level of popularity after several years of hard slog under the unfortunate name of Son Of A Bitch. This pop metal classic would be notable for coming out on Eurodisco label Carrere, even if it didn't contain the immortal words 'For God's sake get those groundlights on'.

FIST's 'Name Rank and Serial Number' These punky tynesiders threatened a north-eastern NWOBHM takeover but in time-honoured sixties–seventies punk fashion they were only allowed one moment of glory, and this rapid fire proto-Minor Threat epic was it.

Sledgehammer's 'Sledgehammer' Despite auspicious origins – hailing from a satellite town of Slough and playing early gigs supporting Motorhead – the irresistible chorus of Sledgehammer's eponymous debut single ('It hit me like a sledgehammer!') would be their only legacy.

Diamond Head's 'Helpless' This inspiring footnote in the musical history of Stourbridge sounds even better with hindsight. Diamond Head were NWOBHM's born stars but they cooked their own goose by being too femme-glamorous (and by taking the name from an obscure sixties melodrama starring Charlton Heston).

Molly Hatchet's 'Flirtin' With Disaster' The Hatchet were not British and certainly not new wave, but their jaunty self assurance showed up the angst of Anglo-metallers in sharp relief. This is a great piece of overheated southern boogie, sort of ZZ Top on Pro Plus.

Six Metal Evangelists

Geoff Barton The Godfather of NWOBHM; when the movement became too big for *Sounds* he gave it the home which would ultimately be its grave by founding *Kerrang* magazine, which survives weekly to this day as a landmark in onomatopoeic publishing.

Bill Laswell Not just for producing Motorhead's *Orgasmatron* but also for his own work with Last Exit, bringing the heaviest of metal's pleasures to an audience which might otherwise have thought itself too good for them.

Rick Rubin He must share some of the blame for The Cult but how much less chromed and lustrous would prime time Def Jam, especially The Beasties' *Licensed To III* have been without his metallic promptings?

Tipper Gore The witchhunting queen of the PMRC censorship lobby with a name culled from Ozzy Osbourne's worst nightmare. With enemies like this who needs friends?

Lemmy Heroically taking it upon himself to embody some of Metal's less savoury aspects – among them incipient Toryism and a fondness for the novels of Sven Hassell – Lemmy somehow managed to remain a ceaselessly urbane individual whose music is a clarion call for worldwide anarchy.

Tommy Vance Those honeyed tones announcing the coming attractions on Radio 1's Friday Rock Show over a real Greek yoghurt of a bass riff put Mr Vance on as magically close terms with his target audience as John Peel or Mike Allen's pioneering electro showcase on Capital Radio.

Six of the Best From Tankard

Tankard are an unjustly obscure and intensely likeable lumpen thrash quintet from Frankfurt who, judging by the picture on their 1991 greatest hits album rise to the impossible challenge of making Uriah Heep look sexy. With these six texts they anticipate and confront the cultural bewilderment of post-unification Germany with fearsone clarity.

'The Morning After' 'Lying in my bed, with a swollen head, what did I do? . . . Oh shit!'

'Zombie Attack!' 'Oh what a boring video . . . what's that noise coming from the door? . . . Aargh!'

'Chemical Invasion' 'Stop the chemical invasion. Pollution – no thanks.'

'Tantrum' 'Tantrum! Who stold my beer? Tantrum! You must die!'

Empty Tankard' 'Empty Tankard! Empty Tankard! Empty Tankard!'

'Shit-Faced' Tankard at their most alarming. The lyrics are inaudible, but the message is clear.

(All these songs and more can be found on the compilation album *The Very Best of Tankard*, resonantly sub-titled *Hair Of The Dog.*)

Psychedelic Ear

'It's the most psychedelic experience I ever had . . . I was never a heavy psychedelics user and I certainly wasn't using them on that occasion . . . but I remember flames and water dripping out of the ends of his hands.'

Pete Townshend on going to see Jimi Hendrix play, in *Crosstown Traffic* by
Charles Shaar Murray

'The function of the brain and nervous system is in the main eliminative and not productive – each person is at each moment capable of remembering all that has ever happened to him and of perceiving everything that is happening everywhere in the universe. The function of the brain and the nervous system is to protect us from being overwhelmed and confused by this mass of largely useless and irrelevant knowledge . . .'

Aldous Huxley quotes the philosopher D.C. Broad quoting the philosopher Bergson,
in *The Doors of Perception*

The Doors of Perception, Aldous Huxley's celebrated account of his 1953 mescalin trip, not only gave The Doors their name (though Huxley's title was in itself a quote from William Blake) it also defined the parameters for future discussions of the psychedelic experience.

The idea that there was a higher level of understanding beyond our usual cognisance – what Huxley rather snootily calls the 'measly trickle of the kind of consciousness that will help us to stay alive on the surface of this particular planet' – to which chemical or other keys might give us access, was not in itself a new one. In the light of hypnosis, the monologues of Ronnie Corbett and sundry other well-documented psychogenic phenomena, the existence somewhere within all our heads of an internal vista of total recall is a matter of common sense rather than visionary speculation.

But how one might gain access to this state of omniscience – and whether it would be desirable to do so even if you could – is another question altogether. In this regard, as so often, the history of scientology has something to offer us. Russell Miller's *Bare-faced Messiah* contains a riveting account of the Californian public meeting in August 1950 where L. Ron Hubbard introduced the first 'clear' to a crowd of over six thousand people. (By applying the techniques of dianetics it was, he claimed, possible to gradually remove the blockages or 'engrams' from traumatic early episodes that cause the mind to shut down like a cerebral thermostat, up to the point where you had totally unlocked the memory banks and become 'clear'.)

L. Ron Hubbard himself had the ability to mould his unique talents and experiences into appropriately mythic shapes – such as his glamorous past lives as a racecar driver in 'Marcab' civilisation, coming back in each new incarnation to beat his own records; or even a more humdrum existence in charge of a factory making steel humanoids which he sold to 'Thetans'. Unfortunately, he had not instructed his chosen envoy to the next level in the art of such imaginative embroidery.

When Sonya Bianca – a Bostonian physics major and occasional pianist – took the stage and informed the assembled gathering that in the course of her attaining 'clear' status, dianetics 'had cured her of a painful itching in the eyebrows' consequent upon an allergy to paint, the public response was understandably muted. But when someone shouted out, 'What did you have for breakfast on October 3rd 1942?' and she was unable to answer, the crowd began to grow restive.

The same thing happens on Chris Moyles' Saturday-morning Radio 1 show, on the rare occasions when Moyles' assistant 'Comedy Dave' loses the uncanny grasp of recent pop history that enables him to identify a rapid-fire selection of mainstream chart hits from the late eighties onwards almost before their first notes have been played. The vituperation elicited by Dave's infrequent lapses into mortal fallibility is not explicable solely in terms of his boss's carefully maintained reputation for grouchiness.

There is something intoxicating about Comedy Dave when he's on song – somehow delineating Gabrielle from Des'ree and The Back-street Boys from N-Sync on the basis of an atmosphere in the studio in the nano-second before the track starts – that you could imagine a man of Moyles' self-confessed spiritual impoverishment struggling to do without. But Dave's gift is a fragile one: when he loses it, he really loses it.

Like Luke Skywalker using the force in *Star Wars* or Keanu Reeves in *The Matrix* appreciating that 'there is no spoon', its survival seems to be dependent on confidence in a higher power – Freud's 'oceanic' consciousness towards which every higher human activity from art to religion seems to direct itself. Like the extraordinary body of musical knowledge on which a great jazz improviser will draw in any moment of supposed spontaneity, Dave's apparently effortless mas-tery of his subject is the product of innumerable hours of hard study.

One of the great selling points of psychedelic – or indeed any, if you're going to get formal about the meaning of the word psychedelic in this context – drugs is that they promise more or less instant access to this higher state of consciousness, without making any reciprocal demands (other than a small financial investment, a willingness to wander the hills at dawn clutching a book about mushrooms, or the duplicity requisite in remaining friends with someone who thinks *Withnail & I* is the greatest film of all time).

There being no such thing as a free lunch – except the one the Hare Krishnas have paid for – a price will always have to be paid at some stage. And whether that price be a lifetime of snakebite flashbacks, permanent damage to the frontal lobe, an increased tolerance for the later works of The Steve Miller Band or someone having a photo of you wearing a snood, is a question merely of scale rather than substance. If psychedelia – at its most intense – offers a rope-ladder down from the sky into a tidal lagoon of pure information, the sad fates of such psychedelic visionaries as Sly Stone, Syd Barrett, Brian Wilson, Sly Stone and Roky Erikson (see below) attest to the real danger of drowning if that ladder gets whisked away.

In the midst of his pioneering mescalin trip, Aldous Huxley decided to put on some music to see how the experience was affected by it. The quote at the very start of this book – 'These voices were a bridge back to the human world' – is derived from his subsequent observations. The author was actually listening to some madrigals by Gesualdo, but it could just as easily – timeslip permitting – have been Country Joe & The Fish's *Electric Music For The Mind And Body* or 'Waterfalls' by TLC. The important thing to remember is, traffic over Huxley's bridge goes both ways.

The Cautionary Tale Of The 13th Floor Elevators

The first mad hot flush of Texas psychedelia, the Rosetta Stone in any authoritative history of jug-blowing and the answer to the age-old question of how to get from Buddy Holly to The Butthole Surfers with only one brief stop for food, water and pseudo-religious psychedelic ecstasy . . . the glorious but tragic story of The 13th Floor Elevators offers conclusive proof that while growing up on a diet of b-movies and horror comics, fundamentalist Christian hysteria and primitive hallucinogens was extremly injurious to the psychic well-being of young American men, it could also provide a lot of first-class entertainment for everyone else.

Austin, Texas; the bright, distant mid-sixties. Teenage Roky (born Roger) Erikson joins a band called The Spades. 'You're Gonna Miss Me', a single written by Erikson, is released on aptly named Zero records without a great deal of success. With the arrival of ex-Kingsman Stacey Sutherland (lead guitar), Benny Thruman (bass and electric violin, replaced before the release of their debut album by Ronnie Leathermann), John Ike Walter on drums and old sociology teacher turned psychedelic Svengali Tommy Hall (lyrics, drugs and blowing into a jug), The Spades mutate into the more happily named 13th Floor Elevators. A new version of 'You're Gonna Miss Me' is released by Austin's International Artists label and, in April 1966, becomes a national Top Sixty hit.

A taut and brutal 2 minutes and 38 seconds of neurotic white r'n'b – 'I gave you a warning but you never heeded it / How can you say you missed my loving when you never needed it?' – 'You're Gonna Miss Me' stood out from the sixties punk crowd by virtue first of the snarling intensity of Erikson's vocal but most of all thanks to a noise in the background – Hall and his magic jug – which suggested the crazed gobbling of an electric turkey.

On the sleeve of *The Psychedelic Sounds Of The 13th Floor Elevators*, the debut album which followed a couple of months later, the band's producer Lelan Rogers extended a word of thanks 'to the many DJs whom we have never met personally, but who kept asking, "What is that funny little noise on that record"?'

The Psychedelic Sounds Of . . . was a revelation, not only because it contained most of the songs – the hurtling 'Fire Engine', the mind-bending 'Reverberation (Doubt)', and the touchingly romantic 'Splash 1' – for which the band would be eternally remembered, but also as it proclaimed them as possessors of vital pharmaceutical and philo-sophical information.

'Since Aristotle', sleeve notes signed simply 'Elevators' observed sagely, 'man has organised his knowledge vertically in separate and unrelated groups.' Now at last, with with chemical assistance, it would be possible to 'resystematize all knowledge so that it would be related horizontally rather than vertically.' The new man would view the old 'in much the same way as the old man views the ape' and 'You're Gonna Miss Me' was not the classic sixties punk kiss off it seemed to be, it dealt with 'the dismissal of . . . those people who for the sake of appearances take on the superficial aspects of the quest.'

The 13th Floor Elevators might have regarded their debut album as a 'quest for pure sanity', but much of the joy of it for those fortunate enough to have elevators which stopped at other floors too was (and is) that it sounds completely deranged. On tracks like 'Through the Rhythm' – complete with tortured shouts of 'Who am I?' – 'Kingdom Of Heaven' ('the Kingdom of heaven is within you') and the deeply scary 'Monkey Island', Erikson comes across as a man wading heroically towards self-realisation through a piranha-infested halluci-nogenic mangrove. The fact that a state of higher awareness finally eluded him did not diminish the thrill of the chase, either for Erikson himself or for subsequent armchair spectators.

By the time of the band's next LP, 'Easter Everywhere', Dan Galino and Danny Thomas had replaced Leatherman and John Ike Walters on bass and drums, but this could not hobble the headlong rush of

'Levitation' or the swirling momentum of 'She Lives (In A Time Of Her Own)'. The second album was more uneven than the first. At its worst – a heinous unprovoked assault on Bob Dylan's 'It's All Over Now Baby Blue' – it was pretty awful, but at their best, The 13th Floor Elevators were true world-beaters.

'Slip Inside This House', cannily recontextualised by Primal Scream on their 1991 landmark *Screamadelica*, was an amazing eight-minute mind-meld, and 'Earthquake' – 'You pull through earth and stone, you pull through flesh and bone' – was the sound of mental as well as metal foundations shifting. When they were really humming, The 13th Floor Elevators went to some of the same strange radiocative places The Velvet Undergorund did. The difference was that The 13th Floor Elevators didn't have a map. 'You've got to open up your mind and let everything come through,' Roky had urged on 'Roller Coaster', but if you actually *did* let everything come through, life could get very hard to cope with.

While a disappointingly tame live album offered few glimpses of the psychosis for which the band have been justly celebrated (though a jaunty canter through Buddy Holly's 'I'm Gonna Love You Too' provided a welcome insight into their Texan prehistory), their rarely heard last LP *Bull Of The Woods* contains some of their strangest and most beautiful music. The introverted hymn-like tone of 'May The Circle Remain Unbroken' recalls Big Star's *SisterLovers* – another supposedly lost masterpiece which turned out not to have been as lost as all that – and wherever the horn section on 'Never Another' and 'Dr Doom' comes from, it's not earth.

By the time *Bull Of The Woods* finally came out, the band had effectively disbanded. Erikson whose impassioned advocacy of narcotic indulgence had not escaped the notice of the authorities, was caught with a small quantity of hashish. Offered the choice of prison or mental hospital, he chose the latter, and after escaping but forgetting to go on the run, was subjected to three years of Thorazine and electric shock treatment.

In the years after Roky's release, a couple of abortive reformations were attempted but most of what remained of his maverick energies were subsequently focussed (if that is the right word) on a stop-start solo career. In a horrific late twist to the Elevators saga, guitarist Stacey Sutherland was shot dead by his wife in 1978. Shortly afterwards, when the journalist Nick Kent tracked Erikson to his lair, he found him lying in a shack behind an Austin porn shop, filled with TV's and radios all tuned – at alarmingly high volume – to different channels.

Northern House Was The New Acid Soul

The ultimate inheritors of The 13th Floor Elevators' mantle of psychedelic madness would not, as Simon Reynolds perspicaciously notes in his excellent book *Energy Flash*, be the legions of earnest paisley-clad revivalists – tramping down the decades with the resigned tread of enlisted men – but the children's crusade that was hardcore, or 'ardkore, according to how you look at it. Just as the juvenile armies of the middle ages attained a crazy momentum by virtue of their lack of conventional weaponry[67], so hardcore's blend of primitive equipment, recycled kiddie TV themes, speeded-up voices and blatant drug references turned infantile regression into first-class art.

Brutal, distorted, critically-reviled (just as sixties punk had been until Lenny Kaye's *Nuggets* and Lester Bangs' inspirational nagging finally woke people up to it), the musical rump left behind when acid house moved on was a safehouse for twisted pop genius. But it wasn't just commentators who were slow to realise this, leading participants struggled too. Why else would Liam Howlett have proclaimed himself embarrassed by cheap and cheerful early Prodigy classics like 'Charly' and 'Out Of Space' when really it was 'Smack My Bitch Up' that he should have been ashamed of?

Reynolds expresses the uncharacteristically dewy-eyed hope that one day 'a future form of techno may reinvoke the ideas and attitudes of 'ardkore, in the same way that the punks of 1976 staged a partial return to the stark riffs and dynamic minimalism of sixties mod and garage punk'. Normally in books or TV programmes on VH-1 when people say, 'hopefully round about now there are four loveable mop-tops just waiting to do it all again . . .' it is a sign that they have no grasp of the true meaning of the events they have just described, but in 'ardkore's case, the music's very aura of disposability and instantaneousness make the idea that it might prove unexpectedly durable profoundly appealing.[68]

As acid house's freshly laundered undergarment has been ironed into history (with no less a static cling of generational triumphalism than punk and the sixties counter-culture before it) 'ardkore still offers a renegade wrinkle of unfulfilled potentiality.

Inside the Luton Hoo estate, the 1997 Tribal Gathering is another consumer-friendly heritage attraction. The themed tents – Equator, Amazon, Sahara, Arctic, Detroit – somehow manage to be closer together than they are at normal festivals with no loss of sonic definition, allowing revellers to tread water on a timeless wavelength with the last fifteen years of dance music history laid out before them like a delicious Masonic smorgasbord.

From techno old-stager Juan Atkins to Roni Size's future fusion debutants Reprazent. From trip-hop chancers the Sneaker Pimps to the magical mystery of the Old Skool paddock, where Roxanne Shante segues into Rakim and BMX bikers practise their ancient craft. It's like one of those absurd Virtual nightclubs made flesh. Except as night falls and blanket sales rocket, the monkeys are not virtual. They are made of real brass.

For all the Gathering's big-name live attractions – from Kraftwerk to Daft Punk – it's inside the Tropic 'ardkore nostalgia tent that the crowd are having the best time. White gloves are de rigeur and a DJ called Mark Smith – probably no relation, but it's hard to be sure – induces mass hyper-ventilation while a mad dancer waves a cutlass. If such a thing exists as a form of music that can only be appreciated with the aid of drugs, 'ardkore is surely supposed to be it, and yet half a decade after its heyday, stone-cold sober designated drivers (well, this one anyway) are still sucked instantly into its delirious hubbub.

Contemporary beat science's endless convoy of proliferating sub-genres comes seductively close to fulfilling Huxley's mescalin vision of 'a perpetual present made up of one continually changing apocalypse'. But it is a mistake to overstate the symbiotic evolution of musical and narcotic technologies. Such equations reduce artist and listener alike to the status of those circuit boxes with a million different wires sticking out of them you sometimes see Telecom engineers puzzling over at the side of the road – 'the red wire, no the blue wire'.

And it's not only the history of music that resists enclosure within tidy mechanistic paddocks, the history of drugs does too. If more evidence were needed on this count, the long strange trip which Ecstasy took would supply it.

From its invention by Russian exile Alexander Shulgin, and early enthusiastic adoption by the American therapeutic community – as Matthew Collin gleefully notes in his definitive acid house history *Altered State*, upwards of half a million capsules were distributed by US mental health care professionals before the drug was finally declared illegal there in 1985 – via gay nightclubs in Texas and New York, through the raucous reunions of loved-up Londoners who couldn't bear to come back to earth when they came home from Ibiza, to its final resting place on the front pages of the tabloids as the scourge of previously law-abiding (ahem) British suburban youth, Ecstasy's ever-expanding allure proved consistently stronger than the determination of each successive clique of aficionados to keep it to themselves.

'No one wants a sixties situation to develop,' arch-LSD evangelist Timothy Leary had observed prophetically in the early stages of MDMA experimentation, 'where sleazy characters hang around college dorms peddling pills falsely labelled XTC to lazy thrill-seekers.' Imagine his later horror at discovering that some of the people who were taking Ecstasy hadn't even been to college!

The dialogue between mass and élite cultures that runs throughout the story Collin tells so well parallels another – potentially more fraught with danger – between purity and adulteration. Of the supposed Ecstasy tablets seized by police at the Fantazia legal rave at Castle Donnington in 1992, 97 per cent were actually made of something else: vitamin pills, hay-fever capsules, paracetamol. Between the millennial dreams of those whose existences Ecstasy has energised, and the grim realities of the far smaller number the drug (or crude imitations of it) has scarred or even ended, lies a wealth of uncharted territory.

Engagingly ill at ease in a self-consciously cool Edinburgh café that one of the characters in his second book, *The Acid House*, professes to hate, Irvine Welsh discusses his fourth and, by his own admission, least well-realised book. Given its title (*Ecstasy*), its cover image (a man with very little hair holding a letter 'e' between his teeth – the publishers wanted Irvine to pose in this guise himself, but he wisely demurred), and the narcotic leitmotif of minds opened by chemical intervention, this book might be regarded as a blatant attempt to cash in on his status as the literary high priest of nineties drug culture.

The truth turns out to be quite the reverse: 'The dilemma I was trying to resolve,' Welsh says pensively, 'and I don't think I have – not successfully anyway – is, if you don't have these feelings and you get them induced chemically, do you have a right to them?'

This seems an unexpected way for him to be looking at things.

'I think it's one of the great unsung dangers of Ecstasy – and it's something I'm very interested in – the psychic damage it can do to people by giving them feelings that might not necessarily be the right ones to have.'

So the author of *Trainspotting* is calling for a drug-free society?

Welsh smiles. 'I genuinely would like for there to be absolutely no drugs at all – tobacco, alcohol, Ecstasy, cannabis, whatever we need to get us into some kind of spiritual relationship. I really would like it if we could get there without needing any of that, but I think the kind of world we live in [by this, he elucidates later, he means 'Western consumer capitalism'] makes it very difficult for that to happen.'

In 1975, around the time the Wigan Casino had its own Leah Betts-style drug death tragedy, the *Wigan Gazette* endeavoured to put its readers' minds at rest about what might be going on inside the soon-to-be legendary venue. 'Observers of the Casino scene from this newspaper describe the all-nighters as noisy, repetitive, sweaty, sexless and sometimes boring affairs. Why, people don't even dance together because of the dangers of physical damage from outflung legs and arms!'

Whoever those observers were, they seem to have been hell-bent on keeping all the fun for themselves. But the oft-remarked parallels between northern soul and acid house did not stop with the dangers of physical damage from outflung legs and arms. 'It was often implied and sometimes said openly that youngsters needed stimulants to dance all night,' Casino DJ Russ Winstanley remembered later. 'This was, of course, a sweeping generalisation and ignored the fact that young healthy people caught up in the excitiement of the music they loved needed nothing but their natural energy to get them through a sweaty six- or eight-hour all-nighter.'[69]

Interlude #1 (Catatonic): 'Do you want anything from the pharmacy?'

'Do you want anything from the pharmacy?' Mark Linkous' manager asks him, in a voice that works hard to conceal an edge of trepidation. 'No thanks,' drawls the thirty-three-year-old Virginian, smiling, and everyone breathes a sigh of relief.

After Linkous' band, Sparklehorse, had made their triumphant British debut at the Astoria Theatre in January of '96, the soft-spoken singer and songwriter opted to celebrate by mixing an unhealthy cocktail of Valium and prescription anti-depressants. He was unconscious in his hotel room for fourteen hours, and when paramedics straightened out the legs that had been trapped underneath his body, the rush of poison coursing through his bloodstream brought on a cardiac arrest that rendered Linkous technically dead.

He still walks with a limp after the accident, but on the evidence of the haunting, tender tunes which fill Sparklehorse's second album, *Good Morning Spider*, its only lasting effect has been to intensify his determination to add to the sum of beauty in the world rather than subtracting from it. A man who lives with his girlfriend on a tree farm in his home state and makes music that echoes with the swing of porch doors and the rustle of falling leaves would seem to have plenty to live for, but ask Linkous if the accident has cured him of his self-destructive tendencies, and he's still not convinced.

'I don't think it's something you're ever really cured of,' he insists.

'Once you know you can swallow something or stick something in your arm and ten seconds later you're content with the universe, it's pretty hard not to do it.'

Interlude #2 (Hydroponic): 'I Remember Every Public Enemy Show'

Chuck D: *All I have now is a memory: I remember every Public Enemy show – 1253 in all – every city, every incident . . .*
Tricky: *I smoke weed, so straight away it's gone . . .*[70]

Interlude #3 (Isotonic): 'How Long Does It Last Before It Goes Away?'

Before taking his seat, iron-pumping punk samurai Henry Rollins reaches down to pick up a vase of flowers on the hotel table and sniff the bouquet. A large gobbet of pollen lodges on his nose. The interviewer doesn't notice this in time to bring it to his attention without embarrassing him, so it remains there – hanging from his nostril like the infamous cocaine dewdrop that had to be airbrushed from Neil Young's snout in Martin Scorsese's *The Last Waltz* – until halfway through the subsequent photo session.

Rollins's ascetic lifestyle renders his limited stock of drug reminiscences a lot more entertaining than the rock-star average (though the formative acid-guzzling experiences sympathetically detailed in James Parker's unauthorised biography *Turn It On* disqualify him from the monastic lustre maintained by his old school friend, Minor Threat and Fugazi founder Ian Mackaye[71]).

'A few years ago,' Rollins remembers, 'I asked a friend if I could share his joint – I honestly wanted to try it out, to see what all those dopeheads were on about. I got stoned, I guess. My friend asked me if I was high, and I said, "Is this it? You pay hard-earned money to feel like this? How long does it last before it goes away and I can get back to real life?"'[72]

The Balance Between Everything And Nothing

In 1986 the cast of the BBC1 school soap *Grange Hill* had a hit with an anti-drugs anthem called 'Just Say No'. The authors of this infectious piece of improving pop music were playing with fire; the urge to say no being the first step along a well-travelled road to social disorder and all-round punk-rock psychosis.

From The Fugs' 'Nothing' – 'Monday nothing, Tuesday nothing . . . Friday for a change a little more nothing' – through Lou Reed's heartfelt wish that 'Heroin' would 'nullify my life', to Iggy and the Stooges' 'No Fun' ('We felt we had some kind of lyrical message to get across and we weren't really sure what it was yet,' Glen Matlock remembers of The Sex Pistols' decision to cover this song, 'but we knew "No Fun" had something to do with it') negation was the foundation stone of punk rock.

At the great moment in Julian Temple's duplicitous after-the-fact Sex Pistols documentary *The Filth & the Fury* when councillor Bernard Brook-Partridge proclaims them 'the antithesis of human kind', he is actually doing Malcolm McLaren's work for him (Partridge's later assertion that 'the whole world would be vastly improved by their total and utter non-existence' is just the icing on the cake).

In *Repossessed*, Julian Cope quotes from a letter written by Carl Jung to a certain Father Victor White, in which the maverick psychologist and philosopher recounts his response to *The Doors of Perception*. Where Huxley is ecstatic about seeing the source of all existence in a vase of flowers, Jung is appalled by the very idea. 'I should hate to see the place,' he writes, 'where the paint is made that colours the world, where the light is created that makes shine the splendour of the dawn, the lines and shapes of all form.'

An arch-hallucinophile like Cope might have been expected to bridle at such an apparently reactionary statement. Instead he pronounces himself 'open-mouthed at Carl Jung's rock 'n' roll', astutely noting that, 'Even in his denial, Jung wrote like the spoken passage on a Hank Williams song – he was a believer.'

Just as any self-respecting punk rocker was actually only affecting nihilism as a cunning smokescreen for an all-out assault on hypocrisy and inertia, so the creative drug-taker walks a thin line between letting it all in and blanking it all out. So also the history of music and drugs – from Bessie Smith's moonshine to Charlie Parker's heroin to Lester Bangs' Romilar cough mixture to the white knuckle puritanism of Minor Threat to 4 Hero's drug-free darkside 'ardkore – is about the balance between everything and nothing. Or to put it slightly less gnomically, to the well-tuned psychedelic ear, music's power to take listeners both into and out of themselves operates independently of chemical enhancement.

Political Ear

'We're the young generation, and we've got something to say.'
The Monkees: 'Hey Hey, We're the Monkees!'

'Greetings and welcome Rolling Stones . . . The revolutionary youth of the world hears your music and is inspired to ever more deadly acts.'
Oakland California, anonymously authored late sixties pre-gig flyer

1968. Paris, Chicago, London. All around the western world, rock music is the soundtrack to youthful rebellion. Just twelve months old, but still susceptible to the influence of 'Street Fighting Man', a young child reaches out of his pram in Sainsbury's in East Ham and hides two tins of baby food under the coverlet.

Revolutionary youth has been inspired to a deadly act. Politics and pop have achieved a synthesis of radical action. Needless to say the person pushing the pram[73] – apprehended on the forecourt and forced to explain their child's gesture to the store detective – does not see things this way.

To anyone not old enough to remember a time when The Rolling Stones were considered to be revolutionary figures, the very idea is absurd. Could these be the same Rolling Stones whose lead singer would one day release a solo single called 'Let's Work', which was basically Norman Tebbit's 'on your bike' speech set to music? The same Rolling Stones who have come to embody every notion of stasis and corporate co-option currently available to the politically aware pop aficionado?

Yes, they could, and a great debt is owed to Mick and Keith for teaching us a valuable lesson. Putting political faith in pop stars, like putting it in politicians, is a fool's game (though what a sad world it would be if no one ever dared to play it). Both, after all, earn their keep by supplying sounds that people want to hear. Politicians only have to be accountable every five years; pop musicians every time they bring out a record. The people no one should ever trust are music journalists, who still get paid by the word however pure the idealism they project.

The puritan left history of pop music and politics sees ideological rigour fighting a brave but ultimately doomed campaign against pop's natural fecklessness, in the vain hope of harnessing its perceived generation-uniting power. Out of this rocky soil grow both the joyless demonology of 'selling out', and the unhealthy notion that musical worth can somehow be equated with political progress achieved, both of which twisted notions institutionalise neglect of the most important business of pop, which is the giving of pleasure.

Such arguments run swiftly aground, furthermore, on the fact that the best records are often made by people – Chuck Berry, Guns 'N' Roses, NWA, Happy Mondays – with regressive opinions and unsavoury personal habits, while transparently decent and worthy human beings (mentioning no names, Johnny Clegg) tend to make appalling music. And isn't this apparently uncomfortable reality in itself what the authors of *1066 & All That* would have characterised as 'a good thing' – an affirmation of music's liberating potential, and a necessary reminder that where politics and pop are concerned, ideological intention and cultural impact are very different things?

How else to explain the fact that The Isley Brothers' politically unimpeachable anthem of hope for the world's hungry 'Harvest For The World' now serves a somewhat less utopian function as an advert for a popular carvery chain (if only they had had the audacity to change the lyrics to 'When will there be a Harvester for the world?' this sacrilege would at least have been funny)? Or that Pink Floyd's superficially reprehensible millionaire's anti-education rant 'Another Brick In The Wall pt2' was banned in apartheid South Africa after being employed as a morale-boosting anthem by protestors in the Soweto school boycotts?

Conversely, it's often when pop stars think they are at their most ruggedly individual and politically audacious that they most clearly demonstrate their unsavoury herd instincts. One example that springs to mind is the rare lapse in good taste made by Massive Attack's usually impeccably well-mannered 3-D in being rude to Fergie (who was – and is – after all, just another showbusiness professional like himself) at the MTV Europe awards in Milan in 1998. Another is the watery assault on John Prescott by Chumbawamba's Danbert Nobacon at the same year's Brits ceremony.

Surely the compromises implicit in Prescott's accession to high political office after many years of trade union activism were no more drastic than those made by Chumbawamba in signing to EMI and having a global hit with a song that boasted the revolutionary hookline 'He drinks a whiskey drink, he drinks a lager drink'? In fact, perhaps this is the nub of the matter: we hate in others what we despise in ourselves.[74]

The strange truth is that when pop stars really want to inspire political action they make right-wing gestures, not left-wing ones. Just as Eric Clapton's drunken pro-Enoch Powell burblings at the Birmingham Odeon not only showed his appropriation of black musical forms in a new and unfavourable light, but also provided the initial impetus for Rock Against Racism, so Morrissey's disreputable flag-waving antics at the first Madstock show at Finsbury Park didn't just get him bottled off the stage but gave fuel to the fire of all those, like Cornershop, who were fed up with the simpering parochialist tendency within British indie music.

If the government was to introduce payment by results for pop-motivated political radicalisation (and this seems no more implicitly ludicrous than trying to introduce it for teaching), then reactionary curmudgeons playing superannuated rockabilly would be collecting all the fat bonuses. In the light of this perplexing state of affairs, perhaps the best way forward is to follow the words of the late John F. Kennedy, and ask not what pop can do for politics, but what politics can do for pop.

'They've Got Wives'

With characteristic foresight, Elvis Presley seems to have had this whole issue pretty well nailed down three decades ago. In the course of 1970's extraordinary secret encounter with Kennedy's successor but one, Richard Millhouse Nixon, Elvis first denounced The Beatles as anti-American, and then offered his services in the fight against drug abuse and Communist brainwashing. Nixon responded with presents of a much-coveted special agent badge for Elvis, and gold key-chains for all his bodyguards. But the King was still not satisfied. He fixed the embarrassed President's gift cupboard with a steely glare and reminded him, 'They've got wives.'

As well as Elvis' special agent's badge (and the title of a Lambchop album), Nixon also gave pop music Gil Scot-Heron's 'H2Ogate Blues', in which, over a gently rambling backdrop of piano, bass and drums, the Washingtonian proto-rapper fashions perhaps the most devastating fusion of music and political invective ever realised. For all the ugliness of the corruption Scot-Heron describes, the dominant emotion conjured up by his poetic wizardry is glee – glee at naming names: 'If Nixon knew, then Agnew but Ag didn't knew enough to get out of jail' – glee at furnishing the justice that society was itself unwilling or unable to administer.

This last is probably the key to all pop's most inspiring moments of explicit political engagement – from Victor Jara's exquisite Chilean agit-paeans to the Sex Pistols playing a Christmas party for the families of striking firemen in Huddersfield. If pop music is really, as Brian Eno has contended, about 'inventing imaginary worlds and inviting people to live in them', what happens at the point where those imaginary worlds intersect with the real one? And how do pop's new models of social and political organisation reflect the make-up of those to which they supposedly provide an alternative?

On 7 June, 1977, a south London new-town balcony comes together for a Silver Jubilee street party – an anachronistic but touching throwback to an ideal of community and popular sovereignty which, in this place at least, has never actually existed. Still, there is cake in red paper napkins, and at least one nearly ten-year-old is delighted to receive a silver-plated commemorative coin.

Just down the River Thames, on a boat opposite the Houses of Parliament, The Sex Pistols have organised a party of their own: a bizarre and touching throw forward to an ideal of community and popular sovereignty which will not exist for all that much longer.

There is some ill-feeling amongst punk's pilgrim fathers about the fact that the bar does not serve doubles.

'They Say Jump, You Say "How High?"'

Fifteen years on, and punk nostalgia is the jubilee mug of a new generation. In front of a young and very enthusiastic Brixton Academy crowd, Zack De La Rocha – singer with upsurgent LA funk-metal quartet Rage Against The Machine – announces the location of a BNP march planned for the next day, and the likely presence there of an unsavoury Holocaust 'revisionist', who needs to be taught a history lesson. This gets such a lusty cheer from the paying public that it seems churlish to remark that De La Rocha has got the villain's name wrong.

For all their anti-establishment fury – and a degree of pissed-offness is inevitable in any group of people who read Bobby Sands' poetry out of choice – Rage Against The Machine have still to come to terms with their status as golden boys of their employers at the Sony Corporation. Does it delight or disturb them to see rows of fans wearing freshly bought £14 t-shirts bounding along obediently to the chorus 'They say jump, you say how high'? Surely if the kids are taking the band's message seriously ('Fuck you, I won't do what you tell me!'), they shouldn't be enjoying themselves quite so much.

'Do They Owe Us a Living? 'Course They Do, Course They Do'

One way around the dilemma of complicity between corporate profiteering and performers' instinctive crowd-control mechanisms is to opt out of the former system altogether. Crass, Britain's best-loved anarcho-punks, industriously set about building a utopian political community, at the same time as fashioning an unforgettable rallying cry for the workshy of the world ('Do they owe us a living? Course they do, course they do . . .').

Releases such as their heroically confrontational Falklands war protest single 'How Does It Feel To Be The Mother Of A Thousand

Dead?' wilfully eschewed all those aspects of the rock process conducive to an ovine mentality. Outside the bounds of respectable society, Crass hit upon contradictions of their own between direct action and non-violence, and split up for fear of becoming what they had set out to destroy. But not before they had hatched an instant diaspora.

The malodorous leather jacket bearing the legends FLUX OF PINK INDIANS or RUDIMENTARY PENI inscribed in primordial Tipp-ex might now seem like the last but two decadal cusp's equivalent of a Billy Ray Cyrus haircut. But there was a prophetic quality to the humane primitivist battlecries of the bands Crass inspired that was entirely lacking in the music which inspired such contemporaneous fashion indulgences as the too-crisp denim jacket with the Saxon patches, Adam Ant pirate-period pantaloons, or the Duran Duran rumpled-look suit.

Listening to *A-sides* – an inspired assemblage of late seventies and early eighties singles on the Crass label – this prophetic quality shines through to almost unnerving effect. Honey Bane ('Girl on the run, attractive and so young: ruining herself coz she detests her mum'), Dirt ('Unemployment is getting too high; they'll find a solution, they'll start a fucking war!') and Captain Sensible ('From rags to riches I'm a self-made chap: I bought everything I can, but it's a load of crap'); these people had the eighties taped when the decade had barely even started. They had seen the future, and they knew it sucked.

Home Taping is Killing Record Companies ... and it's About Time

The Crass empire not only provided a rickety rope-bridge between the outer reaches of the sixties underground and the post acid-house hedonist nomad coalition (captured for posterity in the ludicrous illustration on the inside sleeve of The Prodigy's *Music for The Jilted Generation*), it also acted as a prototype for other, more enduring frontier musical enclaves.

Dutch constructivist avant-thrash collective The Ex set up on a similar basic model and thrive to this day – twenty years on from their original inception – collaborating with Palestinian and Kurdish folk musicians, free-jazz luminaries, Belgian stand-up comedians, in fact any kindred spirit who comes within hailing distance.

'He saw us playing and was amazed by it, and we saw him playing and felt the same way,' says guitarist Terrie, of The Ex's link-up with improvising cellist Tom Cora (the resulting joint album *Scrabbling at the Lock* was one of both parties' most exciting recordings). 'He knows all the theoretical background to music and we know nothing,' Terrie admits smilingly. 'In the beginning, he was quite shocked that I didn't even know which string I was using – he would have to say "second string, third fret", but in the end we made a good basis for him, because when we play together there are four of us, but we are like one person.'

Best experienced live, where the intensity of their playing sweeps the listener up and along with the same exhilarating momentum that drives the band, The Ex formed in response to punk, or more accurately post-punk – The Gang of Four's scratchy agit-prop, the DIY folk didacticism of The Mekons, and Wire's alien musical rigour being their most obvious influences. But their sound is distinctly their own, as is the moral scrupulousness which sustains it. Many bands profess a distaste for rock 'n' roll's traditional ego frippery, but few go so far as to insist that all names on gig posters should be printed the same size.

The Ex's political idealism was a natural outgrowth from the Amsterdam squat scene that was their initial launchpad. 'People were always busy putting out information and we were always doing music,' Terrie remembers, 'so it seemed natural to put the two together.' This band have always understood how nice it is for the consumer to get something for nothing, as the complete archive photo history of the CNT union's role in the Spanish Civil War which accompanied their legendary *1936* double-pack single, demonstrated to lustrous effect.[75]

Their music might not accord with everyone's definition of popular, but its pleasures are still pop's. The sense of fun which seems to run through everything The Ex do – from the poster campaign in which a grimacing executive shows his empty pockets, accompanied by the slogan 'Home taping is killing record companies, and it's about time', to the invocation 'Have a nice listen', which accompanies even their sternest and most forbidding package – is all the more infectious for its unexpectedness. And any band who can release a set of six singles in a dinky carrier bag decorated with an unflattering picture of the Mayor of Amsterdam and the legend 'This is an Amsterdam scumbag', can at the very least be credited with retuning pop's consumerist mindset.

Pop So Loved The World . . .

The link between The Ex's northern European agit-juggernaut and the shiny new British pop of the early eighties might not be apparent at first glance, but both had learned one of the chief lessons of punk. For all their apparently apolitical demeanour, groups like ABC, Soft Cell and The Human League shared with The Ex an appreciation of just how much space it was possible to annex for your imagination if only you had the energy and the will. This was a vision of expanded pop possibility that seemed – in the mainstream at least – to die with Live Aid.

On that fateful night in 1985, the upstairs room of a Chalk Farm pub was responding with such enthusiasm to the racket made by Lancastrian noise refuseniks The Membranes, that the landlady came upstairs and warned that the ceiling was in danger of collapse. Almost as one, the crowd lay down on the floor and danced by waving its legs in the air.

The contrast between this spectacle and the one being played out on the world's TV screens needs a bit of thinking about. On the one hand there must be a certain warped sense of righteousness about opting out of any global ceremony of compassion in which Phil Collins is involved[76]. On the other, it would be crazy to pretend that such aesthetically motivated self-interest does not have a downside.

In his book *The Recording Angel*, Evan Eisenberg writes of the music lover refusing to be a social unit – 'or any other kind of unit besides a listening, enjoying unit that thinks its own thoughts and maps its own emotions' – as if to do this were to make some kind of political statement. As valid a part of pop's joy-giving armoury as such declarations of self-imposed alienation are, it would be wrong to pretend they are acts without social cost. If you ignore a homeless person asking for money because a favourite song is playing on your Walkman, it doesn't actually make any difference to them what you're listening to.

Perhaps it wasn't so uncharacteristic when you think about it, that at a time when in both Britain and America, notions of social consensus – indeed the very idea of society itself – were being dismantled from above, pop music should forgo its status as the ultimate form of escapism to fashion for itself a new image as a community of caring. Even in retrospect, there is something quite irresistible about the idea of world leaders being held over a barrel by the moral rigour of the man who gave the world 'I Don't Like Mondays'.

The tentacles of capitalist career advancement and album repromotion might have – at the very least – crept around the edges of events such as Live Aid, Farm Aid, and the Nelson Mandela tribute, but for all their implicit contradictions, these spectacles still kept alive the unfashionable flames of philanthropy and political engagement at a time when dark governmental forces were striving to extinguish them. A lot of the music might have been pretty dreadful, but even that makes a strange kind of sense if you look at the whole thing as a sort of holy sacrifice – pop so loved the world that it gave its only song . . .

'As Michael and Lionel Have Shown Us, The World is Just TV. If Children are Starving, Let Them Drink Pepsi'

The above couplet comes from Culturcide's answer record to USA for Africa's 'We Are The World', sung to the same tune and entitled, with irrefutable directness 'They're Not The World'. It is all right to quote the lyrics at some length ('They're not the world, they're not the children, they're just bosses and bureaucrats and rock 'n' roll has-beens') because Culturcide came from Texas, and copyright meant nothing to them.

Their classic 1987 album *Tacky Souvenirs of Pre-Revolutionary America* was built on the simple and yet brilliant idea of shouting their own ideas (and adding the occasional horrible squealing noise) over the words of the most anodyne popular songs they could lay their hands on[77]. This technique would later be put to gruesomely effective use by Puff Daddy, but in Culturcide's rough and ready hands it made for an intriguing statement about the political subtexts inherent in sampling.

Hip-hop and House Unite and Fight

In the wake of 'Cop Killer' and other censorship controversies, US rappers would later come to portray themselves – with a fair degree of legitimacy – as engaging directly with the state. Ice T's 'Message to the Soldier' articulated a vision of himself as outlaw hero stepping into the breach left by the destruction of US black political leadership ('They killed King and they shot X: now they want me') whose broad appeal said more about the void left by that destruction than it did about anything else.

The idea of any consituency being reduced to looking to the 2 Live Crew for inspiration is profoundly disturbing, and the vaudeville bloodline that runs through even rap's (or any other kind of music's come to that) most avowedly radical moments is too strong to be ignored. Grandmaster Flash's 'The Message' – that benchmark of authentic social realism so beloved of politically-minded rap fans – was actually the work of lyricist Duke Bootee. Sugarhill boss Sylvia Robinson put Grandmaster Flash's name on it even though the Grandmaster himself didn't actually appear on the record, because she thought (correctly as it turned out) that it would sell better that way.

At the other end of the dancefloor, it's an apolitical gloss that is deceptive. While much has traditionally been made of the politically disengaged nature of acid house's Ecstasy-heightened hedonism, the British Establishment would hardly have mobilised such a weight of resources against nomad soundsystems like Spiral Tribe if they had seen things that way.

And yet neither is this one of those simplistic sagas of state power and cultural resistance so beloved of bearded historians. As Matthew Collin's *Altered States* makes intriguingly clear, the late eighties' unprecedented outbreak of mass communal pleasure-seeking was equally a reaction to and a development of the dominant political ideas of the Thatcher era. 'Echoing its ethos of choice and market freedom,' is the way Collin puts it, 'yet expressing desires for a collective experience that Thatcherism rejected and consumerism could not provide.'

Acid house's original soundtrack – the house and techno sounds of Chicago and Detroit – were made by unlicensed adaptations of the same new technology which had destroyed those American cities' industrial futures. Similarly, the rogue entrepreneurs who delivered the music and its chemical accoutrements to an eager new British audience were adapting the libertarian capitalism that had laid waste to their environment to uses its authors would never have dreamt of.

This logic of appropriation spun off in all sorts of unexpected directions – from party organisers putting the newly privatised British Telecom's brand new voicebank system to good use outwitting the police, to consumptive ravers enhancing their sense of physical disorientation via liberal applications of menthol rub.

'Stop Eating Cheese! Milk is for Little Cows not Human Beings.'

At a brief and already almost forgotten juncture at the start of the last decade, an Anglo-American musical generation weaned on MTV and right-wing governments briefly burst into political life – churning out manifestos and dogmas like there was no tomorrow.

If this new politicisation had a single point of origin, it was probably in the raucous fun-filled polemics of Washingtonian youth propagandists and gangster ideologues The Nation of Ulysses, whose 1991 debut *13-point Programme to Destroy America* was the perfect showcase for a new style of Maoist consumer fetishism – fast and funny and illuminated by flashes of amusingly random ideological rigour, inveigling against the moral evils of earbuds and toothpaste

('Do not wipe the taste of the day away with the false and foreign taste of mint').

A year after this auspicious debut, The Nation of Ulysses released a disappointing follow-up about how attractive they were to women, and then split up, but a vital seed had still been planted.

Rock had been pressed into so many causes – being For Jobs and the Vote and Against Racism and the Rich – that the idea of unifying it behind any single goal, however worthy, had rather lost its novelty. One of the most liberating long-term legacies of RAR was the way it broke up rock's bogus boy monolith – it *wasn't* just rock against racism, it was reggae and pop and punk and jazz, all standing more or less together – and consequently there was a whiff of nostalgic machismo about subesquent attempts to revitalise it.

From pioneering baseball cap, turban and intifada-headscarf-wearing Bradford hip-hop trouple Fun-Da-Mental's 'United Colours of Frustration' tour – a bold if doomed attempt to double dare Benetton's co-option of radical rhetoric into advertising – to the Riot Grrrl ideal of an underground network embodying furious rejection of sexual oppression (albeit one eventually filtered through the masturbatory fantasies of ageing male rock journalists), new visions of political engagement battled to connect with the times.

Inspired by the mood of the moment, *Dirty* – Sonic Youth's election year protest album – forsook their usual self-indulgent lyrical miasma to make a series of unusually forthright political statements. 'Youth Against Fascism' paid unexpectedly sincere tribute to those who bang cans outside the White House in free-form protest while 'Swimsuit Issue' dealt with sexual harassment in the wake of the Clarence Thomas hearings. Thurston Moore's notes say simply: 'We believe Anita Hill', and the song itself snarls 'Don't touch my breast; I'm just working at my desk'.

There was something uplifting about the idea of an American underground generation which had previously looked to Charles Manson for political leadership finding idealistic redemption in the twilight of its years[78]. Unfortunately, it was too good to last. As if alarmed by the new momentum generated by these uncharacteristic shows of political commitment – 'Self-Fulfillment' and 'Sugar Kane' were (and are) some of the best things the band ever did – Sonic

Youth crept back into their shells and have not (at the time of writing) made a decent record since.

For the last word on the millennial radicalism of the early nineteen nineties though, you have to go to Consolidated. In 1992, this high-minded San Franciscan white rap act from the left fringe of the American industrial and hardcore heartland put out an unforgettable live album, supplementing the band's usual impassioned assaults on US gun culture, homophobia and the global fishing industry with selections from their justly notorious open microphone sessions, in which members of the audience either complain about not being allowed to slamdance, or strive to outdo the band in the purity of their ideals and the ferocity of their ideological rigour.

This bold democratic experiment throws up some genuinely subversive ideas. One dangerous individual questions the political propriety of Consolidated's very existence: 'Industrial music is Fascism, come on guys.' Another issues the revolutionary vegan rallying cry: 'Stop eating cheese! Milk is for little cows, not human beings.'

A Manic Street Preachers Odyssey in Four Parts

A. 'Understand We Can Never Belong/Throw Some Acid on the Mona Lisa's Face.'

The London Astoria in 1992. Dressed from a garage sale at the New York Dolls' house, Nicky and Richey pose ineffectually either side of the drumkit. All those who hoped that if they ignored The Manic Street Preachers for long enough they might just go away are obliged to think again.

As with Kylie Minogue post 'Better the Devil', there is something infectiously debased about their desperation to prove themselves. Richey needing seventeen stitches after scratching '4-Real' on his forearm with a razor blade to impress a sceptical *NME* journalist was bad enough, but this band's self-laceration is not just skin-deep. Always the first to acknowledge what sad characters they seem, they implore you to deny the culture of consumption while at the same time purchasing their iconography wholesale from Athena.

Admittedly 'Motorcycle Emptiness' does have quite a good tune, but the Manics' playground nihilism seems like an extension of post-Thatcherite degradation, not a reaction to it. Momentarily tiring of hopping foolishly round the stage, flexing his white drainpiped legs in an assortment of undignified stretching exercises, Nicky attacks a photographer who he deems to be infringing his personal space. Fortunately, his efforts to bring down his guitar on the innocent man's head are about as focussed and successful as his and Richey's attempts ('Understand we can never belong/Throw some acid on the Mona Lisa's face') at writing political lyrics.

B. A Riot of Your Own

It's getting on for 11.30 p.m. in the lobby of a medium-sized Bayswater hotel. The mood is one of mild consternation. Down the road in Hammersmith, trouble has flared outside Le Palais as demand for tickets to the Champions in Action ragga show has vastly exceeded supply. Upstairs, Tiger (the night's main attraction), is without his stage clothes. The suit-man called round earlier in the evening but neglected to drop off the requisite finery. Tiger, left frantically ironing his own shirts, is said to be 'vexed'.

His fellow Champions – Sanchez, Daddy Screw and fresh-faced 18-year-old Terror Fabulous – have suffered no such sartorial mishap, and emerge in their full-suited splendour. Two efficient women with mobile phones usher the four of them into a small convoy of cars, which are driven at high velocity over a speed-bumpy back route to a Hammersmith Broadway that temporarily resembles the Gaza Strip. There, a dreadlocked figure guides them through police-lines and into the back of the venue through crowds of disgruntled would-be punters.

Inside, the steam hits you square in the face. The show has been mightily oversold. The crowd is standing on tables and hanging off the walls. Everyone is dressed up well beyond the nines – to the elevens, the twelves even – in taffeta, sequins, wedding dresses, and diaphonous body-suits. The atmosphere, given the conditions, is remarkably peaceable. If you had Tory MPs in these conditions, there would undoubtedly be a riot.

Daddy Screw is propelled on to the stage with indecent haste. A gentlemanly presence, for all his lascivious dancing, he appears slightly intimidated by the warmth of his reception. The front ten or fifteen rows are composed entirely of voracious females whose intentions towards Daddy are not what the Victorians would have called honourable. When a dancer emerges to bump and grind formulaically with him the music is all but drowned out by the loud sucking of teeth. Terror Fabulous follows, bouncing words and nursery rhyme chants around the wiry rhythms of backing band Ruff Cut with considerable deftness. The two come back on together, hurling armfuls of roses into the seething front ranks.

The violence for which this evening will later be remembered does not 'erupt'. By the time people notice it, it's over. Many don't even hear the shots which leave two people injured; they just see large spaces appear in the crowd where none seemed possible before.

Sanchez, an old-fashioned crooner with a formidable MOR armoury, does a fine job of sweetening the atmosphere after the first of these incidents. The promoter ticks off the troublemakers in a schoolmasterly fashion – 'I want to apologise on their behalf, because they're too stupid to do it themselves.' Woefully underdressed in an emergency plaid waistcoat, Tiger does his best to roar, but his thunder has been stolen. Given his previous utterances on the subject of gun-play (his new single is called 'Nobody Move'), it is hard feel too sorry for him.

Walking home up the Shepherd's Bush road accompanied by an escort of police dogs, it is harder than ever to be impressed by those – The Manic Street Preachers, for example – whose understanding of violence seems to end with the hackneyed recycling of old Clash rhetoric.

C. Sartori in Milton Keynes

Sometimes rock's communal dream comes true, but rarely in the way you'd expect. On the second of Bon Jovi's two nights at the Milton Keynes National Bowl[79] in 1993, gangs of those who can't or won't pay twenty pounds to get in are gathered outside the venue. Some have beer, some have food. All you can see is the searchlights dancing over the hill, but the music sounds fine – for some reason even more emotively Springsteen-esque outside the arena than in.

The best place to be is on the bridge over the ring road, where the cars rushing beneath give the songs extra impetus. Inside the bowl, Bon Jovi still succeed in fashioning a kind of intimacy out of the absurd hugeness of it all. Their every move is replayed on high resolution video walls; no matter that because of the distances involved, the vision gets to you a vital second or so before the sound, as if two songs are being played at once.

There is one magical moment when guitarist (and Cher veteran) Richie Sambora is transported to the top of a mountain in mid-solo, another during the excellent 'Dry Country' when Jon Bon Jovi takes us for a ride on the back of his motorbike. Among the neatly dressed and disconcertingly healthy-looking crowd, a renegade element stands out like the proverbial bruised digit. Sidling uneasily through the burger stalls in feather boas and t-shirts that say 'Molotov Cocktails of Fabulous Destruction', The Manic Street Preachers contingent seem puzzled by their favourite band's choice of touring partners. Their heroes are backstage, taking their 'Bad Medicine' and hurriedly scribbling down notes for an Open University degree in stadium stagecraft.

D. The Bragg/Preachers Toilet Dichotomy

In the immediate aftermath of the 1999 Glastonbury festival, an ugly war of words erupts between old school authenticist minstrel Billy Bragg and new school plastic evangelists The Manic Street Preachers over the latter ensemble's having supposedly reserved a luxurious toilet exclusively for their own use. This disagreement elegantly dramatises an ideological chasm of glacial proportions.

As much as Glastonbury's rough and ready myth has been compromised by wall-to-wall TV coverage and people staying in air-conditioned vans, the enduring horror of its defecatory outlets persists in the public nose as a throwback to its original pioneer spirit. From Bragg's perspective, the ideal of a youthful town the size of Swindon assembling in the vale of Avalon, doing basically what it wants and then dispersing a few days later with no more ill effects than the occasional acid flashback or severe gastric disorder, is severely dishonoured by the prospect of puffed-up rock stars relieving themselves in pampered seclusion.

For The Manic Street Preachers – who after all proclaimed their determination to emulate rock behemoths Guns N Roses from the outset (it just took a while for everyone to realise they meant what they said) – a shameless toilet hierarchy is another means of expressing their alienation from discredited traditions of folk and hippie protest.[80] Since what looked and sounded to uninformed observers in 1992 (well, this one anyway) like careerist nihilism was actually an honest and impassioned response to the grisly demise of traditional social and political organisation in their home community following the collapse of the miners' strike.[81]

Critics have often commented on the seeming contradiction in expressing radical political ideas while using stadium rock moves picked up from Bon Jovi, but this contradiction is the whole point, and not to embrace it is to make the same fundamental misunderstanding as socialist theoretician Walter Benjamin did in 1931 when he wrote that 'mechanical reproduction destroys the ritual value of a work of art'.[82] (What he meant to say was not 'destroys' but 'enhances'.)

As heavy metal prophet Robert Walser observes (and he also has some interesting things to say about the political significance of the chord progressions in Bon Jovi's 'Livin' On A Prayer', but that's another story), 'Mass mediation is typically assumed to be a barrier standing between the art and the audience with the power to corrupt both ... it is just as important to see how it can make available the resources with which new communities are built.' If The Manic Street Preachers' New Year's Eve 1999 show at the new Cardiff International Stadium proved anything, it was the truth of this statement.

Or to put it more simply, pop music needs sociology like a dolphin needs an electric toothbrush: one of the greatest things about it, is that it gives us a glimpse of a world where sociology is no longer necessary.

All-Seeing Ear

'I'm just plain old Mary.'

'Deep Inside' by Mary J. Blige, 1999

'When individuals come together in a group, all their inhibitions fall away, and all the cruel, brutal and destructive instincts which lie dormant as relics of a primitive epoch are stirred up to find free gratification.'

Freud's commentary on Le Bon's *Psychologie des Foules* in *Group Psychology and the Analysis of the Ego*

'Our ears,' notes composer, arranger, multi-instrumentalist and band-leader Nitin Sawhney, 'take in a far greater width of frequencies than our eyes do.'

Music has often been thought of as a portal to worlds beyond the one we can see. Anyone who has ever become one with their car while motorway driving to Rod Stewart's 'The Handbags & The Gladrags' can testify to the way that sound loosens the constraints of our individual selves, to the point where the boundaries between us and the external world seem newly fluid. But there is another way in which music opens up new vistas of understanding, both of others and of ourselves, and that is through our relationship with the performer – both with his or her personality as expressed in the performance, and with the worldview projected by its content.

The philosopher A.J. Ayer's book *The Problem of Knowledge* speaks gloomily of experiences as being 'as such . . . incommunicable': of 'people enclosed within the fortresses of their own experiences. They can observe the battlements of other fortresses but they cannot penetrate them'[83]. One of the things pop does is to lower the drawbridges of those other fortresses and invite us in. It also encourages us to enter turrets in our own fortress which might otherwise have remained unexplored.

Sometimes this happens in a very straightforward way. When Badly Drawn Boy speaks of the thrill of getting his first 12-inch single back from the pressing plant – 'I remember looking into the grooves and thinking, "That's me in there"' – or Elliott Smith says that his job is to 'sing about what it's like *being a person*', the connection that might be made between performer and listener is an obvious and direct one. But where there's more than one person involved (and sometimes even when there isn't) things can get considerably more complicated.

When Freud wrote the words quoted at the start of this chapter, or those a couple of pages earlier in *Group Psychology and the Analysis of the Ego* – 'A group is impulsive, changeable and irritable. It is led almost exclusively by the unconscious ... it cannot tolerate any delay between its desire and the fulfillment of what it desires' – no one (least of all the man himself) could have realised that it was *pop* groups he was talking about[84]. And yet the manner in which these uniquely sensual and childish social units reflect and channel the personalities of the saucy individuals who comprise them, offers a blueprint for all human interaction that is endlessly instructive. How do we learn from them? Let us count the ways[85].

1. How Individuals Express Themselves in Groups: the Collective Gospel According to New Edition and Godspeed You Black Emperor!

In 1983, a fresh-faced quintet of Boston teenagers known as New Edition had a number-one hit with a song called 'Candy Girl'. It was influenced by the Jackson Five's 'ABC' in the same way that Christian Slater's early film career was influenced by Jack Nicholson's – i.e., it suggested that the cultural tradition it had come from had completed its evolution, and that the only future which remained lay in periodic revisitation of key steps along the way.

Thirteen years later, such grim forebodings have, at least in New

Edition's case (Christian Slater is another story), proven unfounded. New Edition have supplied a bridge over hip-hop and electro from America's ancient soul and funk heritage to the thriving R'n'B vocal scene of today. They are also – albeit somewhat less obviously – the Godfathers of Britpop, because without New Edition there would have been no New Kids on the Block and without the New Kids there would have been no Take That and without Take That there would have been no teenagers interested enough in pop music to want to buy records by Blur and Oasis.

Most surprising of all – given the usual sad fates of child stars, from Michael Jackson to Musical Youth – New Edition are still in pretty good shape. Back together with a supremely slinky new top 10 single called 'Hit Me Off', they go through their paces for a record company photo session. Under the watchful eye of a huge salmon, only the day before swimming happily in a highland stream and now lying on a plate with a small bite taken out of its shoulder, they strike a series of amusingly emphatic poses. These gestures, roughly translated as 'Look at my lovely jacket' or 'Hello, I'm surfing now', are backed up by imposing displays of vocal pyrotechnics, as New Edition enliven the posturing ritual by lustily and melodiously singing along with a tape of their forthcoming album.

There are certain obvious logistical problems posed by a six-person interview. (When Bobby Brown left in 1987, in pursuit of solo enormity and – ultimately – Whitney Houston, his place was taken by Philadelphia soul singer Johnny Gill, who rather touchingly keeps his place in today's suave sextet.) Photos done, settled in a circle with matching Timberland boots on the table, New Edition thoughtfully seek to play down their overwhelming numerical advantage by introducing themselves into the tape recorder.

'Hi, my name is Johnny Gill, I'm the überest guy in the group.' 'I'm Ron Devoe' – space-age sunglasses give him a slight air of Christopher Walken in *Communion* – 'remember my voice.' 'This is Bobby Brown, [warmly] peace to all the players and the macks.' A short pause, then the quiet one in the dazzling Moschino sweater: 'Ralph Tresvant . . . What's up?' Opposite him, the man who is having an unspecified difficulty with his trouser-fly: 'This is Rick Bell – [distractedly] Ricky Rick Ricky.' And what would Michael Bivins (the business-like-looking one with the glasses) say if he hadn't just gone to have a word with the video director? Bobby Brown – who has already shown his star quality in the photographer's studio by rolling up his left trouser leg to make himself look like a pirate – impersonates Bivins' guttural Butthead-type laugh to widespread amusement.

1978, Boston's Orchard Park projects. Taken on by manager Maurice Starr after coming second in a talent contest (history does not record what happens to the winners), New Edition began to work their way painstakingly up the showbusiness ladder. Ron remembers 'being out on the road doing three or four shows a night and then getting dropped off back in the projects with $10 after being on tour for a year'.

Bobby grimaces: 'Having a contract with Streetwise Records where the only thing that they gave you for royalties was a VCR . . . in fact, it wasn't even a VCR' – he is triumphantly indignant now – 'it was a Betamax.'

Michael (shaking his head in quiet disbelief): 'It had one of those little remote-control cords that connected to the machine.'

Of the 1996 New Edition album *Home Again*, Bobby observes: 'We feel we created a masterpiece.' And collective *joie de vivre* expresses itself in a hilariously self-lacerating impromptu rendition of 'Candy Girl', complete with shaky-voiced adolescent proto-raps: 'Hey, check out Ricky and Ronnie!' 'My girl's the best and that's no lie.'

Sitting on the floor outside a central London toilet, four members of Montreal guerrilla soundscape outfit Godspeed You Black Emperor! are asked whether their band offers a single means of collective expression or a channel for nine individuals to express themselves separately. 'Those two things seem to be the same,' replies Norsola, strictly. Aidan agrees: 'Yes and Yes.'

2. How Individuals Express Themselves in Multitudes: Mike Paradinas and Susumu Yokota are Your Guides

If you saw Mike Paradinas in the street, you might not give him a second look – except perhaps to reflect on the advisability or otherwise of his ponytail. And yet this apparently unassuming individual is not only the creator of some of the most arresting and imaginative British electronic music of the last decade, he is also warlord of a private army of shifting identities.

As well as the µ-ziq name with which he is most widely associated, Paradinas has recorded under a legion of aliases seemingly designed to illustrate the truth of Walt Whitman's line about the I containing multitudes. But the myriad of moods and textures incorporated within the 1999 µ-ziq album *Royal Astronomy* threatened to relegate the exploits of such pseudonymous incarnations as Kid Spatula, Slag Boom Van Loon and deviant cheesy listening supremo Jake Slazenger to posterity's lonely sidelines.

'Scaling', the album's bewitching opening number, progresses smoothly from a courtly fake string intro, to Yul Brynner's introductory fanfare in *The King and I*, to the sound of Jeremy Paxman being attacked by a hormonally imbalanced seagull. It then fades into 'The Hwicci Song': the march of the elephants from *Dumbo* rearranged for the lost tribes of hip-hop. And from 'Autumn Acid's' pastoral Vietnam flashback through 'Carpet Muncher's' funky testcard shuffle to the woozy vocal atmospherics of 'The Fear', *Royal Astronomy* maintains these stratospheric levels of energy and invention more or less throughout.

Mike Paradinas' feet are not about to leave the ground though. 'What annoys me,' he complains, 'is not the fact that people seem to like this record, but that they can't take the other stuff I'm doing – which I like just as much but can't release because no one will buy it.'

Presumably those multifarious *noms de guerre* have been a good way of expressing different sides of his musical personality?

'I don't put myself into any persona,' he says crossly, 'that would be a crap thing to do. It's just a tradition in techno: a device whereby different record companies can market music in a variety of styles without stepping on other record companies' toes.'

A polite enquiry as to whether different tributaries leading into a single river might be a good analogy for the way each aspect of what he does relates to the whole elicits the following response: 'Work on that one . . . it could turn out to be interesting.'

'Maybe a river,' Paradinas continues more encouragingly, 'and then, what are they called? Docks – where different things are off-loaded . . . I'm getting away from that now anyway, though. In the current climate where nothing is selling very much, you have to have one brand name to market.'

If Paradinas' career still seems somewhat overshadowed by that of his friend and sometime musical collaborator, Aphex Twin, that's probably because while the latter has cloaked his music in a sumptuous raiment of myths and stunts, the former, well, hasn't. 'I could've,' he insist, 'but I knew people would only accuse me of copying him, so I thought, "No, I'll be pure".' The funny thing about this absence of pointers and subtexts is that it makes μ-ziq records more intriguing rather than less.

Despite his claim to be 'not very good with language', Paradinas' album titles alone (*Tango 'N' Vectif, Bluff Limbo, Salsa With Mesquite, In Pine Effect* and *Lunatic Harness*) display more verbal facility than the entire oeuvres of many a celebrated rock lyricist. *Royal Astronomy* turns out to have come not from the anticipated lame millennial or eclipse-related conceit, but a James Thurber short story about an astronomer who told a king the stars were disappearing when in fact he was going blind.

What relevance this tale might have to the life of a former architecture student who lives in a nice Victorian house in Worcester with his girlfriend and young son Caleb is for him to know and us to find out. Does Mike Paradinas think his music is communicating something about himself? 'I don't know if it's something about myself,' he allows himself a rare smile 'but it's definitely something.'

The idea of an ambient recording that stops you in your tracks might seem to be a contradiction in terms, but Susumu Yokota's *Image 1983–1998* does exactly that. The packaging for this exquisite half-hour selection incorporates some rather bewildering samples of Mr Yokota's multimedia artwork, and notes proclaiming his work's affinity with *Kona* – a Japanese word for an assemblage of white grains which, once scattered, 'can never be replaced in their original form . . . Like the vagueness of memories'.

All of which is somewhat off-putting. Until you actually listen to the music. Too often in the past the ambient tag has been an excuse for laziness; why bother putting any effort into what you do if people are always going to be doing something else while they're listening to it? Any reprobate and their monkey can leave a tumble dryer on for half an hour, drop in some spoken word samples from daytime TV, and wrap the whole thing up in a nice picture of a cloud in the hope that some drug-addled loser with an Apple Mac will call it a subliminal masterpiece.

But there is another, higher ambient tradition – the one to which Yokota's record belongs. This tradition goes back to Brian Eno and before him Erik Satie, and involves the painstaking creation of music designed to seep into your everyday existence through the cracks, and change the character of day-to-day life from within. In Yokota's case, it's not just the sounds he makes which seem to crystallise previously intangible emotions, his working methods do so too.

Image 1983–98 is not a conventional compilation. The first five tracks – deceptively simple guitar and organ sketches, vaguely reminiscent of Jim O'Rourke or some other downbeat charmer from Chicago – turn out to have been recorded in 1983–84. The other eight, picking up the earlier themes and opening them out like a daffodil in a speeded-up nature film, were done a decade and a half later.

In between times, Mr Yokota – previously best known in this country for more generic electronic dance releases such as *Frankfurt/ Tokyo Connection* on Sven Vath's Harthouse label – claims that his 'life became techno'. To find out what he means by this, it is necessary to enlist the help of an e-mail interpreter. Judging by such earlier Yokotan verbal coups as his likening of acid house to 'shrimps jumping up and down' the imprecise nature of this means of communication is an asset rather than a liability.

If Yokota 'became techno' in the years after 1984 (proof of his devotion to the form being, apparently, that 'rhythms were repetitively ticked off even while sleeping'), did he have to 'un-become' it in order to go back to work again on the music he made before his techno awakening?

'For a while I only had time for various forms of House – I was especially into the futuristic flow of Detroit music and the mentality of Trance – but in the mid to late nineties it all became boring, and at this time I realised the New Wave which had initially inspired me around the end of the seventies (Young Marble Giants, Joy Division, etc.) was still fresh. I think these bands are my roots and *Image* was an opportunity for me to express that.'

Joy Division are often cited as a musical influence, but it seems especially gratifying that the magically quiet and evocative music of obscure welsh trio Young Marble Giants (whose album *Colossal Youth* was originally released on Rough Trade in 1980) should have travelled half-way round the world to warp the mind of a Japanese techno-head.

'The Young Marble Giants have affected me the most of all musically,' Yokota maintains gravely. 'I can feel deja vu from them.' The tune on *Image 1983–98* which most strongly bears the Giants' mark is the enthralling 'Nisemono No Uta' (roughly translated as 'Counterfeit Song'). This hypnotic song fragment also quotes Gloria Gaynor's karaoke standard 'I Am What I Am' to persuasive effect, as a disembodied voice emerges from the mix to proclaim 'I am my own special creation'.

Yokota has released music under a lot of different names – among them Stevia, 246, Prism and, bizarrely, Ringo. Are these separate identities a reflection of different parts of his personality, or are aliases just a practical means of getting round the problems caused by working with different record companies simultaneously?

'Both of these are true. I wanted to make myself more chaotic, I thought I could find something new from mixing myself up . . . but now I only release music under my real name.'

Yokota's is the sort of music you put on while you're doing the washing up only to find it has taken possession of your very soul. Could he tell his listeners what he feels is the difference between *Image 1983–98* and the later *Magic Thread*, which seems to join the dots between his techno and ambient personas?

'Image is me looking back at the past with a sense of nostalgia. *Magic Thread* is the sound of human evolution – weaving ever more intricate patterns from an initial thread of hemp.'

3. 'Oh Well, Let Jimmy Take Care of it.'
(Smog and Will Oldham present *Individuals Spurning Social Containment.*)

In comparison with previous Bill 'Smog' Callahan releases, 1999's *Knock Knock* is an impossibly upbeat record. The line 'For the first time in my life I let myself be held, like a big old baby' is representative of the generally revelatory lyrical tone, and the fact that this album features not one but two songs showcasing the Chicago Children's Choir is fair warning of the scope of its territorial ambitions.

'Have you ever heard a song with children's voices on it that you *didn't* like?' demands Callahan. Bill is a somewhat forbidding individual, who will never use words when silence is available, so the image of him in the studio surrounded by tiny acolytes is more or less irresistible. It turns out that *Knock Knock*'s choral segments were not recorded live, but with Callahan lip-syncing the main vocal through a glass studio partition ('They wanted to see me sing,' he says proudly). Perhaps this was something their guardians insisted on.

Having released some of the strangest, loveliest, records of the nineties under names that were variations on palatial themes (Palace Music, Palace Brothers, Palace Songs, etc.), it made a crazy kind of sense that Will Oldham should bring the decade to a close by rebranding himself in tribute to the son of a deposed monarch. The unweildiness of Bonny 'Prince' Billy's name is in sharp contrast with the increased accessibility of his music.

Previously a man who seemed to carry the weight of the world in his forehead, with *I See A Darkness*, his debut album as Bonnie 'Prince' Billy Oldham admits that 'pleasure was more on the agenda'. He hopes this record will 'enable the listener to consider as a victory things he or she would previously have thought of as a defeat'.

Ask him what brought about this sudden upturn in his emotional fortures and Oldham will tell you about the three weeks he spent in the winter of 1997, touring Europe with a group of improvisational musicians, playing live soundtracks to an experimental black and white film about the hardships of life in an Alaskan fishing village. The funny thing is, he will not be joking. You can even find the original soundtrack and two records of the tour, if you look very carefully (the one I've got is *The Last Place To Go* by Boxhead Ensemble Atavistic LP96CD) and share this experience for yourself.

Callahan also has surprising new sources of inspiration to tell of. A trip to see Wu-Tang Clan bad-boy Ol' Dirty Bastard perform last summer seems to have made a big impression on him. 'It was really great, you know? He had a posse – eight other rappers came out first and did three songs without him – and it was like watching a party. What I like about music is to get the feeling that you're spending a day talking to somebody. I like Funkadelic a lot too, you get that sense from them.'

It may be that earlier Smog records, 1996's mesmerising, borderline catatonic *The Doctor Came At Dawn* for example, were heavily influenced by Funkadelic too, but if so, that influence was very discreet. When Will Oldham said in a recent American interview that he hoped people would listen to his records in the same way his New York neighbour listened to Mariah Carey, a trend became discernible. To understand it, you have to go back in time a little.

Oldham and Callahan first played live together in Britain in 1995. With Britpop at its brazen height and America still trying to fill the void left by the death of Kurt Cobain with clump and grind grunge pretenders, the ancient quietness of their music was a marvellous revelation. By 1999, the reconnection with the well-springs of American folk pioneered by Palace and Smog had become a commonplace. *Mojo* cover stories, Radio 1 *Newsbeat* reports and free CDs given away with *Uncut* magazine celebrated the commodification of that reconnection under such sweeping umbrella headings as 'alt.country', 'Americana' and 'the new roots explosion'.

Such marketing ruses are inevitably anathema to ornery frontier individualists like Oldham and Callahan. 'Calling the music Americana is ridiculous,' the former says sensibly. 'What happens to the rest of America?' The suggestion that he might be part of a wider musicianly society goads Callahan to unheard of heights of annoyance. 'I don't know if anyone in their right mind . . .' he checks, as if surprised by this own ardour, 'it's not for me, at least, to be part of a community. My music changes so much it's ridiculous for me to be lumped in with other people. I guess I'm pretty lazy and if I felt I was part of a community I would just think, "Oh well, let Jimmy take care of it".'

The two men's determination to set themselves apart from their burgeoning would-be peer group has had some hilarious results. In conversation, Oldham persistently pronounces the name of his inexplicably revered fellow troubador Mark Eitzel as 'Mark Asshole'. Where he once peered out at his audience with a look of child-like bemusement, Bonnie 'Prince' Billy's 1999 London Astoria show found him rocking out in a sweat-soaked vest and belching loutishly into the microphone. He later amazed a packed King's Cross Water Rats with a testosterone-crazed cover of AC/DC's 'Big Balls'.

Callahan meanwhile styles *Knock Knock* as 'an album for teenagers'. For the cover art he chose lightning and wildcats, on the basis that these are 'things teenagers identify with', therein exhibiting an intuitive rapport with the youth of today that is little short of frightening, and which he develops to even more priapic effect on 2000's wet and wild *Dongs of Sevotion*.

All of this repositioning would be no more than an idle diversion if the music it had produced wasn't so fantastic. Call it what you will – and 'the alt.country frontlash' is the designation all the smart money's on – Oldham and Callahan's rebellion against received wisdom is an example to us all. Neil Young once wrote that on feeling his music becoming middle of the road, his only option was to head for the ditch. Bill Callahan puts it even better in *Knock Knock*'s exquisite 'River Guard'. 'We are constantly on trial,' he sings. 'It's a way of being free.'

4. 'We Were the First All-Night People, and Not Everyone in This Country Liked That' (or How Individuals Excluded From Communities Sometimes Band Together to Make a Better World For Everyone, by Dennis Bovell)

Tabby Cat Kelly's haunting and beautiful 'Don't Call Us Immigrants' sets the bitter-sweet tone perfectly for the landmark collection of British roots reggae to which it lends its title. 'Find some other way to amuse yourselves,' Kelly counsels his unnamed tormentors, with an authority born of bitter experience, 'because what's a joke to you is death to me.'

Perceived as second-class citizens – musically as well as socially – these UK reggae pioneers fought back with music whose spirit and quality still shines through three decades on. Some, like Black Slate and Aswad (whose 'Sticksman' and 'It's Not Our Wish' are two of this fine compilation's highlights), went on to achieve crossover infamy. Others, like the one and only Pablo Gad, didn't. But all made a scandalously unsung contribution to Britain's musical heritage that with the advent of this record can now claim its long overdue place in the sun.

'Shops like Sound Seven in Dalston or Don Christie in Birmigham,' remembers Adrian Sherwood, whose Pressure Sounds label is responsible for this vital musical document, 'could sell five hundred copies of one single on a Saturday afternoon.'[86] The halcyon days of British reggae seem a long way off now, but the music on *Don't Call Us Immigrants* still sounds brand new.

Visionary producer Dennis Bovell would go on to have a hand in a lot of great music – from Orange Juice to The Slits to Janet Kay's 'Silly Games' (of which more later) – but his early days with UK roots trailblazers Matumbi have a special place in his memory.

Driving up the M1 and then the M6 to Birmingham and on to Manchester or Leeds, Bovell felt like a pioneer of the Old West. 'There was a lot of rivalry between London and Birmingham in particular,' he remembers. 'It was, "This is going on." "No, *this* is going on" . . . kind of like the Northern Soul versus disco thing. In the early days we had to have two different sets – one for inside London and one for outside.'

As connections were made and new groups and sound systems sprang up all across the country, British reggae soon felt the hand of the law on its collar. 'We were the first all-night people,' Bovell continues, 'and not everyone in this country liked that. Wherever there was a reggae dance the police would be looking for people who were going to "cause trouble". You'd play a new club and go back three weeks later and it would be closed down. Reggae was being hounded, and then the punk generation came up and said [assumes comedy punk voice], "We *like* this".'

Persecution reached its zenith after trouble at a soundclash between Sufferers Hi Fi and Sir Lord Koos at the Carib Club on Cricklewood Broadway, when police surrounded the venue and administered severe beatings to homebound revellers. Of the twelve people subsequently tried at the Old Bailey under the archaic law of Riot and Affray, Bovell himself was the most severely punished, and served six months of an outrageous three-year sentence before the verdict was finally overturned. 'When you're in prison you're furious and you're thinking, "When I get out I'm gonna do this and I'm gonna do that,"' Bovell remembers, 'but once I was released, I was so glad to be out that I just got on with it.'

The impact of the music he got on with is still being felt anew a quarter of a century later. 'The legacy of this stuff,' Adrian Sherwood enthuses, 'the frequencies, the tone, the approach to the radical treatment of sound – has been handed down, almost like a griot thing, from r'n'b through Soul II Soul to Massive Attack to the drum and bass and UK Garage people. It's almost like the blues now, and we're just trying to get it taken as seriously as it should be.'

One of the key differences between British and Jamaican reggae was that British groups tended, in Sherwood's phrase, to be 'gangs of mates' rather than session musicians, as in Jamaica. A greater accent on live performances rather than sound-system clashes demanded technical innovations – such as Bovell's pioneering live dub guitar technique – which would echo down through the subsequent development of British pop.

As Bovell explains the rhythmic backdrop to Janet Kay's gorgeous falsetto rhapsody 'Silly Games', you can hear musical history unfolding. 'What I was trying to do there was change the style of reggae drumming. There was a style we used to call "Go deh", and that had progressed into "The flying cymbal" [Bovell makes a flying cymbal noise] "*pea-soup, pea-soup, pea-soup*" – the whole disco lot grabbed that – then it moved to Rockers, when the bass drum was on the floor on all four beats, so I came up with this drum pattern where instead of having the hi-hat open, you would close it up and roll it. Angus Gaye [aka Aswad's Drummie Zeb] was the only one who could play it. He was the best drummer around at the time. We went in and cut the track and it was so successful that I didn't dare make another tune with the same drumbeat.'

That's not always been the way of things with reggae's sonic innovations, has it?

'People hit on a formula and they stay there – that's been one of the music's greatest downfalls. As any inventor will tell you, once you've invented something, you want to invent something else.'

5. It's Not Where You're From, it's Where You're At: Overthrowing The Tyranny of Cultural Determinism, the Stefan Betke Way

Upstairs in a converted Brixton church, a 30K sound rig is working its own electronic epiphany. The noise of hungry mice nibbling through an electric cable gives way to a strange whooshing pulse. Fragments of melody float up from the speakers and out over the top of the crowd's heads, and a giant clock starts ticking in their innards. The volume of the bass stops just short of being frightening – imagine being picked up by a giant's hand and gently shaken so your kidney ends up where your liver used to be.

One man is behind this disorienting but undeniably spiritual experience. He is, in the finest tradition of dub reggae, a German, and his name is Stefan Betke. Recorded under the name of Pole, Betke's debut album (entitled, with characteristic understatement, *CD 1*) was one of the most quietly captivating records of 1998: a digital susurration that sweeps up the unwary listener into its gossamer babble. The tradename Pole is no phallocentric battlecry, but a tribute to the Waldorf Pole Filter, one of the numerous obscure pieces of electronic equipment with which Betke comes into contact in the course of his day-job as a tape operator at the Dubplates and Mastering studio in Berlin.

It's a sample from a broken Waldorf Pole Filter that supplies the constant, oddly reassuring clicking sound which suffuses the whole recording. (It also, clicking sound fans will be pleased to discover, looms large on the equally beguiling follow-ups *Pole 2 & 3*.) Betke – a jovial individual with very well-organised hair – obligingly fills in some historical background.

'I started out with a group playing avant-garde jazz in the early eighties. We were using lots of samples and delay effects, and I was very impressed with the space echo.'

For the less technically minded among us, what does the space echo do exactly?

'It's very simple – you don't need to know much about electronics. There is a tape inside, the sound is recorded and repeated – *ding ding ding* – you can change the speed and for how long it's repeated: that's all.'

That *ding ding ding* is not the only aspect of Betke's work that will ring a bell with dub aficionados: his recordings have the same depth of field as a classic King Tubby or Keith Hudson reissue on Blood & Fire. The extraordinary thing about *CD1* is that Betke actually recorded it while living in Cologne, with no knowledge of any reggae tradition beyond Bob Marley. When he moved to Berlin and played it to his new workmates at Dubplates and Mastering they said (and you really have to enunciate this in Germanically accented English to get the full effect) 'OK, that's dubstyle!'

Has his subsequent crash course in dub science changed the way Betke makes music?

'For me or for the audience?'

For you, because everyone else knew about it before.

'I suppose the main thing listening to dub taught me was that I am not alone in the studio with my crazy mind and this *bing bing bing* [Betke's echo chamber impression is getting more uncanny with every moment that passes.] Also, now when I find a melody and I think it's a bit like Augustus Pablo, I put it away.'

Anyone who thinks it strange that a reformed German jazz musician should find himself unknowingly echoing the innovations of Jamaican producers of a quarter of a century earlier should consider the overwhelming influence of Kraftwerk on the beginnings of hip-hop. 'So many styles of European music have been influenced by dub,' Betke explains patiently, 'that it makes perfect sense to go the other way. At first sight it seems strange that a man should come from where I do and make sounds like this, but it isn't: it's quite normal.'

6. It's Not Where You're At, It's Where You're From: Adjusting to the Tyranny of Cultural Determinism With Style and Dignity, Like Bessie Smith and Shaun Ryder Did

In *Empress of the Blues*, Chris Albertson's biography of the great blues singer Bessie Smith, he describes the attempts of clubowner Charles Bailey to enforce the racist convention of the time whereby black performers went to their dressing room through the back entrance, to save white audiences the pain of having to look at them. 'If they see you before the show,' he argued spuriously, 'they won't find you as interesting. 'I don't give a fuck,' Bessie responded. 'If you don't like it, kiss my black ass.'

Seventy years or so later, a clipped Mancunian voice cuts through the babble of a posey Hampstead watering hole. 'I don't want any profile shots,' insists Shaun Ryder, the Edward Lear of British Ecstasy culture. Perched uneasily on a seat by the wall, he takes the photographer on a guided tour of his face. 'I'm all right on this side . . . no wait a minute, it's the other side that's OK.'

7. 'There's Still Love There, but Business is Business.' The Rights and Value of the Individual in Contemporary R'n'B, Destiny's Child and Mary J. Blige Tell it Like it Is

When Texan close harmony quartet Destiny's Child released their fine second album *The Writing's On the Wall* in the summer of 1999, no one realised just how prophetic the album's title was going to be. Surfing the post 'No Scrubs' wave of female r'n'b empowerment in grand style, the first two singles – the courtly, harpsichord-powered 'Bills' and the infectiously jittery 'Bugaboo' – were deservedly substantial hits. At some level, though, this sleek and industrious outfit was deemed to be underperforming.

Two group members – La Toya and La Tavia – were summarily replaced and Destiny's Child's merciless promotional schedule continued without a pause.

As a third single (the again aptly titled 'Say My Name') throws Destiny's new Children Michelle and Farrah in at the deep end with some of the most intricate vocal arrangements imaginable, the group's leader Beyoncé is asked about the line-up changes on MTV News. 'There's still love there,' she says crisply, 'but business is business.' Within a further six months, Farrah is gone too.

From Florence Ballard's brutal extirpation from The Supremes, to the realisation when En Vogue came back with *EV3* that one of them had gone, the individual has often seemed to be expendable in female r'n'b vocal groups. And yet it's this very vulnerability to forces stronger than themself which makes the individual's contribution so precious. Just as the fact that armies of writers, producers and stylists contribute to the creation of a single identity makes that identity more powerful rather than less.

On 'Deep Inside' – the third track on her epic 1999 album *Mary* – hip-hop diva Mary J. Blige explores these apparent contradictions to mesmerising effect. 'Deep inside I wish that they could see,' she demands plaintively, 'that I'm just plain old Mary.' Beneath the apparent disingenuousness of the multi-platinum soul queen who wants people to love her for herself, there is something extraordinarily touching going on. While Elton John – who presumably knows a thing or two about this kind of anxiety – pounds away at a pub piano on the backing track, Mary outlines her dilemma.

Because she's lived her life publically for so long, it's hard for her to find a man she can really trust. She doesn't have a lot of friends, and even though material things – the cars, the clothes, the diamonds, the furs, the house (Mary is not stinting with this list, but that's exactly how it should be) – 'don't make the woman', she worries that they're all people see when they look at her. She's not happy to have such a cynical view of humanity, it's just what experience has taught her, and when Mary J. Blige sings 'Don't judge me or think I'm bitter, for the evil god's allowed me to see', no one is really going to argue with her.

The eerie thing is that the backing vocalists sing 'I wish that *you* could see' (that she's just plain old Mary) while Mary herself sings 'I wish that *they* could see', as if they had a closer connection than she does with the world at large, simply by virtue of not being Mary. 'All day, all night, I'm Mary,' Blige bellows, like it's half a blessing and half a curse, before embracing her ultimate destiny with a defiant – not to say heroic – 'MJB, Yeah!'

8. 'All Humanity is Some Kind of Restrictive Limitation': Leaving the Twentieth Century With Elvis and Sun Ra

When the critic Duncan Smith wrote, shortly after Elvis' death in 1977, of the great man as being 'not the author of Elvis' and, worse than that, 'ex-centric to his own Elvishood' it seemed a shocking thing to read. Almost a quarter of century later, in the spring of the year 2000, Elvis' original TCB band – and never had the Presleyan soubriquet Taking Care of Business been better lived up to – appeared live on stage at Wembley Arena. In what was billed as 'the multimedia event of a lifetime', James Burton, Glen D. Hardin, Ron Stutt, and backing singers The Stamps and The Sweet Inspirations were live onstage, while Elvis himself was 'live on screen'. In one sense this demonstrated the truth of Smith's observation, in another its falseness. Either way, the question remained of whether – and if so, at what point – Elvis would actually be leaving the building.

On the occasion (in late 1992) of their penultimate British live appearance, Sun Ra and his Omniverse Ultra 21st Century Arkestra meet no earthly resistance to their celestial aspiration. At least thirteen of them cram the stage at Ronnie Scotts. Some standing, most seated, they beat out strange dense rhythms on a variety of drums while taking it in apparently random turn to blow horn solos of dazzling virtuosity.

Dressed in his habitual spangled head-dress and modest sequinned cape, Sun Ra is helped out to his piano by two trusty retainers. It takes him long enough to negotiate a passage to the piano stool to lend credence to his claim to be three thousand years old – if not to support the contention that he hails from Saturn. Finally settled at his

Steinway, he unleashes incandescent trickles of notes with hands that don't appear to move.

Sun Ra's face doesn't give much away and neither do the official records of his time here on earth,[87] though history does note his formative experience with ailing big band leader Fletcher Henderson, whose music echoes joyfully throughout the Ra oeuvre, alongside the nursery rhymes, avant-garde dissonance and occasional dash of bossa nova which fill innumerable fantastic albums with titles like *My Brother The Wind II* or *The Nubians of Plutonia*.

The shocking accessibility of the sounds the Arkestra are making is initially shrouded in an all but impenetrable cloak of intergalactic mysticism, but gradually seeps through by what you call a process of cosmosis. The exhilaration comes not just from the gleeful abandon of the playing as from its iron discipline. Individual egos – even of a great soloist like John Gilmore – are not allowed to intrude upon the collective effort.

The obvious glee of the drummer, bouncing up and down as he plays, might initially be hard to square with the fiercely puritannical co-operative regimen within which this music is conceived, rehearsed and recorded, but Sun Ra himself gives the best explanation. 'I tell my arkestra that all humanity is some kind of restricted limitation,' he once said mischievously, 'but they're in the Ra jail, and it's the best in the world.'

9. How *Stars in Their Eyes* Ought to Be Quite Depressing But Actually Represents an Unlikely Triumph of the Human Spirit. Additional Dialogue: Matthew Kelly and Underworld

That the most popular music programme on British TV (a grand final will be watched by as many people as watch *Top of the Pops* and the FA Cup Final put together) should be a show in which members of the public are judged on their ability to impersonate the star of their choice, might easily be seen as a symptom of a culture in the terminal stages of decline, but that would be a mistake. Authenticity is an over-used notion, and yet – as anyone who saw the man who was

Philip Bailey from Earth, Wind & Fire will tearfully testify – there is something acutely authentic about the emotional content of *Stars in Their Eyes*. To the stars themselves it would be a job. To the contestants it is a dream come true.

'I think people want an idea of something rather than the reality,' is presenter Matthew Kelly's more earthbound explanation for the programme's huge appeal, as he waits for his lunch in a chintzy Bournemouth hotel.

Does he think *Stars in Their Eyes* is camp?

'Oh hardly at all [laughter], especially the Christmas specials. Those are fantastic. You stand at the side of the set thinking, "What the fuck is going on?" They've deforested half of Norway for the pine trees, there's about £2000 worth of false snow coming down, there are lookalikes of every single singing star you could possibly imagine, reindeer that look like they've been nicked from a shopping mall, ten-foot nodding snowmen, a choir of schoolchildren and a twenty-eight-piece orchestra, and the whole lot is covered in sequins. You think, "No, this isn't camp at all."'

Now in its second decade, the show might have been expected to decline after the first wave of Elvises and Karen Carpenters had spent itself.

'I think the reason the opposite's happened,' Kelly enthuses, 'is that all the people who wanted to do it have done it, and now we're getting the *real* real people. We've gone through the semi-professionals and the show-offs and now it's people who've never sung in public. People whose parents don't even know they can sing are making their singing debuts in front of an audience of thirteen million.'

There is a poignantly stark contrast sometimes between the paucity of opportunities real life seems to offer *Stars in Their Eyes* contestants and the extravagant ideal of glamour the show is built around.

'A lot of people seem to think it's going to be the best thing that ever happens to them,' Kelly says worriedly, 'but I sincerely hope it isn't.'

At this point Matthew's tomato and mozzarella salad arrives. It is not the best thing that has ever happened to him. The cheese is a scary brownish yellow and tastes like grated trainer insole. 'That's never mozzarella,' he exclaims, understandably outraged.

Did Granada come to him when they realised that the obvious solution to the problem posed by original *Stars in Their Eyes* host Leslie Crowther's car accident – a Leslie Crowther lookalike – would have been in very poor taste?

'Oh yes. The kind of show I do, you wouldn't actually really pursue, would you?' A shocked pause. Matthew Kelly's habitual self-deprecation has landed him in deep water. 'No, but I mean you'd set your sights . . .'

A bit higher?

The Granada press officer chokes on a prawn.

Kelly laughs good-humouredly. 'I didn't say that.'

In view of this position does Kelly have any qualms about accepting what he himself describes as 'absurd amounts of money' for presenting *Stars in Their Eyes*?

'I'll have to think about that word "qualms",' he replies with a hint of mischief. 'Look at these hands [he holds them up] they're like silk. They haven't done a proper day's work in their lives.' And with that we move through to the lounge. Two respectable-looking people in late middle-age vacate their window seat with much giggling so that Matthew Kelly can have his photograph taken in decent light. One of them is a man dressed as a woman.

It was a shame Underworld didn't keep faith with their professed intention to call their third album *Tonight Matthew, We Are Going To Be Underworld*. Not because borrowing a catchphrase from *Stars in Their Eyes* was the best joke in the world. Not because the title they chose instead (the supposedly less unwieldy *Beaucoup Fish*) was, to put it diplomatically, crap. But because the *Tonight Matthew . . .* business would have gone to the heart of why if you were going to bury one British art-techno ensemble in a lead-lined capsule and ask them to come out in thirty years time to remind us what it was like to be alive in Britain in the mid-late nineteen nineties, Underworld would be your only option.

Karl Hyde, Rick Smith and Darren Emerson come through Matthew Kelly's magic doors everytime they make a record. It's clear that people who go on about dance music 'lacking personality' are really only talking about themselves – if you don't want to take that beat and let it twine itself around the vertebrae of your life like a climbing plant around a fence-post, then that's up to you, but it's your problem, not the music's.

In the sulphurous streams of consciousness Karl Hyde sends bubbling up through the magic geology of the mixing desk, new identities can be taken on and discarded almost at will.[88] In Hyde's magnetic mumble, Underworld have found a personal voice every bit as compelling as their music's endlessly shifting sequenced underlay.

10. How the Comeback Special Is Not a Travesty But a Test of Strength, With Malcolm McLaren and Madness

From the moment in Elvis' *'68 Comeback Special* when the leather-clad King essays a trademark sneer and jokes, 'There's something wrong with my lip,' the reunion (either of a band or an individual – reconciling their new self with their old) has been an essential pop tradition. But, enjoying a quiet *al fresco* cappuccino in a sun-drenched Charlotte Street, Malcolm McLaren begs to differ.

'I wish I cared more,' he says of the Sex Pistols reformation which will take place a few days later. 'I try to but I can't. I suppose it's because it's antique, it's in a vacuum, it's in a frame – it's part of a compilation of oldies. If you think about it, is it really any different from a Gerry and the Pacemakers reunion?'

Surely McLaren must derive some perverse enjoyment from the fact that, while being globally reviled as the ultimate Fagin/Svengali figure, he is the only one not making any money out of the exploitation of the Sex Pistols' legacy?

'It is hilarious, really,' Malcolm relents. 'When it comes to actually answering the question, "Who killed Bambi?" – he smiles, almost wistfully – 'I'd have to say that *I just don't know.*'

An earlier reunion in John Lydon's old Finsbury Park stamping ground: troops of geese wheel overhead. They're getting ready, somewhat prematurely, to fly away south, which is what Madness did, which is why the park beneath – never the loveliest of London's green spaces – is now fenced off with corrugated iron, and a landscape of par-boiled English flesh, big boots and plastic beer cups stretches as far as you can see.

A large part of Madness's piquancy, right from the beginning, was nostalgia for things that could never have been quite as sweet as they made them sound.

'If we'd struggled on for years playing the George Robey,' Suggs says, a few weeks before their first Madstock reunion in 1992, 'we probably wouldn't have ended up in the bizarrely rose-tinted situation we're in now. But because we stopped when we did, after a while there seemed to be some strange thread running through everything that was written about us; it would all be couched in these strange holy overtones of dewy-eyedness.'

'It's all very well being flattered by this sort of thing,' says record company executive Carl Smyth (aka Chas Smash), 'but who wants to be a British institution? The category we fall into in terms of British institutions would have more to do with red phone boxes and double-decker buses, and all the other things that disappeared through lack of interest.'

By the time they finally get around to recording new material (and the single 'Lovestruck' manages to be worthy of both their early and later selves, even though the album's not much cop), Madness reunions have become annual events. Far from a betrayal of the band's founding charter, this nostalgic ritual would seem to be entirely in keeping with the band's remit.

Just as the number of times a skimmed stone bounces off the surface of the ocean is testimony to the strength, not the weakness, of the initial throw; so how far an individual or collective persona can get from its original template and still mean something, is proof of its enduring power rather than the extent of its decline.

In this context, there's no difference between The Velvet Underground leading each other off the main stage like four wise old elephants at Glastonbury in 1992, Alex Chilton breathing life into the legend of Big Star with two moonlighting whippersnappers from middle-ranking US college rockers The Posies a year later, cousins Ron and Ernie Isley still upholding the legacy of The Isley Brothers ('Whenever we go onstage,' says Ernie simply,[89] 'it feels like we're all there'), or Lynyrd Skynyrd continuing to dedicate their most famous song to 'All the Freebirds up in heaven' a full fifteen years after lead singer Ronnie Van Zant and three other band members were killed in a plane crash.

All are trying to live up to ideals of how they should behave – both in relation to each other and everyone else – which, while they have been defined by music, extend into every corner of the world beyond it. These ideals don't always work as a guide to how you should live your life, but they sometimes do.

The Last Paragraph

In the midst of The Teardrop Explodes' demise, one of the band's members began to speak unmythologically. Julian Cope's disappointment expressed itself as follows: 'Suddenly I perceived that I was a great being, staring down at some vastly lesser molecular structure known as Dave Balfe.'[90] At this pivotal moment, Cope had become the pop psyche's living embodiment. The opportunity to inhabit this 'great being' is open to all, but the commitment and energy required should not be underestimated. A former guitarist with eighties John Peel favourites Tools You Can Trust puts it best, fondly recalling his band-leader's constant post-gig strictures: 'You were smiling again. Don't fucking smile. We're Tools You Can Trust. We don't smile.'

The Whistling Appendix

'Between thought and expression', sang Lou Reed in The Velvet Underground's 'Some Kinda Love', 'lies a lifetime'. If he had reflected a little more carefully, he might have been driven to observe that between thought and expression lies the whistling bit. As well as being the perfect vehicle for those parts of a song which can't – or shouldn't – be put into words, the whistling bit is the physical embodiment of everything about the mysteries of human communication through music that this book has endeavoured to celebrate.

When Captain Beefheart called the human whistle 'the flesh horn' he not only supplied a more resonant alternative for those who find the dictionary definition – 'to produce (shrill or flutelike sounds), as by passing breath through a narrow constriction most easily formed by the pursed lips' – a little lacking in romance, but also located this most idiosyncratic of instruments squarely (and accurately) between the voice and the brass section.

Like the saxophone and the harmonica, the whistle can be deadly in the wrong hands (if Roxy Music's 'Jealous Guy' is the 'Baker Street' of whistling, does that make Peter Gabriel's 'Jeux Sans Frontieres' the 'Will You?'), but in the right ones it's a marvel. Sometimes a respite, and sometimes an intensification, but always a pleasure and never a chore. What follows is partly an informal Top 20 (not arranged in any divisive order of merit, but sequenced to beguile the ear) and partly a journey into the heart of the whistle . . .

The Rule – the sound must be entirely and incontrovertibly human in origin: there's no room for referees' cast offs.

The Rub – due to space restrictions, there is no room for Bob Crosby's 'Big Noise From Winetka', Elvis Presley's 'I Love You Because', 'Hello Mabel' by The Bonzo Dog Doo Dah Band, 'Whistle In' by The Beach Boys, The Nightingales' '(Keep On) Carrying On', 'Lazy Sunday Afternoon' by The Small Faces, Syd Barrett's 'Maisie', 'I Was Kaiser Bill's Batman' by Whistling Jack Smith, the song on Robert Wyatt's *End of an Ear* that has whistling in it, or whichever other landmark of air-based improvisational endeavour sprang straight into your mind the moment this topic was broached.

The Results

1. 'Inga' by Victor Jara on *Canto Libre* (Movieplay 1978)

A supremely jaunty revolving guitar figure, some bongos and a lot of people laughing in the background would have captured the momentary optimism of the Allende takeover poignantly enough on their own. But factor in the gleeful chirrup of the doomed Chilean folksinger (part jovial extrapolation, part conceptual throw forward to the wolf whistle on the first New York Dolls album) and you've got a heartbreaker of continental proportions.

2. 'I Just Got Back From The Fantasy, Ahead Of Our Time In The Four Winds of Ellet' by Parliament on *Up For the Downstroke* (Casablanca 1974)

Previously less celebrated than the other great Clintonian sidemen Bernie Worrell, Bootsy Collins and Eddie Hazel, Peter Chase here makes a successful bid to join the ranks of the élite with perhaps the most extraordinary piece of whistling ever recorded. Virtuosity is an over-rated quality, but Chase's heroic determination to establish himself as the Yngwie Malmstein of the flesh horn takes on even greater resonance in the unlikely lyrical context of paternal responsibility against the odds ('I knew I had to come back and raise you kids', he proclaims mournfully, amid sidelong glances at a more convivial alternate reality of heads down, no-nonsense psychedelic excess). Imagine the soul of Kenny G possessed by a demented skylark and you're just about in the ballpark.

3. 'The Whistling Song' on *Meat Puppets II* (SST 1984) by The Meat Puppets
A unique verse/whistle/verse format is just one of the distinguishing features of this lovely last track on Chris and Curt Kirkwood's classic second album. The chord progression ascends dustily in the manner of a John Ford hero climbing into his bunk. The whistling has the sort of magical sun-baked quality accessible only to those who spend a lot of their spare time hanging around in the desert.

4. 'Maiden's Milk' by The Meat Puppets on *Up On The Sun* (SST 1985)
A more complex piece of work than its predecessor in the Kirkwood whistling canon – foreshadowing the band's imminent drift away from the clear prairie of hardcore/bluegrass crossover towards the marshy lowlands of psychedelic sludge – this starts out abstract (thick bass-strings played as if they are trying to escape) and gradually revs up through some fine chiming desert guitar figures to pull off the most daring of all musical feats: the two-part whistling harmony.

5. 'Sweet Georgia Brown' by Rahsaan Roland Kirk on *Simmer, Reduce, Garnish and Serve* (Warners 1996)
Celebrated among other things for playing three wind and brass instruments at the same time, the great Roland Kirk calls upon a whistling specialist (William Eaton of the Eaton Family of Whistlers from Durham, North Carolina) to help out with this gleefully sarcastic reinvigoration of an apparently exhausted standard. Much merriment is induced by his brave attempts to outface Fred Moore's frenetic washboard ('Is he whistling Dixie?'). At the end, the police come.

6. 'Black Satin' by Miles Davis on *On The Corner* (Columbia 1974)
Described by Jon Hassell as the quintessential Fourth World composition on account of its improvisation combining Indian classical music, Stockhausen and Sly Stone, this imposing proto-fusion landmark is actually best remembered for it's whistling: which replicates the effect of a gang of angry blackbirds turning on a pensioners' outing.

7. 'General Plea To A Girlfriend' by Arab Strap on *The Week Never Starts*

Round Here (Chemikal Underground 1996)

As if its lyrical content were not sufficiently to the point ('I make no boasts about my body, the workmanship is somewhat shoddy . . . sometimes I overwork my gob, can't buy you gifts, I've got no job') this supremely rough and ready love song has a whistling break that gives Boston terriers anxiety attacks. Also looming large in an exquisite arrangement is the sound of someone banging a child's drum in the room next door.

8. 'Mellow Doubt' by Teenage Fanclub (Creation 1995)

The more melodious face of Caledonian romanticism. In the same way that this band's three different lead voices all express the group's collective personality with equal clarity and spirit, Norman Blake's whistle speaks for all of us.

9. 'Red Eyed & Blue' by Wilco, on *Being There* (Reprise 1998)

What could have been just one more song about musicians sitting around failing to be creative, turns out to be something much more valuable. It starts by lowering the listener gradually into a pit of melancholy, only to extract itself from the mire with a transcendental whistling bit and finish up enthused at the infinite possibilities for good humour and self-expression offered by an old piano in a dusty room.

10. 'Sissyneck' by Beck (Geffen 1996)

This pneumatic *Odelay* country-funk jam kicks off with the kind of whistle an especially ornery cowhand might do just after spitting out a big lump of chewing tobacco, then goes on to map out its author's next two directions (the ragged rhinestone glory of *Mutations* and the shameless Prince revivalism of *Midnite Vultures*) simultaneously in an overlaying mesh.

11. 'Boops (Here To Go)' by Sly & Robbie (Fourth & Broadway 1987)

Science-fiction disco dub on the digital cusp. The second part of the epic whistling bout pays tribute to the pseudo-classical heritage of *Saturday Night Fever*'s 'Fifth Of Beethoven' with a rollicking rendition of Rossini's 'The Barber of Seville' (de-de di-ya, de-de di-ya, de-de di-ya, de di-ya, de di-ya), familiar to all transvestite cartoon rabbit fans as the musical backdrop in front of which Bugs dons a dress in Chuck Jones's 'The Rabbit of Seville'. The origin of the first part is – even after lengthy research – still shrouded in mystery. In fact the first person to identify it (via the publisher's address) will receive an exclusive tape of this appendix and possibly a Kit-Kat Chunky.

12. 'Regulate' by Warren G (Def Jam 1992)

You would not want to stake your life on this whistle being of human origin (there's the odd moment where it sounds like one of those tricky West Coast synthesisers) but such rules are made to be broken. For all the big talk of g-funk, guns and girls, the real subject of this song is getting your stuff nicked ('I can't believe it's happening in my own town!') and the show of bravery in the kid-on-their-way-to-their-first-day-at-school whistle is one of its most affecting features.

13. 'For A Few Dollars More' by Ennio Morricone on *The Very Best of Ennio Morricone* (Music Club 1992)

In *A Fistful of Dollars* – the first part of the epic Clint Eastwood/Sergio Leone spaghetti western soundtrack trilogy that would be such a seminal influence on dub reggae and hip-hop – there are a piccolo, a bell and a whip, and the whistle is first answered and then overtaken by a bird call and some pan's pipes. In this crisper, more contained second instalment, it's a jew's harp that acts as a counterpoint, allowing the whistle more space to grow until the bells and the chanting come in with the riding noise. The third part, *The Good, the Bad and the Ugly,* was not Morricone's last involvement with the whistle – he also used it to potent effect in the 'Farewell To Cheyenne' segment of his *Once Upon A Time in the West* suite.

14. 'How Soon Is Now?' by The Smiths (Rough Trade 1985)

Morrissey's big tongue – subsequently revealed to such distressing effect in so many solo live performances – proved its worth with this unexpected and limber whistling segment. Worryingly acclaimed by US music business legend Seymour Stein as 'The "Stairway To Heaven" of the nineteen eighties', this song somehow turned out OK.

15. 'Step On' by Happy Mondays (Factory 1990)

'Call the cops' indeed. Shaun Ryder and the band he would later (a few years before they got back together) describe as 'a bunch of talentless arseholes from Salford' are on such transcendent form here that you don't notice that the tune is The Beatles' 'Come Together' with a wig on. One of those whistles you do with your fingers brings in Ryder's maniacal laugh and a big Italian house piano, and then a classic whistling coda takes it back out again, but not before his gleeful expostulation ('You're twisting my melon man!') has twisted Led Zeppelin's original appropriation of Willie Dixon's lemon into a balloon animal.

16. '(Sittin' On) The Dock Of The Bay' by Otis Redding (Atlantic 1967)

Wave noises, seagulls, melancholy, Steve Cropper's nautical guitar twirls: Otis Redding's posthumous number one is the biggest moment in flesh horn history and that's all there is to it. As that sublime whistled coda rolls out across the baseline like a gently retreating tide, it might be the great singer's soul ascending to the hereafter.

17. 'Everlasting Arm' by Mercury Rev on *See You on the Other Side* (Beggars Banquet 1995)

Another vision of the afterlife. This time the whistle supplies a vital sense of human agency – like the hand that touches God's on Michaelangelo's Sistine Chapel ceiling – in an ethereal world of single exhaust clarinets, arhoolie flutes and strange stereo water effects.

18. 'Piggies' by The Beatles on *Anthology 3* (Apple 1996)

It's not hard to hear what Charles Manson liked about George Harrison's misanthropic madrigal, but the chirpy whistling interlude that follows the song's ugly narrative climax points the way to a more sympathetic interpretation. Perhaps the lines Harrison seems to be making up as he goes along – 'You will see them out for dinner with their piggy wives . . . forks and knives . . . to eat their pork chops' – are a subliminal prophesy of the dangers of unnatural feeding practices in intensive farming.

19. 'Harry Irene' by Captain Beefheart on *Shiny Beast (Bat Chain Puller)* (Virgin 1979)

At first, this gently spiralling tale of canteen-owners whose tuna sandwiches could turn the dark into day sounds like it could have come from one of Captain Beefheart's attempted sell-out albums of earlier in the decade, but a sublime whistling break – deftly contrasted with a boulevardier's accordion – makes the connection to his earlier, more experimental work (whistling was sometimes used to teach the Magic Band how to play *Trout Mask Replica*). And by the time 'what does this mean?' has turned into 'what's the meaning of this?' the listener's head has been well and truly messed with.

20. 'Epitaph' by Badly Drawn Boy on *The Hour of Bewilderbeast* (Twisted Nerve/XL 2000)

'I hope you never die, there's no need to say why,' Damon Gough proclaims reassuringly on the last track of his lovely debut album. His girlfriend joins in on backing vocals, there's a chorus of birdsong, and the whistling's pivotal function is clearly set out in the lyrics: 'Cements the melody, to signify we're free.'

Copyright Acknowledgements

Call Him George by Jay Allison Stuart (Jazz Club) © Dorothy Tait

Charles Manson in His Own Words by Charles Manson with Nuell Emmons (Grafton 1986) © Nuell Emmons/Grafton Books 1986

Crosstown Traffic by Charles Shaar Murray (Faber and Faber 1989) © Charles Shaar Murray 1989

Dead Elvis: A Chronicle of a Cultural Obsession by Greil Marcus (Viking 1992) © Greil Marcus 1991

Divided Self, The by R.D. Laing (Pelican 1987) © R.D. Laing 1969

Dolly: My Life & Other Unfinished Business by Dolly Parton with Buddy Sheffield (HarperCollins 1993) © Dolly Parton 1993

Doors of Perception, The by Aldous Huxley (Flamingo 1994) © Mrs Laura Huxley 1954

Energy Flash by Simon Reynolds (Picador 1998) © Simon Reynolds 1998

Exotica by David Toop (Serpent's Tail 1999) © David Toop 1999

Faber Book of Pop, The eds Hanif Kureishi and Jon Savage (Faber and Faber 1995) © Jon Savage and Hanif Kureishi 1995

Get In The Van by Henry Rollins (2.13.61 1994) © Henry Rollins 1994

Group Psychology, Civilization and its Discontents and Other Works Freud: group analysis etc

Head On by Julian Cope (Magog 1994) and *The Modern Antiquarian: A Pre-Millennial Odyssey Through Megalithic Britain* (Thorsons 1988) © Julian Cope 1994 and 1998

History of the Blues, The by Frances Davis (Secker & Warburg 1995) © Frances Davis 1995

I Dream of Madonna by Kay Turner (Thames and Hudson 1993) © Kay Turner 1992

I Need More by Iggy Pop with Anne Wehrer (Karz/Cohl 1982) © Pop/Wehrer 1982

Invisible Man by Ralph Ellison (Penguin 1972) © Ralph Ellison 1952

It's Not About a Salary: Rap, Race & Resistance in Los Angeles by Brian Cross (Verso 1993) © Brian Cross 1993

Jelly Roll Morton observations from the Library of Congress recordings, reprinted in Ralph Gleason's *Jam Session* (see above)

Lynch on Lynch, ed. Chris Rodley (Faber and Faber 1998) © David Lynch 1997

More Brilliant Than the Sun: Adventures in Sonic Fiction by Kodwo Eshun (Quartet 1998) © Kodwo Eshun/Quartet Books 1998

Ocean of Sound by David Toop (Serpent's Tail 1995) © David Toop 1995

Private Parts by Howard Stern (Pocket Star 1994) © One Twelve, Inc, 1993

Problem of Knowledge, The by A.J. Ayer (Penguin 1984) © A.J. Ayer 1956

Psychotic Reactions & Carburettor Dung by Lester Bangs ed. Greil Marcus (Serpent's Tail 1996) © Lester Bangs, Greil Marcus 1987

Notes

Introduction

1 See John F. Szwed's *Space Is the Place: The Life and Times of Sun Ra.*

2 In Greil Marcus' *Dead Elvis: A Chronicle of a Cultural Obsession*, a professor of English at Middle Tennesee State University asks a class of second and third graders who Elvis was and receives the immortal reply: 'This big black guy who invented the electric guitar,' which casts the supposedly clear-cut racial divide in the Presley story in an intriguingly uneven light. Unfortunately, posterity has not always been so playful, and Marcus' predictions as to the enduring nature of Albert Goldman's slurs on the good names of Presley, Sam Phillips and other 'pioneers of racial decency' have up to now proved sadly accurate.

3 Quoted in Dave Marsh: *Before I Get Old – The Story of The Who.*

Radio

4 Jimmy Savile's own account of the momentous events at the Belle Vue Road branch of the Loyal Order of Ancient Shepherds simply cannot be bettered. Any house which does not possess a copy of his autobiography *As It Happens* cannot really be called a home.

5 There is a troubling side to it though. A rather odd TV programme broadcast as part of Peel's sixtieth birthday celebrations celebrates his oft harped upon exasperation at his eldest son's inability to keep his room tidy. But why is John Peel penalising his firstborn for exactly the sort of behaviour he has indulged – nay encouraged – in the rest of the nation's young people for the past three-and-a-bit decades? Surely he can see that his son is merely aping their behaviour in a bid to win his

father's love, while Peel himself adopts the sort of disapproving Victorian manner he found so difficult in his own father. It is all a bit sad and very much along the lines of the relationship between Dr and Scott Evil in the Austin Powers movies, but with Mark E. Smith as Mini-me.

6   Ulf Poschardt's *DJ Culture* takes this idea several steps further by mixing up academic language with fragments of jive talk and rap lyric in the hope of undermining the pernicious snobberies of the Frankfurt School. Grumpy Marxist grand-wizard Theodor Adorno and hip-hop seer Greg Tate must, Poschardt insists, 'fertilise one another by communicating and ceasing to be alone'. This is all very well, but Poschardt's claim that the DJ exists 'to interrogate and partially destroy archaic notions of artistic authorship' would probably come as news to Pete Tong. On second thoughts, perhaps it wouldn't.

7   For those who can take a large dose of Stern's personality, Howard's autobiography *Private Parts* is riveting stuff. His divorce came through just too late for its impact to be assessed in this volume.

8   See Nelson George's *The Death Of Rhythm & Blues*.

9   He didn't win, but it was worth a try.

TV

10   This story took a rather sinister turn in 1999, when UEFA signed a secret charter obliging British league clubs to play no song other than Robbie Williams' 'Let Me Entertain You'.

11   Matthew Collin's *Altered State* sheds valuable new light on several enduring Ecstasy myths, most notably that of the drug's role in the decline of football hooliganism in the late Eighties and early Nineties. Collin contends that while some terrace hardmen no doubt forgot their petty hatreds in the delirium of the dance, others saw the money-making opportunities and moved in to run things. Collin turns an admirably steely investigative eye on the criminal takeover of the Ecstasy infrastructure – the switch, in the memorable phrase of one of the participants, 'from double-barrelled name to double-barrelled shotgun'. The only problem with what Collin appealingly terms 'pirate utopias' is that pirates tend to want to live in them.

12   From William Burroughs interview with Jimmy Page, published in *Very Seventies: A Cultural History of the 1970s from the pages of Crawdaddy (Simon & Schuster 1995)*

Film

13 *Seventies Soul Top 10*: Channel 4 2000

14 You can take this too far though. The natty critical designation 'a soundtrack for a film that hasn't been made yet' has been so overused that it has become actively pernicious. 'That one's a real death knell,' says Chemical Brother Ed Simmons. 'It just means you have to watch something else to divert your attention from the boredom of the music.'

15 In allowing the star in question to be not just everything they are, but everything they ought to be, the cameo is arguably the perfect cinematic vehicle for the canny pop luminary. While it would be hard to countenance Billy Idol in a gruelling two-hour drama about pan-handlers in the depression, no-one could deny he was great in *The Wedding Singer*. The parameters of the cameo form as we know it today were defined by Alice Cooper's epoch-making contribution in *Wayne's World* – instructing a bewildered Wayne and Garth on the delights of his home state of Milwaukee.

Director Penelope Spheeris had learnt everything there was to know about compressing the whole of a pop persona into a very small space from her interaction with Lemmy and Ozzy Osbourne in making the classic heavy metal documentary *The Decline Of Western Civilisation pt 2: The Metal Years*.

From the everyday (The Ramones and just about any other band who ever existed turning up on *The Simpsons*, Robert Smith of The Cure on *South Park*) to the unforgettable (The Wu-Tang Clan's appearance on *Larry Sanders*, where Hank Kingsley welcomed them with the immortal line, 'Which one of you is Old Dirty Bitch?'), to the downright embarrassing (the episode in the otherwise impeccable *My So-Called Life* where Buffalo Tom played a gig in a local hall and everyone was supposed to think it was cool), the cameo now rules on TV as well.

16 It is interesting that the nineties' other major Beatles picture – Christopher Munch's *The Hours and the Times* (1992) – approached the band's legend from a similar angle, and not only in casting Ian Hart as Lennon. A claustrophobic, no-budget, black and white chamber piece where *Backbeat* was a brassy pop product, it's again set before before the band went supernova, and again describes the young Lennon's journey to cultural enlightenment through a close male friendship (this time with Brian Epstein) whose clear homoerotic overtones were of as much interest to him as they were to everyone

else. Whether this says more about Lennon's concerns or those of his cinematic biographers is probably a moot point.

17   This superstar pick-up band methodology was also used to imposing effect in Todd Haynes' glam rock fantasy *Velvet Goldmine*

18   A film also notable for a memorable seduction scene in which Frank Sinatra whisks Mia off her feet with the lusty imprecation 'Let's do it My Way'.

19   Strangely, Courtney Love's muse Madonna also found her finest role as herself (though – tellingly – in Madonna's case, she was in control). *In Bed With Madonna*'s American title *Truth or Dare* reflects the requirements of a nation which understands the true value of celebrity and values a superstar who is prepared to reveal herself to this extent. Alex Keshishian's film somehow manages to make Warren Beatty appear as a paragon of propriety ('Why say anything off carema? What would be the point?'), even as it dwells on Madonna's rather double-edged concern for her dancers ('I think I've unconsciously chosen people who are emotionally crippled in some way') and appalling treatment of her girlhood idol (now grown up unsuccessful), who is driven to observe, 'What a bitch!'

20   In the marvellous *Scooby-Doo*-style denouement the villianous scientist Devereux earns the immortal epitaph 'He created Kiss to destroy Kiss, and he lost'.

Video

21   Obviously video is recorded on tape rather than film, so it doesn't have frames and can't be frozen. But as the audio-visual oeuvre of The Stereophonics (especially their magical *Apocalypse Now* tribute for 'The Bartender & The Thief') so eloquently testifies, video so badly wants to be cinema that it would be cruel to deny it its little fantasy.

22   While these four sample categories of early video endeavour might seem irretrievably old school to the sophisticated twenty-first century eye, they live on like a well-designed pair of Adidas. Readers with time on their hands might like to match each of the designations to the following modern video landmarks: George Michael's LA toilet epic 'Outside', that Limp Bizkit (or was it Korn? It is always so hard to be sure) video where the bullet goes through the wall, Mel C and Left Eye's 'Never Be the Same Again' and The Bluetones' footballing fat-suit tableau.

23 I can't actually remember where this quote came from but people who are too lazy to read footnotes will never know that.

24 In his ludicrously titled *Intelligent Person's Guide to Modern Culture*, Scruton wrote gloomily of a tidal wave of pop culture 'drowning out the unconfident murmurs of the fathers as they trudge towards extinction'. Without wishing to spoil the plot of *Beavis and Butt-head Do America* for anyone who hasn't seen it yet, that is more or less exactly what happens in it. In a pleasing historical footnote, Scruton's supposedly devastating critique of popular culture was hoist on its own petard when he was successfully sued by the Pet Shop Boys for implying they did not play their instruments.

25 In *Time Travel*, Jon Savage shrewdly places *Beavis and Butthead* within a punk heritage of assumed stupidity. This tradition goes way back, cf. Anatole Broyard's 1955 essay 'A Portrait of the Hipster': 'Since articulateness is a condition of if not actually a cause of anxiety, the hipster relieved his anxiety by disarticulating himself.'

26 Anyone who doubts this should try to get a look at Ronin Ro's grisly but gripping *Have Gun Will Travel: The Spectacular Rise and Violent Fall of Death Row Records*, and, for intriguing parallels with an earlier golden age of American gangsterdom, the voracious reader is directed to Shawn Levy's super snappy *Rat Pack Confidential*.

27 Quoted in *Lynch On Lynch*, ed. Chris Rodley.

Books

28 Similarly literature aspires to the condition of literature – when it aspires to pop music it fails. This is seen as clearly in Kureishi's own canon as anywhere else . . . The impressionistic musical backdrop of *The Buddha of Suburbia* being beautifully observed, the craven Prince fetishism of *The Black Album* being rather less successfully realised.

29 The journey from the gleamingly cynical dissection of Leonard Bernstein's party for the Black Panthers in *Radical Chic & Mau-Mauing the Flak Catchers* to the embarrassing rap affectations of *A Man In Full* is one best expressed in terms of visual art – as a progression from an exquisite pointillist landscape to the kind of large cat portrait much favoured by Home Counties tea shops.

30 The Phil Collins and Huey Lewis stuff in *American Psycho* is certainly pretty funny.

31 There are intriguing parallels between the careers of the rock-star-

turned-novelist and the soap-star-turned-pop-singer (though more work remains to be done on the aesthetic nexus between Nick Cave and Martine McCutcheon). Like an apple core thrown from a speeding car, both are launched with the full weight of pre-existing personas but generally have difficulty maintaining their initial momentum.

32 If only this were true of more of the 'club fiction' boom which followed in Welsh's wake like the seagulls pursuing Eric Cantona's trawler.

33 Though Lydon's generally scathing tone does render his occasional warm enthusiasm – for Jose Ferrer's film performance as Cyrano de Bergerac, or the time he spent as a teenager building a sewage farm in Guildford, for his brief career as a London daycare worker ('I still feel I could have become a teacher if I'd followed through on it') – strangely touching.

The Prism / The Souls / The Choir

34 The strange thing about Air's music is it sometimes seems to do better in places it's not supposed to be. In an environment specially designed for it – for example, as the soundtrack to Sofia Coppola's *The Virgin Suicides* – it can sometimes get a bit claustrophobic.

35 Gough's own artistic roots are somewhat less conventional. He identifies seeing Bruce Springsteen performing 'Thunder Road' on TV as the pivotal happening in his creative evolution. 'Everyone's got one moment where music really grabbed them for the first time,' he recalls proudly, 'and in terms of wanting to capture the magic that someone else has given you and give it to other people, that's mine.'

36 In a neat twist of fate, Bargeld later became better known for playing guitar with Nick Cave than for his own endeavours. 'I had to find a way to react to the whole symbolism of the guitar, which I hated; so I built a repertoire for myself – fifty ways of playing guitar without playing guitar.'

37 It might be possible to get the impression that this man lacked a sense of humour if you didn't know that Neubauten once co-headlined with Showaddywaddy.

38 When *The Marshall Mathers LP* comes out, it proves him to be as good as his word.

39 Except among that portion of the public in the know about the sort of things he used to get up to in the Robert Fripp years.

40 Also one of Captain Beefheart's favourites.

41   The images of Efrim's dog Wanda swimming underwater are exquisite,
     though. This fine animal was given a fitting send-off in *He Has Left Us
     Alone But Shafts Of Light Sometimes Grace The Corner Of Our Rooms*,
     the bewitching 2000 debut album by Godspeed spin-off trio A Silver
     Mt. Zion: one of a select group of great albums – oh, all right then, Janet
     Jackson's *Janet* is the only other one I can think of – dedicated to dead
     or dying pets. *He Has Left Us Alone* . . . offers far more than just a
     small-screen version of Godspeed's mighty sensurround. Its haunting
     piano, violin and found sound loops are supplemented on track four by
     an actual lead vocal, outlining a political position slightly to the left of
     the great Dennis Skinner, and poignantly delivered by Efrim in a voice
     which makes Mercury Rev's Jonathan Donahue sound like Meat Loaf.

42   After its first showing on *Top of the Pops*, Jamie Theakston observed,
     'It's OK fellas, you can come out from behind the sofa now, she's gone.'

43   For the historical background to the turn of the century golden age of
     Kelis, Missy Elliott, TLC and Destiny's Child, Harmless records'
     superb 2000 compilation *I'm A Good Woman* brings the great aunts of
     today's sex-war gladiators dancing out of the bin-liner of history with a
     gloriously defiant swagger. There are not one but two answer records'
     to the Isley Brothers's 'It's Your Thing'; there's the fearsome Betty
     Davis, whose uptight jazz legend husband Miles wouldn't stand for her
     dalliance with a certain Mr Jimi Hendrix; and – arguably best of all –
     there is Ann Winley, who in the midst of her ferocious 'Watchdog'
     warns her recalcitrant male associate, 'I'll hit you where the good lord
     split you.'

44   What Leila terms her 'comedy' surname has a neat ironic twist to it:
     'The funny thing about it is that Persians are obsessed with *not* being
     Arabs, so a Persian being called Arab is like an IRA man being called
     John England.'

45   Nervously questioned about this dubious (but no more so than the
     nomenclatural choices of New Order, Joy Division or Spandau Ballet)
     predilection on *Jo Whiley* in early 2000, Lemmy advances a defence
     straight out of Susan Sontag: 'It's not my fault they made the best
     stuff.'

46   Daughter of the legendary ELO and Move manager Don Arden, Sharon
     once said something very amusing about unbearably pompous Sabbath
     copyists The Smashing Pumpkins, but unfortunately I can't remember
     what it was.

47 Ozzy had a Yorkshire terrier in quarantine once that ran away as soon as it got home: 'I thought,' he reminisces sadly, '"Bye bye, six grand".'

48 A great Pet Shop Boys song (and there are many) offers an elegant vision of economy, self-awareness and and emotional truth. This is not an effect necessarily enhanced by ten dancers in electric-blue suits prancing round with pig masks on their faces.

49 For an alternative – and somewhat more salacious – take on the sacred and the profane, Ray Charles' autobiography *Brother Ray* is a work of genius.

50 He has yet to follow his wiry Electronic associate Johnny Marr into the gym, though – 'All those sweaty genitals hanging out in the changing rooms, it doesn't quite grab my fancy ... Johnny seems to like it, though.'

51 There are several more complete New Order records – the nervy whirl of *Low Life, Technique*'s Ibizan rhapsody, even the uncertain, elegaic *Movement* – but this one's blend of fabulous pop songs ('Age of Consent', 'Leave Me Alone', 'The Village' and 'Your Silent Face') and formative doodles somehow seems to represent them better than any other.

52 Considering Paul Weller's solo career with reference to the major population centres of the East Midlands, if *Wild Wood* suggested Nottingham – engagingly lively and revealing new pleasures at every visit – and the third, *Stanley Road*, was more like Derby (there's something worth getting at in the middle but the ring road goes on a bit) then *Heavy Soul* was getting dangerously close to Loughborough. By 2000's *Heliocentric*, the prospect of a cup of tea at Leicester Forest East services was an extremely welcome one.

53 Neil has an electronics development company hard at work on alternative forms of sound reproduction. This he refers to – only half joking – as 'the beginning of his life's work'.

Sample Ear

54 KRS-1's aggressive promotion of an anti-gang agenda is best characterised in the formulation 'Stop the violence or I'll hit you'.

55 Cross's title is actually borrowed from KRS-1's 1988 single 'My Philosophy'. When you fill in the second part of the KRS-1 quote – 'It's not about a salary, it's all about reality' – you get a paradox. The reality of rap, and LA rap in particular, is that a salary is exactly what it

generally is about. And why shouldn't it be? As Chuck D once put it in conversation with Tricky in *Vox* magazine: 'The whole ghetto concept of getting paid is more a *concept* of getting paid than actually getting paid.'

56   Further evidence as to the carefree nature of Horace's youth is furnished by his achievements in the field of paternity. 'I guess when you're young the record's playing everywhere and girls get pregnant,' he explains, with as much innocence as a father of sixteen can be expected to muster.

57   In the introduction to his 1937 'Imaginary Landscape No. 1 For Manipulated Turntables' Cage proclaimed, 'Given four film phono-graphs, we can compose and perform a quartet for explosive motor, wind, heartbeat and landslide.' That was pretty much the formula for the first couple of Cypress Hill albums too.

58   A few months before, Public Enemy are performing a full Security Of The First World-accompanied set at Nottingham Rock City, at their formidable *It Takes A Nation of Millions* peak, on an awesome Def Jam package bill which also features Eric B & Rakim and LL Cool J. DJ Graeme Park is playing house records in the changeovers and – the fickle British public being what it is – they're going down better than the main acts. Eric B has words to say about this, and they aren't words you'd use to a child.

59   Ice-T used to be the proud owner of a pit-bull called Felony. LL Cool J had a dachshund called Penny.

60   When Al Green says he's going to to sing all night long, you can always be sure he'll be back in his dressing room within ten minutes.

61   This is in Kodwo Eshun's book, but I think he got it from David Toop.

Metal Ear

62   As Jim Derogatis' Lester Bangs biography notes, the whole Seattle Sound was basically an attempt to deliver the second album Bangs had imagined for the Count Five (a record 'so grungey that . . . you could barely distinguish anything except an undifferentiated wall of grinding noise and intermittent punctuation of glottal sow-like gruntings'). The thing about prophecy is it's the confidence and imagination entailed in the act itself that are interesting rather than the actual outcome. Had he lived to see the early nineties Bangs would have no doubt have found

the tidal wave of post-Nirvana corporate rock sludge an offence at the very deepest level.

63 Megadeth's version of 'Anarchy In The UK' has more ideological thrust to it than the one The Sex Pistols do at Finsbury Park. 'Anarchy?' muses singer Dave Mustaine poetically. 'Yes, someday, maybe.'

64 As South African jazz pianist and bandleader Abdullah Ibrahim observed in 1990, 'Where does music that's *not* world music come from?'

65 Whatever your circumstances, the decision to become a professional musician entails a willingness to cut yourself off from the mainstream of respectable society. This holds true from Charlie Patton to Johnny Marr. ('The deal I made as a kid,' remembers the level-headed Mancunian guitarist, now showing some natty metal moves with his new band The Healers 'was for the musician's life – good or bad. When I was sleeping on Matt Johnson's couch trying to get a deal with The Smiths, Muddy Waters was on my mind.')

66 Braithwaite's distinctive personal style won him sponsorship from Kappa, the Italian clothing line, whose distinctive naked-women-sitting-back-to-back logo has been hailed by many authorities as the epitome of sartorial degradation. ('I swear to God I think that's what draws me,' Braithwaite expostulates, 'the sheer obtuseness of it.')

Psychedelic Ear

67 For a fascinating account of this disturbing phenomenon, read *In Pursuit of the Millenium* by Norman Cohn (spookily enough, Nik's dad).

68 Observers on the West Coast of America have already noted teenagers turning up to rave functions in white gloves and facemasks: encouraging evidence that 'ardkore might be going to ground there in the same way that punk and ska did (though hopefully not with such disastrous long-term musical consequences).

69 There wasn't just the danger of the drugs to be considered, there was also the food . . . As recounted in Russ Winstanley and David Nowell's aptly-titled *Soul Survivors: The Wigan Casino Story:* 'Hardened pies and pasties seemed to linger in the heated display cabinet for ever and those brave few who tried them usually drew strange looks.'

70 That conversation between Tricky and Chuck D again. How did Chuck D make his solo album *The Autobiography of Mistachuck* 'an album

for somebody who doesn't smoke pot to think how somebody who smokes thinks'? 'I spun around fifteen times and got dizzy.'

71 Somewhere in the big black sack full of tapes behind the sofa there is a fascinating unpublished interview with straight-edge Godfather Mackaye. Unfortunately I have never been able to find it.

72 There is – as he is perfectly well aware – a peculiar irony in Rollins' asceticism and highly disciplined, almost martial, demeanour. The samurai lifestyle he embraced at the dawn of the Reagan era, in the Washington hardcore scene and then with Black Flag, was in itself an escape from military indoctrination. Henry Garfield, as he was then, not only went to Naval school ('"Shut up, sit down" – seven years of that stuff will do a number on you') but was also tormented by an abusive ex-Army father obsessed with making him salute and sing the national anthem.

Does he find anything amusing in the inappropriateness of his military bearing to his status as punk-rock icon and high priest of principled individualism? 'I think it's hilarious. I think *I'm* hilarious, and not just when I mean to be. If you listen to the way I speak and watch the way I conduct myself, there's nothing about me that's rock 'n' roll. It's like, "Hello, I'm in a rock 'n' roll band." "No, you're a narc."'

Political Ear

73 Oh all right then, it was my mum.

74 It's hard to know quite how 3D being rude to Fergie fits in to this, but it must do somewhere. Either way, both pop miscreants got their just deserts: 3D was embarrassed when his mum told him off in the tabloids, and all Chumbawaba's subsequent recordings sank without trace.

75 There's one especially fine photo in this collection. It shows a man getting a terrible haircut and rejoices in the caption 'Victim of a collectivist barber'.

76 As if robbing *South Park* of the Best Song Oscar it should have got for 'Blame Canada' was not crime enough for one year, in 2000 Collins also sued two members of Earth, Wind & Fire on the grounds that he had paid them too much for some session work, which is like Sir Walter Raleigh taking a Native American casino to court because he dropped a pound coin at the salad bar.

77 Among the other selections are hilariously scabrous appropriations of Bruce Springsteen's 'Dancing In The Dark' and Pat Benatar's 'Love Is A Battlefield'.

78 This move was prefigured some years earlier by the great New York noise band Pussy Galore, whose classic 1988 album *Groovy Hate Fuck/Feel Good About Your Body* contains, in 'HC Reb', what still sounds like the most eloquent punk rock plea for sexual equality ever, even when you find out that it's actually Julia Cafritz reading from the letters page of dog-eared US punk bible *Maximum Rock 'n' Roll*.

79 The Milton Keynes Bowl is not the dramatic, deep-sided natural arena the name implies – the reality is more like the Milton Keynes Saucer – but elemental forces are still at work there, and the veneer of civilisation which the Bowl's proprietors have worked so hard on occasionally gets stripped away. At a Guns N Roses show in 1992, some very drunk men in Stranglers t-shirts somehow get hold of the remains of a cooked pig, and begin playing a gruesome game of American football. Their antics progress in outrageousness until finally one throws the carcass to the ground and has sex with it.

80 The tradition of straightforward political engagement that was available to, say, Billy Bragg or The Specials or The Three Johns or Paul Weller having been discredited – in the Manics' eyes at least – by its apparent failure in the Thatcher epoch.

81 I know this is true because I saw it on a BBC documentary.

82 It's also to be as small-minded as Peter Guralnick is at the point in *Lost Highways*, his celebrated paean to the American folk tradition, when he says 'Entertaining people on a mass level is no longer genuinely popular culture . . . but a pathetic dilution of a rich cultural tradition.' The only reasoned intellectual response to this particular viewpoint is a lusty shout of 'Hey, c'mon Grandad, get with the programme.'

All-Seeing Ear

83 This view was originally attributed to the Vienna School: a group of Austrian academics with a fatal weakness for Ultravox.

84 Though in a rarely cited but prophetic pamphlet *Massenpsychologie und Appleton-analyse*, Freud would later compare All Saints' 'Pure Shores' dance routine to 'the flight of a flock of linnets', in the way it seemed to express the will of a single mutant organism rather than a group of disparate individuals.

85 The Nightingales' 'Elvis, The Last Ten Days' – a poignant survey of The King's final unreleased final diary entries ('Day 10: Tomorrow I'll start my diet, and answer some of that fan mail') has been very influential on this chapter's somewhat unorthodox structure.

86 From Cymande to Craig David, and Loose Ends to A Guy Called Gerald, such networks of independent entrepreurial endeavour have always been crucial to the development of British black music. 'We built our own crowd up from the clubs,' explains Jazzie B, when asked about the origins of Soul II Soul's sumptuous north London enterprise culture. 'Those were our people, the people who respected what we were doing, and we fed those people with what they wanted: they paid for the entertainment, they bought the clothes, and one thing just led to another.'

87 *Space Is the Place* recounts him refusing to put details of his parentage, place of birth and 'real' name on his passport, and being allowed to get away with it because the relevant official was intimidated by his strangeness.

88 When 'Shudder/King of Snake' tests the primal pulse of Giorgio Moroder's 'I Feel Love', you remember that it was European synth-pop's infectious anaemia that gave Detroit's techno pioneers their first route map. Which is why it's so weird when people make out that Underworld's prehistory in early eighties electro-pop tarts Freur is somehow a skeleton in their cupboard. Actually, it's their trump card.

89 On Channel 4's *Seventies Soul Top Ten* in early 2000.

90 Cope's subsequent travails as a solo artist would amplify this dilemma. ('I understood how Lawrence of Arabia felt,' he would later observe, 'when he came back to London and was compelled to dress as his legend.')

Index